TRIAL
AND
ERROR

TRIAL
AND
ERROR

David Jessel

Foreword by
Michael Mansfield Q.C.

HEADLINE
in association with
Channel Four Television

First published in 1994 by
HEADLINE BOOK PUBLISHING

10 9 8 7 6 5 4 3 2 1

ISBN 0 7472 7836 9

Phototypeset by Intype, London
Printed and bound in Great Britain by
Mackays of Chatham PLC, Chatham, Kent

HEADLINE BOOK PUBLISHING
A division of Hodder Headline PLC
338 Euston Road
London NW1 3BH

To Sir Ludovic Kennedy
in friendship and respect

Contents

Acknowledgements

There are a lot of people I need to thank – mostly the people who did the work.

Sieving and selecting the casework is principally the work of Steve Haywood and the research team of Bob Duffield (who I have persuaded to write one of the chapters), Nina Davies and Sue Walker. Olwyn Silvester, with the help of Emma Coghlan and Laura Carter, who has been tireless in tracking down the photographs, forced me to make time for this book and make the most of it. Stephen Phelps, apart from producing half the programmes, has been a great encouragement, as well as being the cause of some of the more absurd things that happen when a television crew is let loose on real life.

Channel Four has been a strong and consistent ally – and you need allies when you are doing this sort of awkward television; David Lloyd in particular gave us all the chance to do this work, at a time when 'high-ups' at the BBC had led me to believe they were bored with miscarriages-of-justice programmes. Thanks to both organizations for their part in creating Just Television, the most exciting and fulfilling time of my professional life. My gratitude, too, to Justice for its advice and support, and to our redoubtable advisory group for their inspiration, backing and wisdom.

Roger Houghton of Headline has pushed me off the worst pinnacles of pomposity, but then one person can only do so much. Jan Tomalin is my favourite solicitor, among other reasons because she appreciates my pathetic attempts to stay this side of the law of libel.

Above all, thanks to the good people who had the courage to help us, even if it meant alienating neighbours or stirring up bad memories. It is a constant refreshment to discover how many people believe in justice – and in their responsibility to see it done when the system fails.

David Jessel
Just Television
July 1994

Foreword

As a celluloid child, propelled into the legal profession by the dramatic and persuasive images of the American television law serial of the 50s – *The Defenders* – I am in no doubt about the power and the responsibility of the small screen.

Over the last decade there have been notable examples of programmes making a substantial contribution to the cause and course of justice in the United Kingdom by alerting the public and the authorities to the serious shortcomings in the criminal system – *World in Action* (Granada), *Rough Justice* (BBC), and now *Trial and Error* (Channel 4). Their particular strengths have been commitment, perseverance, careful research, application of resources and, most of all, courage. Rarely thanked, barely recognised and often the butt of judicial venom, this book is a timely revelation of how they have filled an enormous gap and provided hope for those who have been isolated and neglected.

The sad fact is that far from the system recognising the extent of its faults there has been hypocrisy and circumvention by passing the buck from top to bottom. There has been little real heart searching and the Royal Commission, born out of the obvious disquiet about the gravity and quantity of miscarriages, has provided no protections against the clear risk of repetition. Instead the scene has been set by the Government through Michael Howard's current Criminal Justice Bill and by the Opposition, through Tony Blair's policy of abstention, to mislead the public into believing that justice is about a law and order bandwagon containing more prisons (even for 12–14 year olds), longer sentences, no right to silence, no legal requirements for corroboration and, worst of all, a diminution of the democratic freedom to protest under the guise of criminal trespass.

All this needs to be spelt out because the role played by responsible television programmes in this struggle for basic rights is now even more essential. The real agenda is quick fix, cheap, market-led justice: minimise and remove jury trials; re-emphasise the value of confessions by removing the right to silence; encourage plea bargaining; emasculate legal aid – the result being coach loads of the vulnerable being shepherded on day trips to the judicial *hypermarché*.

Resourcing and funding are vital to ensure that there is equality of access and equality of arms if citizen's freedoms and rights, let alone charters, are to be enforced. What is not appreciated is the void into which the wrongfully convicted fall.

If you have the misfortune to be convicted of a serious crime, unless you are able to mount an application for leave to appeal within 28 days your chances of redress diminish to nil. Thereafter the case can only be reopened via the Home Secretary sending it back to the Court.

The problem starts with legal aid. Fresh evidence (either material that previously existed but was not discovered or material which has come into existence subsequently) may not arise for months or years after the trial. The painstaking work required to uncover such material – tramping the streets, blind alleys, forensic tests – consume enormous quantities of time and effort. Most solicitors, especially those specialising in crime, who are already under pressure from serious underfunding, are unwilling to undertake such tasks when there is little prospect of reimbursement, unless a future Home Secretary can be persuaded to refer the case back to the Court of Appeal. It is only at that point the solicitor can hope to recover some costs. Persuading the Home Secretary is a lottery and only a small percentage of petitions succeed. Even if a reference is made, the Court of Appeal has displayed a reluctance to order retrials and to allow appeals in 'fresh evidence cases', construing their powers in a narrow fashion.

Voluntary and non-statutory agencies cannot cope – Liberty, Justice, Amnesty, Innocent. They are dealing with thousands of approaches. Proposals for change even here are stillborn.

There was a broad consensus, including previous Home Secretaries Baker and Hurd, for a new review body to replace the Home Office even before the Royal Commission set about its Brief. Instead of spending its two years of research compiling a prototype, the Commission did little more than endorse the concept. Since then (June 1993) there has been a lapse of more time while a consultation document has been circulated by the Home Office, attempting to seek answers to questions of principle and mechanics established from years ago.

What should be the powers of any new body (Criminal Cases Review Body); how should the powers of the Court of Appeal be reformed; who should serve on the body; what investigative resources should it have? It is already clear that there is a predeliction for a model not dissimilar to the Police Complaints Authority, and that substantial funding required at the initial stages to investigate the merits of the many applications is not going to be forthcoming.

Until the need for more radical change is recognised, once more individuals will be dependent on the goodwill and vigorous independence of journalists, researchers, producers and directors – like the *Trial and Error* team – willing to invest resources and energy in pursuit of freedom from injustice.

Michael Mansfield Q.C.
July 1994

1
Mark Cleary
A Murderer's Victim

Mark Cleary was the victim of the most appalling, cunning, vindictive and manipulative miscarriage of justice. In the end, I think, we managed to prove it. As I write, his case is making its way to the Appeal Court, and his barrister says he'll hang up his boots if he doesn't get the conviction quashed.

At first, I admit, I didn't want to touch the case.

It was an old case, and a loathsome crime, and as such it triggered two prejudices, one journalistic, the other personal; because the crime was committed as long ago as 1985, I was afraid that the case might seem a little whiskery. And because it involved the killing of a child, my own parental sensibilities were outraged. It was only when I overcame those prejudices and began to countenance Mark Cleary's innocence that I could translate those reservations into outrage; suddenly it wasn't a nine-year-old crime, but nine years of wrongful imprisonment, and, although nothing detracted from the horror of the crime, it seemed unbearably wrong and wretched that a miscarriage of justice should be added to something as terrible as the murder of a schoolboy, for which Mark Cleary was convicted.

The telephone rang on my desk, probably because everyone else was busy on their own line. Sean Webster, a journalist with the *Solicitor's Journal*, had for some time taken a kindly interest in us; he had written a friendly piece about Just Television when we left the BBC's *Rough Justice* programme, and he was a welcome ally in the face of the barrage from the Corporation's massed artillery of plump press officers. The BBC had not taken kindly to our leaving, and had briefed media journalists about us in terms so clumsily vitriolic as to prove counterproductive. There

1

was a solicitor in Nottingham, Sean told me, who had been nursing a murder case for years. He didn't know much about it, but it concerned a body in a canal, and the solicitor wouldn't let the case go.

The case struck several totally arbitrary chords. Steve Haywood, one of my colleagues and a former editor of *Rough Justice*, came from the East Midlands and knew the waterways well – he lives for his canal-boat, which he has christened *Justice*. But a stronger reason for following up the case at this early stage was the evident conviction of the solicitor involved.

The provincial solicitor lives at the drabber end of the law, a long way and an InterCity day-return away from the elegant fireworks of Appeal Court QCs. It is a tedious round of attendance at magistrates' courts, and chivvying the legal aid board to stump up the niggardly money grudgingly accepted as the rate for the job. Once a case has exhausted the judicial system, of course, the money dries up. Any solicitor who carries on the fight is either heroic or obsessive, and, on either score, worth talking to. Ron Birkett, of the Nottingham firm of Cleggs, is one of this unsung breed – among whom I'd certainly count Mark Hancock, solicitor for the Darvell brothers in Swansea, whose convictions for murder another of my colleagues, Stephen Phelps, and I helped to overturn in 1992. I rang Birkett, and arranged for Bob Duffield, our research consultant to see him.

It was guaranteed to be an intriguing encounter; for although we all become absorbed in the work, Bob has a unique passion and a tenacity about the cases he adopts. There's little he likes more than to comb through mountains of witness statements, cross-referencing them on a vast and expanding chart; I swear his heart leaps at the prospect of confronting an electoral roll, searching for one key name hidden among a non alphabetic list of fifty thousand. No one kills a potential case more quickly or more decisively than Bob Duffield; but when he begins to get a sniff of a miscarriage, no one fights harder. And, because of those misgivings, Bob had to fight hard to win our commitment to the case of Mark Cleary and the drab and sordid crime of which he was wrongly convicted.

The crime was committed on the Wednesday before Easter in 1985. That afternoon, ten-year-old Wayne Keeton left his grandmother's house on the Bestwood council estate for a spin on his pride and joy, the red-and-yellow BMX bike he had been given for Christmas. He did not return home. Over the next four days, the community mobilized in a search for the child. Since the closure of the local pit the Bestwood area has declined; the heart has gone out of the place. But on this occasion, hundreds of people gave up their holiday weekend to walk the rain-swept moorland and reclaimed slag heaps.

One of these volunteers was Philip Atherton. He was twenty-one. He'd asked his friend Mark Cleary, to come with him. A strange thing happened while they were walking along a part of the embankment of the disused pithead railway, where the boy's BMX had been found abandoned. Atherton was very anxious that they make a thorough search of the area. They both walked, side by side, slashing at the springtime undergrowth with sticks; then Atherton suggested that they swap sides, and double-check the embankment. Although the area had, for obvious reasons, been extensively searched by police only minutes earlier, Atherton found a child's shoe. He showed it to Cleary who, given that police had only minutes earlier completed a fingertip search of the area, assumed it had been discarded as irrelevant. Cleary was also puzzled because he'd combed that very stretch himself without finding anything; it was only when Atherton had suggested that they search again, swapping sides, that the shoe was 'found'. The two left the site at 6 p.m. Less than an hour later, for reasons we can only guess at, the police descended once again on the scene and discovered the shoe for themselves. It was Wayne Keeton's. Had the police really missed the shoe? It seemed unlikely. But why had they come back – had someone tipped them off? If so, it could only be Atherton or Cleary – but why?

On Sunday, Easter Day, four days after Wayne's disappearance, a team of police frogmen searched the nearby River Leen, a narrow stream which runs down from a fishing pond, over a weir, and through a low tunnel before meandering off to swell the Trent. A few yards into the brick tunnel, wedged under water, they found the body of Wayne Keeton.

Philip Atherton was arrested the next day. He confessed almost immediately, his words properly and, as far as we know, accurately minuted. He said he had met Wayne on Wednesday evening outside a row of local shops where the youth of the local Bestwood estate would gather to gossip, giggle, or, like Wayne, whizz up and down the muddy hillocks nearby – all that remained of the old pithead railway embankment. Philip Atherton introduced himself using the name 'Adey'. Who knows what story he spun, to entangle and enmesh the child; some say there was talk of a midnight raid on a local factory, to steal bottles of pop. Whatever the enticement, the two set off along the route of the old railway track on their bikes. It began to get dark. Wayne, his common sense presumably beginning to get the better of his sense of adventure, asked Atherton to walk him home. Atherton refused. Then, Atherton admitted, acting on a sudden sexual urge he grabbed the child round the throat. Wayne bit him on the thumb. The youth lashed out in pain and fury, felling the child to the ground. As his victim screamed, 'Mum, help me', Atherton tried a forcible sexual assault on the boy, but said that he could not muster an adequate erection. Through terror or exhaustion the boy became passive. Atherton then loaded him, quietly moaning, on to the crossbar of his bike and wheeled him back along the embankment. But they didn't go back to the shops. Atherton left the embankment, to reach the main road that runs parallel to it. The child fell off the bike as they negotiated the precipitous, forty-five-degree slope. Loading Wayne back on, Atherton pushed him across the road and down a track which leads past a bone mill to the River Leen. The child by now was silent. Atherton said he thought he was dead, and tried to wash some blood from his face. Then he heard a shout, and fled. He was back home, he said, by 9.30 p.m. when he had his tea and went to bed.

Such was his confession, and bloodstains on his bicycle confirmed the miserable story.

Atherton was remanded in custody. But some seven weeks later, there was a strange development. His father, a local JP, visited Philip Atherton in the cells, and told him that there was talk around the village of a second person having been involved in the killing. According to Mr Atherton's statement to the police, 'Philip said nothing for about two minutes, then said, "OK, Dad." I said "I want a name." He replied, "Mark Cleary." '

After this conversation, Philip Atherton produced a version of the fatal night's events similar in many respects to his original confession, except for one addition; this time Mark Cleary was with him – and it was Mark Cleary who was responsible for the worst aspects of the attack. It was Cleary, for instance, who kicked the child when he was helpless on the ground (a new detail in the description of the attack). 'It was really vicious the way Mark put the boot in,' said Atherton. It was Mark's suggestion to 'fuck Wayne'.

The day after this new statement, Mark Cleary was arrested. He worked as a cleaner at the Shire Hall in Nottingham, which, by a strange irony, housed at the time the city's principal courts, as well as a police station. It was part of Mark's job to make sure the imposing mahogany of the law was properly buffed, and to clear up the legal detritus at the end of trials, as well as swabbing the station floor. He also had to look after some of the grislier departments of the Shire Hall complex – like the flogging room where the easel still stands, with its buckles and restraints, and the sink provided for the man with the birch after he had done his bloody and sweaty work. The old, medieval condemned cells are still there; tiny, rat-ridden holes in the wall, after which the fresh air of the scaffold, behind the tall brick prison wall, must almost have been a relief. On that day, however, Mark was asked by his supervisor to go to the staff room, a snug, dusty boxroom furnished with the sort of friendly old armchairs the council bureaucrats chuck out, but which never quite reach the skip. He was told that two officers wanted to talk to him. Mark Cleary was totally unprepared for what was to follow.

He was taken by car to Hucknall Police Station, on the outskirts of Nottingham. Mark Cleary was interviewed four times. We cannot be absolutely sure about what happened, because no contemporaneous notes were taken. Yet, strangely, some of the conversations are written up apparently verbatim, every exchange detailed, even down to the inclusion of dialect words, some twelve days later. There is one major omission: none of the strenuous denials which Cleary says he made during the first two hours are noted down. The interviewing officer, Detective Superintendent Newton, told Cleary that he believed Atherton 'because he has no reason to tell lies, he's already admitted what he's done.'

Under pressure – Cleary claims the police persistently accused him of being a homosexual killer – and without a solicitor present, Cleary eventually began to make halting and limited admissions. Yes, he had gone along with Atherton and the boy. Wayne began to get on the nerves of the two youths; Atherton hit him and Cleary went home. Two hours later, the police suggested to Cleary that he would feel better if he could only bear to unburden himself fully of his guilt. Cleary apparently replied: 'I know what you mean, I just haven't been able to talk to anyone about it.'

It makes a refreshing change; most 'confessions' usually start – according to the police – with the contrite cliché 'I am so glad to get this off my chest at last.'

The police asked if Cleary kicked the boy. Cleary said he may have struck the boy, to shut him up. The police persisted, asking if it was a hard and deliberate attack. Cleary continued to deny such an assault before admitting that he may have kicked the boy once. 'Only once?' asked the police, who at this stage knew there had been two kicks. Cleary obligingly volunteered that he may have kicked the boy twice. Then – and we have only Cleary's word for it – he told the police that everything he had told them about that night was 'a load of bollocks' and that he had only submitted under pressure. He was held overnight and charged with Wayne's murder.

There are many reasons why people confess to things that they have not done. A cottage industry of forensic psychologists could give you a catalogue of them. In Cleary's case, it was almost certainly a matter of naked vulnerability; a stuttering, ill-educated lad, charged with the most heinous crime in the criminal calendar by officers convinced of his guilt. There was something touchingly understandable in his own simple explanation of why he felt he had to offer the police a confession. 'They took my shoes away,' he told us. No question of rubber truncheons, bright lights and the third degree; they just took his shoes away.

The trial was conducted in an atmosphere thick with anger and recrimination. Nottingham's Number One court, whose antique benches, jury box and dock Mark Cleary had polished so often, was thronged to the gallery. 'There was a Roman circus atmosphere,' said one onlooker; 'every detail drew gasps of horror and hatred from the audience.' Atherton, his co-accused, did not give evidence and so could not be cross-examined about his accusation of Cleary. Cleary relied on a rather feeble alibi that he had been listening to records at home with a friend called Mick Ryan.

There are two problems with alibis, as far as the law is concerned. For a start, most of us find it hard to remember what we were doing on any particular day. Where were you, at half past six on this day seven weeks ago? Your life may have a regular rhythm and routine. If so, one day seems very much like another. For a young man in a regular and monotonous job, one evening is very like another. Most people manage to dredge up a recollection of a particular day from what was on the television that evening, but Cleary didn't watch much television. The second weakness in most alibis is that, almost by definition, there are usually only friends or close family around to support them. This gives the court a problem; your mother may be the person most likely to know where you were on Tuesday night, but if she found you soaked in blood she is also the person most likely to want to protect you – by supporting a false account. The very people in the best position to give you an alibi are also the people most likely, from the court's point of view, to want to shield you.

The only independent witness was Mick Ryan. But Ryan had even less reason than Cleary to remember a Wednesday already some months distant. Ryan made a stuttering appearance. With the best will in the world he could not be certain about where he had been so long ago. Both men, Atherton and Cleary, were convicted of murder. Cleary's counsel, Desmond Fennell QC, advised that there was little hope of a successful appeal.

And there, but for a dedicated solicitor, a couple of coincidences, four months' leg work in Nottingham, and Channel Four's money, the case would have ended. Cleary, found guilty of a terrible crime while refusing to admit his guilt, would have had to reconcile himself to facing the best part of a lifetime in jail.

Bob Duffield made his first research trip to Nottingham in late November 1992. Over the next four months there were to be fifteen more, most of them in the company of producer Stephen Phelps – like Steve Haywood, a former editor of *Rough Justice* who left the BBC so that he could devote himself more intensively to this sort of work. It was a brief, exploratory contact; Bob didn't expect to advance the state of the case beyond the scholarly case assessment that he always prepares from the original documents – studded with meticulous footnotes and references. He went to meet Mark's parents.

These are notes from his casebook.

BD Notes on meeting with parents

The overwhelming impression is one of sadness. She chain-smokes nervously. He looks very ill. They tell us how they had to move from Bestwood after Mark's arrest. Bricks through the window etc. Michael Cleary – older brother – lost leg after being rammed off motorbike by a car driver who hasn't been traced. Discussed Mark's childhood, background, interests. No known gay tendencies. Mad keen on his new moped at the time. They keep reassuring him they're looking after his helmet. Impressively, they've never given up hope. Deeply committed. Sadly, minimal evidential value.

Bob then went to meet Ron Birkett, Mark's campaigning solicitor, and then did the one thing which, in my view, would contribute most to the minimizing of miscarriages of justice; he went to the scene of the crime. The law glories in its dispassionate detachment from the mundane details of life – hence those wigs, those arcane rules of evidence, the collusive, collegiate, senior-common-room, dry-sherry wit of the courtroom. If members of the legal profession could only put on their gumboots and traipse across a few sodden fields they would realise that the crisp, starched version of events with which they are presented is – more than metaphorically – a world away from the creased and tangled truth. Bob saw at once the physical impossibility of wheeling two push-bikes (Atherton's and his victim's) as well as Mark Cleary's moped along the thorny, overgrown railway track. He saw the steep embankment down which Atherton claimed he wheeled his victim; it was virtually unnegotiable even on foot. (When we came to film the site, members of the film crew had to act as a sherpa chain gang, passing the tripod, camera and so on up the slope.) Solicitor and researcher walked across the road, then down the track to the River Leen and found that the path, which we had always assumed was a rutted track, was a metalled road passing through a residential area. Would Atherton really have taken the risk of taking his victim past the illuminated, nine o'clock windows of so many households?

Bob came back with the conviction that something was very wrong about this case. At the heart of it was the deeply implausible notion that a man weak enough to make an immediate confession to killing and attempting to bugger a child would wait for seven weeks before implicating an accomplice. He reported his news about the site visit at a case conference we were holding to determine the next programmes we were going to make. But most of us, apart from our reservations about Cleary being an old and distasteful case, were more interested in a complex conviction involving police malpractice in the North East.

Bob listened to the discussion with concern and bewilderment growing by the minute. He couldn't understand why we weren't going for the Cleary case. Here, he said, was prima-facie evidence of the most appalling and cruel miscarriage of justice. We knew about the treatment supposed sex criminals received in jail: routine physical assault, and revolting interference with their food. We were impressed that Mark Cleary had not invoked prison Rule 43, which grants such a prisoner the sanctuary of voluntary segregation. (Later, we learnt that we were wrong: Cleary had gone on to Rule 43.) I remember Bob saying that, however much Cleary lacked gangland glamour or the journalistic excitement of police corruption, 'this is exactly the sort of case Just Television should be taking on . . . and if we don't, we should pack it all in.' He was right. The glossy, high-profile cases, those with a rolling campaign bandwagon, may be better box office; but we went for Cleary.

The investigation entered its most exciting and unpredictable phase. You knock on a door and don't know what you will find behind it – except, almost certainly, that you'll get a lead to another door you'd never dreamed of knocking on. It is the journalistic equivalent of a cab-driver's day, never knowing where your next fare will take you, a random, pin-table voyage of discovery and disappointment. Those days and nights spent on the Bestwood estate provided the key to the case – the character of the true murderer, Philip Atherton.

Atherton's principal hobby, we soon discovered, was CB radio. It was very much an enthusiasm of the period, where the

9

excitement of being able to communicate made up for the fact that there was nothing of great significance to say. As an activity, it rivals train-spotting for the passion with which its devotees pursue it, and the bafflement of those who are not party to its arcane attraction. CB-ers have their own private vocabulary, originating in the tangled etymological undergrowth of truck-driving middle America – they 'request eyeballs' when they want to see someone. Atherton's call sign, his 'handle', was 'Track Marshal', we were told by another enthusiast who rejoiced in the handle of 'Collywobbles'. It became a running joke with the team, as we dreamt up appropriate handles for each other: Stephen Phelps, plagued by a continuous cold, was given the nickname 'Night Nurse'; Bob Duffield, who occasionally reverts to the donnish persona of the postgraduate Oxford anthropologist he once was, assumed the notional soubriquet 'Professor'. Penetrating the CB fraternity opened up a network of contacts. We soon learnt that Atherton had been beaten up for supposedly boasting on the air about having had sex with an under-age girl; it turned out, however, that he was innocent of both the deed and the boast – someone else had misappropriated his call sign.

Through contacts on the estate we began to build up a picture of Atherton. We learnt that he had difficulty being accepted by people of his own age, and compensated for this isolation by seeking the company of younger children. A young man called David Evans told us of the almost magical sway Atherton held over the youngsters of the neighbourhood. 'You'd follow him anywhere,' he told us, 'he used to tell us scary stories, do weird things.' One of the weirder games of this Pied Piper involved visiting the disused pit buildings and decapitating the pigeons who roosted there; 'he'd wring their necks and watch them flutter to the ground.' Among other things, we also heard that Atherton had a belt festooned with the tails of squirrels killed with a catapult. He would often offer to baby-sit for friends; but on one occasion he locked his charge in the boot of a car, and on another he set fire to some plastic model soldiers and flicked them, flaming and molten, at the children he was meant to be looking after. One of his acquaintances told us how he had once poured bleach into a tank of treasured tropical fish. The fish had died.

It was another tale of animal cruelty that took us closer to the heart of the case. Maxine Tulson had always been worried about the conviction of Mark Cleary. Maxine was a friend of Atherton's girlfriend, Theresa Monte. The Montes used to have a little dog, which would wake up the household whenever Atherton brought Theresa home late. One day, the dog disappeared. Atherton found it, wrapped in a plastic bag, drowned in the River Leen. He had taken a friend, John Jackson, with him on the 'search'. We found out that Jackson had since been imprisoned at HMP Stocken, and Bob made a special trip to confirm the tale.

It was a sombre and unnerving story, given the eventual fate of Wayne Keeton, but we know well the tendency in any community to demonize the guilty, and were therefore sceptical at first. At every turn, however, we found new instances of Atherton's amazing capacity to 'discover' things that had gone missing. Steve Snow told me how Atherton had run over his cat, and then offered to go looking for it. Maxine and her friend Stephanie Rawden told me how Atherton 'was always finding things,' such as a radio and a car which had been stolen from the Montes.

And this was the man who had 'discovered' the shoe of the murder victim.

We uncovered further, macabre aspects of Atherton's behaviour in the days after the murder and before the body was discovered. It seems that he took Cleary down to the very bridge under which the body was at that very moment secreted, and played a game of pooh-sticks – throwing twigs over the upstream side, and seeing which was first to emerge downstream. He took another friend to the same bridge and pondered aloud how strange it would be if the body, for which everyone was searching, was in fact only inches away. The day after Wayne's disappearance, Atherton even offered to sell a BMX bike 'for a tenner' to an acquaintance called Rob Smith. But when Atherton went to fetch it, the bike had disappeared. This was almost certainly Wayne's bike. Atherton seemed to be deriving some strange but pleasurable excitement from his secret knowledge of the boy's death, tempting suspicion, flirting with fate. We were later to learn more of this extra dimension of sensation sought by the psychopathic.

Intriguing as these stories were, all they did was to confirm Atherton's acknowledged guilt; they did not help to exonerate

11

Mark Cleary. We did, however, discover an early attempt by Atherton to point suspicion at the innocent. David Evans, who followed his pigeon-strangling exploits, was induced by Atherton to take part in blowing up a £30,000 bulldozer. After a satisfactory bang, Atherton abandoned the young man to carry the blame alone.

Even so, it's fair to say that spirits were pretty low. There comes a stage with any investigation where you have to make a fine calculation of the odds of success – and when to pull the plug. Fascinating as all this local colour was, we weren't getting any closer to the sniff of a clue pointing to Mark Cleary's innocence. Then, we had one of those lucky breaks that make up for months of tedious tramping through inhospitable estates. We were puzzled about Atherton using the name 'Adey' or 'Adie' – we had no more idea than the police how it was actually spelled – at the time that he met young Wayne. The police had obviously been concerned, too, because they had interviewed almost every young man called Adrian for miles around. For reasons Bob still can't remember (but he must have been getting fairly desperate to embark on such an expedition) he decided to inspect the allotment Atherton used to work. Maybe he'd find a neighbour who could tell him more about the man.

On the next-door patch was a large, awkward man wearing a windcheater and a baseball cap, as he forked away at some recalcitrant bindweed. Mr Rhodes wasn't easy to understand; his words came haltingly through a thick accent and a speech impediment. But yes, he remembered Philip Atherton. He certainly remembered the murder of young Wayne Keeton, for, shortly afterwards, the police had received a tip off that he, an epileptic with learning difficulties, was the murderer. 'If I see Atherton again, I'll smash his head in,' Rhodes told us, because, as he claimed and we were subsequently able to prove, it was Atherton who instigated the call, asking his girlfriend, Theresa Monte, to ring the police with Rhodes' name.

As Bob left, thanking him for this piece of information, he shook his hand and, for the first time, saw the blue letters tattooed on Rhodes' knuckles. Many people have the words LOVE and HATE inked into their flesh. Adrian Rhodes' knuckles were engraved with his own nickname – ADEY. Philip Atherton had pretended to be 'Adie' or 'Adey' at the time he picked up young Wayne. At first we thought he was picking a name at random; we could see it now as a terrifyingly cunning, calculated and manipulative act. Mr Rhodes was lucky – the police were able to eliminate him from their inquiry. In less fortunate circumstances, he might have suffered the fate of Stefan Kiszko, another man with learning disabilities who spent years in jail wrongly convicted of a child murder.

Meanwhile, Bob and Steve were scouring the CB fraternity in search of a witness who had made a strange statement which the police did not seem to have followed up. The witness, Reece Packard, had said that he'd seen a shadowy figure round about midnight lurking outside the Atherton family home. By midnight, of course, Atherton, by his own account, would have been home and in bed for two hours and more. The problem was that Reece Packard was not to be found. That most valuable researcher's tool – the phone book – yielded nothing. There was nothing for it but the laborious comb through the electoral rolls. In the local library at Eastwood – D. H. Lawrence's birthplace – the team began the tedious chore of checking through the lists of local residents. Electoral rolls are listed street by street, house number by house number, so there is no alphabetic short cut. It took three hours before Phelps found the name Derry Packard, who turned out to be Reece's sister. Bob and Steve set out for the address. Just as they were approaching the house, a car nosed out of the driveway. Having put so much effort into finding their quarry, the team were not about to see it slip away. For several miles they gave chase to the bemused, and of course entirely blameless, Ms Packard. When they had caught up with her, and after a sticky few moments while they had to explain their somewhat overenthusiastic pursuit, Derry Packard proved to be a charming and helpful lead. Within minutes, we had found her brother Reece.

Reece told us that what he had *said* to the police was a lot more definite than what *appeared* in his statement. This cuts both ways. Sometimes, it's best to be wary about a witness who develops a clearer picture, years later, than the statement offered at the time; sometimes, on the other hand, you find that the witness has never seen his own statement, and is shocked at

13

the partial, selective, biased, or inaccurate way his views have been represented. Reece Packard told us he was quite convinced that the midnight figure he had seen was Atherton. Indeed, he had met some policemen a few days later who told him that a man had been arrested in connection with the Keeton murder. 'Is it Atherton?' Packard had asked without hesitation. This is what led to Packard making his statement. The police, quite properly cautious about a 'fleeting glimpse' in the dark, asked him if he could be 100 per cent sure; equally properly, Reece Packard said that he couldn't be.

At this stage of the investigation two things were happening; Atherton was emerging as more devious and manipulative than we had imagined, and, to Bob's puzzlement, there seemed to be some confusion about Atherton's timetable of the terrible events that night. The time of the attack was beginning to slip later and later than that which Atherton had always claimed. But neither the police nor the defence had ever queried that timetable. Was this, then, to be another blind alley? Or could the emerging discrepancy somehow hold the answer to the case? Arguments about timing seldom add up – in our experience witnesses can be hours out – but it was something Bob didn't abandon.

Which was just as well. Timing was indeed to provide the key to the case. Within days, there was a breakthrough moment when we visited the home of Mr and Mrs Burgess.

We are always astonished at the open-heartedness with which strangers – after a few moments' understandable suspicion – are prepared to welcome us into their homes at odd hours of the day and night to ask them awkward and sensitive questions. A few, a very few, are abusive and violent, and, it has to be said, the area was polarized between those who supported Atherton's story, and those who stood for Cleary's innocence. Between the two camps there were threats of lighted cigarettes to be put through letterboxes, of undefined harm that would be done to the other side's children. But Mr and Mrs Burgess were kindness itself – even though we were invading the privacy of passionate Nottingham Forest supporters at a time of the Club's impending collapse from Premier League status. None of our subsequent meetings went ungarnished with mighty plates of meaty sandwiches, flagons of tea. Without demur, the Burgesses let us trample all over their house, conducting arcane experiments from their bedroom as we measured how much they could have heard from the embankment behind their home. The couple sat serenely in front of their majestic array of video-recorders and satellite-decoders as we made free with their hospitality and their home. The Burgesses were great television fans; we hope they still are, after having a television crew tramp its equipment over their carpets.

The reason for our curiosity had been buried in a statement Mrs Burgess had given. On the night of the murder, Mrs Burgess was on the edge of sleep when she'd heard a cry, 'Help me, help me,' from outside her bedroom window. The sound was unusual and distressing enough to make her leave her bed and go to the open casement. Her husband – a man used to the precision involved in setting his video – logged the time at 11.23 p.m. We knew that her evidence was significant, because it so accurately echoed what Atherton had described in his first statement to the police: the boy pathetically crying, 'Help me, mum, help me.' But at the time of the trial, no one had thought it important to ask Mrs Burgess to come to court; her statement had merely been read.

As a result, the court didn't understand what we had begun to realize was the crucial significance of this statement. Indeed, not only was its importance overlooked, but its value as evidence had been entirely discounted. When Mrs Burgess wrote that she'd heard the shout from the banking outside her window, she'd meant the disused railway embankment, just feet away. But the judge thought she had meant the bank of the River Leen, in completely the opposite direction, more than a quarter of a mile away, across a main road, from which a shout would have been inaudible. Obviously, if she was claiming to have heard a shout from there, she must have been wrong, or the cry must have been that of somebody else. If, of course, she had been asked to give evidence in person she could have tidied up the misunderstanding. But she wasn't. No one corrected the judge.

So, the evidence of Reece Packard and the Burgesses – plus a dog in a nearby farm which, according to its owners, barked around half-past eleven in a way it only did when strangers were around – all began to point to a later time for the murder.

But where did that get us? Evidence relating to timing is always fairly unreliable, although a discrepancy of as much as two hours did seem strange . . .

January was turning into a witheringly cold February. It was cruelly cold on the road as we traced and retraced Atherton's murderous journeys through the brambles of the overgrown track. The team returned to the Queen's Moat House hotel in Mansfield Road – we were to get to know the place so well that we would specify the room number when we booked – and, over coffee and warming brandies from the night porter, tried to make sense of the new pattern that seemed to be emerging. Atherton was a liar; but why, when you've admitted complicity in a killing, do you lie about the time you did it? The answer was not to come till later, but meanwhile we began to realize that a later time-frame did point to Cleary's innocence. After all, the only evidence against Cleary was his partial, and later withdrawn, confession. And it could only be valid if it matched the version of his supposed accomplice. In other words, if A says he committed a crime in January with B, and B is induced to agree, and then it turns out that the crime was in July, some doubt is bound to arise in the minds of the sceptical and dispassionate observer.

The Nottinghamshire Police had not been sceptical enough. They had secured an easy arrest in Atherton, and his implication of Cleary must have seemed a bonus. They had broken their own Chief Constable's guidelines for interviewing, by not taking proper contemporaneous notes, even though Atherton, the self-confessed killer, had enjoyed the privilege of scrupulously anno-tated interviews conducted by a different officer. And yet they purported to have had total recall when they came to writing up the interviews, even down to the precise turn of phrase and use of dialect idiom – sometimes Cleary says he has done 'nothing' wrong, and a few pages later he is protesting that he has done 'nowt' wrong. On one page he talks of 'me Dad' and 'me tea', but a few exchanges later he refers to 'my Dad'. We went to Birmingham University and showed the interview to a language expert. He told us that the record – written up as a script with dialogue from police and suspect – was a 'script'; it could not be what it purported to be, a verbatim record of what had gone on.

The idioms, explained Dr Malcolm Coulthard, gave 'a kind of playwright's veracity to the text' – not exactly the quality you are looking for in a police statement. I asked him how much of our two-hour conversation I would remember in twenty minutes' time, when the taxi would be taking me back to Birmingham New Street Station; if I tried to recall the conversation word-for-word, I'd get only one per cent of those words right. Food for thought for the reporter, and for those who claim to have been misquoted.

If there had been irregularities in the interviewing of Mark Cleary, it suggests that the police would not have been particularly interested in discrepancies in evidence that tended to cast doubt on his guilt, such as the possibility that the crime may have been committed later that night. The evidence of a much later time began to take concrete and incontrovertible shape. Buried in the statements were four individual pieces of evidence which were to provide the clinching argument. No wonder the defence and the police overlooked them, since each on its own didn't seem to add up to much. Susan Brealey and Teresa Cole were aged seventeen and fourteen when the murder took place. The statements they gave to the police at that time confirmed that they saw Wayne showing off on his bicycle between 9.30 and 10 p.m. on the night in question. (By Atherton's account the child would already have been dead for an hour or so by then.) Susan clearly remembers thinking that it was late for a little boy to be out, and that she had warned Wayne that there were nasty men about, and to be careful. Tears welled up in her eyes as she recalled her thoughts, presumably blaming herself for not having done more to protect the child. Susan and Teresa are no longer gawky teenagers hanging about the shops, but responsible mothers. We asked them what else they could remember about that sighting. Susan told us something intriguing; she herself had been worried about the lateness of the hour. She didn't like walking home in the dark. So she'd asked a local youth to walk her home to safety.

The problem was she couldn't remember his name. If we could trace this person, we might find independent confirmation of the teenagers' story of how much later Wayne was still alive. The seed of doubt about Atherton's first account, first sown by Reece

17

Packard who had seen the shadowy midnight figure he took to be Atherton, was beginning to grow. With Susan and Teresa's evidence, the suspicions about timing were building; the only problem was that we didn't quite know what it all meant, and we still needed some independent corroboration.

Back to the pile of witness statements – never, of course, heard in court, or deemed important by the authorities. Bob found the evidence of a young man called Stephen Barnett to the effect that he had walked two girls home but that *he* couldn't remember *their* names. At once, the pieces began to click into place, but first we had to find Stephen Barnett.

He was to prove elusive, probably because he did not want to be found. We traced his uncle, who made it clear that Stephen did not want to get involved. We knew he was a window cleaner. We toured the area asking for recommendations for local window cleaners, and his telephone number was among those we were given. By a mixture of fairish and foulish means, we managed to get Stephen's address. He was not pleased to see us, complaining that we were harassing him. This is, of course, a sensitive point for any investigative journalist. We work on the principle that it is acceptable to make every endeavour to trace someone. If, having heard our proposal, we are refused any cooperation, we must walk away and leave the person in peace. An honourable journalist will take 'No' for an answer if it is the refusal of a considered proposition. That's why we value people on our team who have the skill and charm to defuse antagonism, suspicion and distrust. We may follow up an initial approach with a letter; continued refusal means we must accept defeat. Harassment, involving camping outside someone's house, persistently ringing doorbells, and so on is not acceptable. It's all too easy to justify such actions because of the justice of the cause, but other investigators have come spectacularly unstuck by applying that justification; it certainly gives the enemies of our work a convenient stick with which to belabour our awkward activities.

There is also the moral dilemma of raking over what is inevitably, for someone, a family tragedy. We don't believe that innocent people should be kept in prison to spare a family's feelings; but we make it a priority to inform the family concerned before the news of our interest reaches them through cruel local rumour or a splash in the evening paper. We write to tell them what we are doing, apologize for any pain that may be involved, ask them if they wish to speak to us at all, and tell them that we understand entirely if they do not. We do not pretend that this does anything to assuage the hurt, but we think it is the right thing to do. I think the most dignified response we had was from the husband of a murder victim who told us that we should go ahead only if we really believed that there was evidence of the convicted man's innocence. It is, we were able to assure him, the *sine qua non* of our business. We simply would not pursue a case where we had severe doubts – though, as we'll see later, that can bring its own problems.

A reasonable explanation usually works, and it worked with Stephen. He agreed to meet the two girls he had so gallantly escorted home eight years earlier. When they met, the threesome recognised each other – a giggly reunion after so long. This strengthened the story of the later sighting. The girls had seen Wayne around 10 p.m., and Steve Barnett had walked one of them home. The three confirmed each other's stories. What would make things watertight would be an independent sighting of the three.

We uncovered it in the unlikeliest of places; we found the statement a fourth person had given to the police – disregarded at the time because it did not match Atherton's confessed version of the time of the assault. This person remembered meeting his friend Steve Barnett that night at the time that corresponded with the other three's stories. What's more, he remembered seeing Wayne doing his wheelies on his new bike at around ten at night. The young man who had given the statement was Michael Cleary, Mark's brother. But we didn't have to be fearful of any misplaced family loyalty – Michael had volunteered this statement very close to the time of Wayne's murder, weeks before any suspicion was to alight on his brother Mark. Michael's statement locks those of Stephen Barnett, Susan Brealey and Teresa Cole together, proving, we believe, that Wayne was alive at ten o'clock and that the murder happened much later than the version given by Atherton and agreed to by the police and the jury.

The only evidence against Mark Cleary was his own confession. It had only stood up because it matched the story of the self-confessed killer. But that story was wrong in one significant detail – the timing, designed in Atherton's story to give him the chance of an alibi. We added that to the catalogue of doubt: the absurdity of the weak-minded Atherton waiting seven weeks before incriminating a genuine accomplice; the impossibility of Cleary manhandling his moped along the track; the authentic ordinariness of his own alibi; Atherton's devious tendency to seek ways to put the blame on to others . . .

Not all the discoveries were made on location. Much of our work involves talking to specialists – such as the language expert in Birmingham. By definition, much of this expertise also concerns the grisly details of human pathology. Wayne Keeton, we knew, had died of drowning – he was still alive when he fell in the river. The presence of tiny organisms, which live in water, in the tissues of the recovered body confirmed this; anyone entering the water alive breathes in these micro-organisms, which would then be found in the lungs and even the brain. But Wayne's body was also found to have considerable damage to the spleen – an organ that mystifies most of us, but which generally supervises the body's immune systems. The wound must have been inflicted – according to Atherton – by the kick Cleary was supposed to have delivered to the boy.

The spleen bleeds very freely when injured. We took the post-mortem results to Professor Alistair Wilson, an accident and emergency specialist attached to the London Hospital, who routinely goes to the scene of major accidents to tend to trauma patients. Many times we have looked out of the Just Television windows, across the London skyline, to see a distinctive orange helicopter clattering purposefully across the capital; it belongs, in fact, to the London Hospital, and is usually carrying Professor Wilson and his team of trained paramedics.

Professor Wilson could not square the bleeding from the spleen (relatively minor) with the story of the boy being kicked some time and distance away from when his body fell into the River Leen. He was deeply unconvinced by Atherton's account of transporting the boy from the scene of the attack to the banks of the river; he would have expected a much greater loss of blood from the spleen as a result of such an agonizing journey.

We do spend rather more time than is good for our health with pathologists. In our library we have a couple of illustrated textbooks of forensic pathology which we insist are kept locked in a filing cabinet; there are pictures in it no one should have to see. However, much often turns on a pathological detail, and, as with any piece of evidence, we argue fiercely among each other over it. One day, on another case, the argument had become quite heated as the three of us sat at the table of the pavement cafe for a lunchtime sandwich. One of us was convinced that we could get access to some samples used at a trial several years earlier. Another of us feared that the police would either have destroyed them or lost them, or that the integrity of the original specimen would have been corrupted by reacting with xylene, the compound used to fix them to the microscopic slide. The third suggested that at least we could prepare an experiment to measure the decay of tissue fragments (the case revolved around the length of time the corpse had lain undiscovered). We became engrossed in the mechanics of such an experiment and the way in which the developing larvae of the blowfly can be used, in conjunction with meteorological data, to estimate the time of death. We were involved in elaborate conjecture about the disposal of bodies, when we were aware of the waitress hovering at our side. It became clear that she had been waiting for some time for a break in the heated debate. 'I don't know who ordered the prawn salad sandwich,' she said, 'but whichever one of you it is, I'm glad I'm not your girlfriend.'

In the case of Mark Cleary, another medical man helped put the case into a more plausible context. Dr Jeremy Coid is the forensic psychiatrist at the Secure Unit at Hackney Hospital. I have two principal memories of the day we spent with him: the constant jingle and clatter of locks and keys of the double-doored security airlocks; and the vague unease that came over me, as I watched an animated game of snooker, when I was told that several of those engaged in the game were killers.

Dr Coid reviewed the evidence in the light of his own experience of forensic psychiatry, warning us quite properly that, without access to Atherton, his observations had to be general ones. He was intrigued at the shift in Atherton's statements; the earliest were full and comparatively detailed confessions, while the later slid much more of the blame on to Cleary for initiating both the sexual and physical attack and were strangely muted when it came to detail. Did the discrepancy in the second statement – the one where he suddenly blamed Cleary – lie in the difference between the immediacy of a first-hand experience, and the inevitably mistier description of a fantasy...? Certainly, had two people been involved in the murder, it seemed odd that not a hint of the cooperation, the relationship between the two attackers, had come out in the version where Atherton put the blame on Cleary.

What Dr Coid made clear was that a murder such as this was a crime of control; the killer had derived pleasure from the vulnerability of his victim. Dr Coid guessed – correctly – that Atherton would have enjoyed the sense of power that came from knowing where the body was, while others searched for it; those macabre games of pooh-sticks all made sense to him. Did Atherton, even behind prison walls, still derive pleasure from the one element of control he could still exercise – the power over Mark Cleary's destiny? He and Cleary once met in prison; according to Cleary, Atherton taunted him with the power he held – the power to speak or stay silent, the power to free his former friend or leave him to rot.

The medical and psychological evidence meshed in with what we'd absorbed on the ground. Let's imagine what could have been going through Atherton's mind, at the time when he learned the details of the coroner's report, particularly the fact that, even though Wayne died of drowning, the injury to the spleen would have, nevertheless, been fatal. It had been agreed that there was insufficient physical evidence to support a charge of buggery – and, to help spare what was left of the family's feelings, it was decided to make little of that aspect of the attack in the report. Armed with this information, Atherton suddenly drops all references to the sexual motive he'd previously admitted to. And now that he knows that the boy was alive when he left him on the river bank, he retracts his original admission, 'he was dead when he fell in, I'm positive.' Now that he knows that the boy was suffering from a fatal injury to his spleen, he places the blame for the kick squarely on Cleary. He sees the chance of a lesser charge for himself – perhaps manslaughter – by heaping his guilt upon Cleary.

His own role in the terrible events of that night is thus made to dwindle significantly, and the onus is transferred to his alleged accomplice. It is a cunning and vindictive plan. We have heard – and had the statement independently confirmed – that Atherton has said that Cleary will stay in prison until he, Atherton thinks fit. It is the last, precious vestige of power that Atherton has as a prisoner – the power over an innocent man's life.

And the discrepancy in the timing? We believe that Atherton, even before deciding to implicate Cleary, had always had the notion of a makeshift alibi at the back of his mind, a notion which survived even as he made his admission to the police, placing the crime much earlier in the evening. By the time he realised that he could transfer the guilt to Cleary, he was stuck with this false timetable, which Cleary, knowing no better because he wasn't there, innocently echoes in his 'confession.'

We made the programme. Some details will always stay with me. There was the courage of Mick Ryan, the alibi witness for Mark Cleary who said, honestly and fatally, that he couldn't remember what he'd been doing that evening. He had proved very hard to find. We left message after message for him. But either he wasn't contactable, or didn't want to be contacted. So we were astonished, one evening, to hear that he was waiting for us downstairs in the hotel foyer. Downstairs, indeed, was a shy young man with a speech impediment aggravated by the obvious stress he was under in coming to see us. At this stage, we had given up hope of locating him, though he would have been useful in demonstrating the flimsy thread on which Cleary's guilt or innocence hung. Mick didn't want to take part in the programme, mainly because of his embarrassment about his stammer. We didn't push it, but tried to assure him that he wouldn't be made to look foolish. In the end, with great dignity, he returned to the courtroom and re-enacted his nervous ordeal. He gave a wonderfully graphic account of the terror of the ordinary mortal facing the majesty of the law. 'In the end, when it was over', he said, 'I got out of the witness box, but couldn't open the door to get out of the court . . . my hands were too sweaty to be able to turn the brass handle.'

Mick Ryan spoke movingly, and it took courage to help us. It made up for those darker moments – like the time we toiled up thirty-eight floors of the Victoria Centre council flats, only to get a door slammed in our faces by someone who 'didn't want to get involved'.

Turning the research into a television programme had, as ever, its moments of absurdity. Filming is a constant compromise between the demands of exposition, and the imperative of making a watchable programme. It's also an agonizingly cooperative exercise. The sound department was not happy when a passing airbus rumbled across the sky during an outside interview, whereas I didn't want to spoil the flow; there was always too much or too little light for the cameraman; the director liked the take of a piece-to-camera where the dappled sunlight fell artistically across my face, whereas I would rather use the version when I succeeded in remembering my lines. And we were always hungry. As ever, we would try to cram in too much filming, too many interviews; the neat daily schedule, which looked so promising at breakfast, had begun to look positively fictional by lunchtime, and, by three in the morning, a mere fantasy – especially when the 'wrap' time was listed as 6 p.m.

One particularly low point found us all looking for somewhere to have lunch at four in the afternoon in Arnold, a suburb of Nottingham. It took all our investigative skills to find anything at all to eat; eventually we found the customers' cafeteria at the local Asda supermarket. I am sure that, at lunchtime, Asda has a veritable banquet on offer; I am sure that, by mid-morning, the all-day breakfast is a sight to savour. But when the all-day breakfast has been around all day, and what's left of the lunch is what Asda's clientele have scrutinized and thought better of, only sheer hunger gets you through the meal. Hunger, and the comforting certainty that, wherever you are, somewhere, in the small hours, there will be a late-night curry waiting.

One disastrous sequence involved the attempt to recreate the progress of a body floating downstream. There was, I hasten to say, an evidential purpose to the exercise, to show that a submerged object, deposited in the river at point A, could not have made it to point B. So as not to disturb any casual passers-by, we had decided to film this sequence late at night. Discretion was indeed the watchword; we intended to film the operation as sensitively as we could; there had, after all, been a real murder, a real tragedy. We had brought up from London a body of the appropriate dimensions. The camera was set to film the delicate dark ripples of water on the moonlit surface.

Unfortunately, you need light even to film darkness. And when you are lighting a considerable area of rural Nottinghamshire, you need quite a lot of light to provide the merest shimmer of implicit moonlight. So we turned up at our discreet location to find a colossal crane, a throbbing generator, and a lamp of a size which Cecil B. de Mille might have considered somewhat on the vulgar side. That night we turned night into day. For miles around, puzzled cockerels cock-a-doodled, and predatory owls returned early to their nests. Only the deployment of teams of loudspeaker vans could have made our sensitive filming more overt. But there was worse to come. When it came to the filming, our body wouldn't sink. It floated, grossly, into shot. The problem was that it wasn't sufficiently waterlogged. We tried again, but still it failed to sink, and instead sailed triumphantly along and over a weir. Eventually, the camera assistant, Theo, was deputed to see what he could do to make the body heavier. Theo waded out into the freezing stream, retrieved the dummy, and tried to hold it under, so that it would absorb more water. Unfortunately, the natural buoyancy of the thing made it pop out from under Theo's grasp, like some gigantic trout snapping at a midnight fly. Theo wrestled with it again, plunging it back beneath the surface of the water. The dummy, however, seemed to have acquired a life of its own. For some time the two were locked in epic struggle, until Theo subdued his rubber adversary.

Fortunately, no one came our way. Otherwise, I'm not sure how we'd have explained the sight of two figures grappling, mid-stream, in the darkness, one clearly intent on submerging the other, while the rest of us looked on in helpless, silent laughter.

It was strange to present the programme from the Shire Hall, from the very court – now decommissioned – where Mark Cleary had himself stood trial and which, in happier days, he had polished and scrubbed. The programme was broadcast in June 1993. It was well received, most importantly by senior officials in both the Home Office and the Court of Appeal, who asked for a copy of the programme. The barrister David Martin-Sperry has since taken up the case, on the basis of our research, only a twentieth of which actually reaches the screen. Interestingly, when we took him up to Nottingham to look at the scene of the crime – a rare encounter with reality for most of m'learned friends – he said it was one of the most useful days he could remember in his professional career.

At the time of writing I received the following letter from Mark Cleary:

> I thought it only right that I should write to you, because the response since your programme has been overwhelming. If the last bit of information that I've had is right, which is 'the case is likely to be heard before the end of the year, and would probably take place before the Christmas recess' then it shall give me even more to celebrate, as I intend to get engaged in December to a person I thought I'd lost forever thirteen years ago. Maybe one day I shall get the chance and tell you the story. But until then I'm praying and hoping that this year will be the year of all years. So once again, thank you for all that you've done.

It was good of him to write; it is good for us to be reminded that, at the heart of a detective story, there is the genuine tragedy of two lives – one, a child's life, lost, and the other shattered by the failure of justice. But things, as we shall see in chapter Twelve, were to change dramatically.

2
Mary Druhan
A Down-and-Out Injustice

Mary Druhan arrived in a couple of large cardboard boxes. Most cases do. Habitually we refer to the casefiles simply by name – 'where's the rest of Druhan? I've lost half of her?' – which can be a little unsettling for those unfamiliar with the protocol. The state in which the boxes arrived – battered, crumpled, and held together with heavy-duty tape on its last adhesive gasp – was an apt reflection of the ragged life that Mary led, before British justice sent her to prison for two murders we believe she did not commit.

Justice – with a capital J – had sent us the case of Mary Druhan. The law reform group is the pre-eminent organization dealing with miscarriages of justice. Justice's reputation, its grandiloquent title – officially the British Section of the International Commission of Jurists – and its erstwhile Chancery Lane address belie the fact that the charity can barely keep its own head above water, let alone provide a lifeline to the hundreds of prisoners who write in every year pleading for help. Justice – in those days at least – was located up three flights of stairs in the Dickensian clutter of two-and-a-half rooms leased on a peppercorn rent from the National Westminster Bank. The photocopier was a museum piece, and when it seized up it had to be galvanized into action by a manoeuvre specifically warned against in the manufacturer's handbook. Shelves buckled and tottered under the weight of files. The small but dedicated staff, many of them volunteers or law students, picked their way through the formidable paperwork of a thousand manila-clad claims of injustice.

Trial and Error has a special arrangement with Justice, who send us cases which they think can benefit from the on-the-ground research and forensic investment in which we specialize. They are just one of the sources of our cases. Many, written on that familiar regulation-issue blue-ruled paper, come from prisoners, or from prisoners' families; others from concerned probation officers, even from prison officers, as well as from solicitors and barristers. Nearly all of them start with the sentiment 'in all my professional career there's only been one case which really worries me . . .'

As a Justice case, we knew that Druhan was bound to have some merit. Justice has a no-nonsense nose for plausible miscreants with too much time on their hands, and trying to trade on the woolly goodwill of penal liberals. They, like we, are sceptical about the professional criminal's frequent outrage at being rightly convicted, but for the wrong reasons. It was a case, from the outset, that we were bound to take seriously.

There is always a thrill of anticipation as you open the first file of a new case. Could this be the one – the one in fifty – that will make it to the air and, more importantly, back to the Appeal Court? In fact, although it turned out to be a fascinating case that helped put us on the map after we'd left the BBC's *Rough Justice*, there were many times we would wish we'd never touched it.

It wasn't just that the case stank. So, regrettably, did most of those involved. And, by the end of each day, most of us couldn't wait for a hot bath with half a capful of Dettol in it. It was a case which took us to the desperate edge of the life of the dispossessed, and into the territory of the manic and deranged. Most people will have had the experience of seeing a ragged, lurching drunk heading their way on a pavement; usually, we try to give that sort of person as wide a berth as possible.

To crack the Druhan case, we lived with them for months.

For Nina Davies, the researcher who undertook most of the investigative work, a particularly low point was when she had to change the knickers of an incontinent, and totally incapable, female alcoholic, while her two drunken male colleagues screamed abuse. I will always associate the case with the scent of menace and strong cider, being threatened with an imminent head-butt by people who were weaving on the borderline between aggression and maudlin acquiescence.

Mary Druhan herself lived on that borderline. She was fifty-three, a drifter staggering from council bed-and-breakfast accommodation, to hostels, to squats. Her unlikely territory was the prim purlieu of Surbiton – self-styled 'jewel of the suburbs' – and the Royal borough of Kingston on Thames. The area supports about thirty such vagrants. There is an ecology of deprivation, we were to discover, which sets fairly definite limits on the numbers who can survive in any particular location. Mary was a familiar face in this little clan of the dispossessed, who huddled together for companionship and a share of each other's weekly giro cheque. At least once a day a core of them would gather in Claremont Gardens, Surbiton: 'StarryEyes' Bob Smith, Joe 'Dancer' Neary (so called because of his lethal habit, when drunk, of waltzing with cars in the four-lane Kingston one-way system), 'Winkle' (who never told us his name in case his mother found out about him; he used to be a getaway driver for a criminal gang) and 'Rubberlegs' Kenny Roberts.

Rubberlegs Roberts was Mary's lover. They were a turbulent couple, bickering at each other with the desperate devotion of the mutually dependent. One June night in 1988 Mary Druhan burnt her lover to death, in a fire which consumed his squat and also took the life of another vagrant, Dick Duddy. There was no chance that it was an accident; the fire had been set in three places – and therefore deliberately, maliciously, murderously. That, at least, was what Reading Crown Court accepted as the truth, and was the basis on which the jury convicted her. There is only one sentence for murder, and that is life.

What life actually means is usually governed by a semi-secret little convention, by which the trial judge writes a recommendation which is later discussed between the Home Office and a senior judge. What also makes a difference – at least to any hopes of early release on licence – is whether or not prisoners admit the crime, and so display due penitence as well as satisfying dour prison therapists that they have confronted their own guilt. When you are not guilty, this poses something of a dilemma. Should you go through the motions of remorse, in order to shorten the injustice, or continue to protest your innocence – at the cost of prolonging a sentence which you should not be serving? Sir Ludovic Kennedy, my friend and mentor, always maintains that prisoners who persist in proclaiming their innocence should be taken seriously for that very reason. I always used to think his view the one soft spot in his philosophy – after all, aren't prisons full of 'innocent' people? In fact, he's right: most people stop protesting their innocence after a couple of years or so. They have either realized their campaigns are getting them nowhere, and have decided to buckle down to their sentence, or they have calculated that protest is only going to induce the Home Office to prolong their imprisonment.

In late September, 1992, in her first assignment as a researcher for *Trial and Error*, Nina Davies began the task of reconstructing the events of that fatal night from the Druhan paperwork. The best way to get an overall view of a case is to read the judge's summing-up; whatever their faults, the British judiciary are good at pulling together the strands of a story into a workmanlike précis of events, providing a reasonable narrative of how the case unfolded in court. It's as good a way as any of judging how strong the evidence was on either side, and how reliable the witnesses. The next step is to look at a much shorter document – the grounds for appeal which the prisoner's barrister has cobbled together, which could involve new evidence that has come to light since the original trial. More often, the grounds of appeal are tedious details of legal technicality. These are not so interesting to us; for better or for worse, we are not interested simply in people who have been wrongly convicted; they have to satisfy a stricter criterion – that they are innocent of the crimes for which they have been convicted. To lawyers, this is a less important distinction than it is to laymen – that's why we are not lawyers. It does help, when you are cold, wet, tired, hungry, and waiting for a contact who never turns up, to believe that you are doing this on behalf of an innocent person.

Within a few days, Nina had pieced together the bare bones of the Mary Druhan case, and it looked fairly unpromising. That is, of course, the usual state of affairs at this stage; what you have read is the official record of how a person was convicted by due process of law, and the account is the same as that which persuaded the jury that the accused – in this case Mary Druhan – was guilty beyond reasonable doubt of the charge of murder. Evidence of a startling miscarriage of justice is hardly likely to leap out from such a source.

The evidence was that Mary and her lover, 'Rubberlegs' Kenny Roberts, met up one evening with 'StarryEyes' Bob Smith. Bob, for once, was in the money, having recently come out of prison and collected the back benefit owed to him by the DHSS – some ninety-pounds-worth. (The judge remarked acidly to the jury: 'Ladies and gentlemen, that, it seems, is what we pay our taxes for.') Well-stoked with cans of export-strength lager, the trio repaired to the Kingston Mill pub by the riverside. It is a pleasant enough place, particularly favoured, these days, by students from the nearby university. Before long, however, a drunken argument began. Mary Druhan accused her lover, Kenny, of carrying on with another woman, called Patsy. Voices were raised in a jealous fury fired by alcohol. According to another man in the pub, Keith Fludgate, Druhan threw beer, and slammed her can on the table, saying she would kill Kenny.

This was all too much for StarryEyes, who had hoped that the evening would turn out to be a celebration of his freedom and his financial windfall. He left the couple arguing. He has no idea about what he did for the next few hours, but later that evening he went round to Number 15 Canbury Park Road, a residential street close to Kingston station, where Joe 'Dancer' Neary and 'Rubberlegs' Roberts dossed, along with a shifting population of other down-and-outs. Mary stumped off to the station, in a huff; there, she was seen by the British Rail ticket collector, who knew her well – Mary would often spend the night in the waiting-room on the platform, until disturbed by the arrival of the dawn commuters.

According to the admittedly drunken Bob Smith, when he returned to Number 15 he found Mary had come back from the station and turned up at 15 Canbury Park Road to continue her furious row with Kenny. Kenny was rolling on the floor while Mary hailed a welter of kicks on him. StarryEyes separated the couple, trying to pacify Mary while Kenny went off to seek refuge with Joe Neary – 'Dancer' was trying to get some sleep throughout the racket. Mary then left, according to StarryEyes.

The next thing Joe Neary says he remembers is hearing the downstairs door open, and the clatter of a pile of paint cans in the hall as someone blundered into them in the dark. There was electricity at Number 15, but all the bulbs had burnt out and no one had bothered to replace them. A few minutes later, he was aware of thick, acrid smoke curling into the first-floor room where he was trying to sleep. The house was on fire.

Joe tried to wake up Kenny, but, true to his Rubberlegs nickname, Kenny was too far gone with drink. He rushed upstairs to the second floor, where another vagrant, Dick Duddy, was asleep, but Dick, too, was in a stupor from which he could not be shaken awake. Joe then came down to the first floor landing, smashed his way out of the window, and went down a ladder conveniently parked against the back of the house. Rather strangely, he then went off to sleep in the municipal gardens, as if the conflagration and death of his friends were no more than an irritating and inconvenient interruption of his nocturnal routine.

Bob Smith, meanwhile, had left Number 15 to continue his night on the razzle, until he was alerted by the sound of the fire engines. Staggering back to the house, he seems to have made enough of a nuisance of himself to get arrested; certainly he was initially suspected of involvement in the fire. Having taken in the situation, he had gone to another pub, by no means the closest pub, supposedly to raise the alarm. He shouted, in slurred and ambiguous terms, that it was all his fault, he was responsible for the deaths of those inside the house. Perhaps he felt guilty for having funded the fatal pub crawl. He also blamed an unspecified group of glue-sniffers for having set the house ablaze.

Mary Druhan, too, was among the crowd which gathered to watch as the fire ripped through Number 15. At or around midnight, two bodies were brought out. The scene-of-crime photographs – always the part of our investigation which calls for a stiff drink – showed that Druhan's lover Kenny had been charred almost beyond recognition, while Dick Duddy, the man upstairs, had died of asphyxia, choking on the smoke.

Surrey Police immediately registered the tragedy at 15 Canbury Park Road as a probable crime. Their suspicions had been alerted when they detected the remaining taint of inflammable liquids – white spirit, most likely – in the hall, the presumed seat of the fire.

It was, for Mary Druhan, a fatal assumption.

It is a lot easier to be wise with hindsight, of course. But the police might not have been so convinced that the fire was deliberately started if they had known of two important facts. First, the house had belonged to a painter and decorator called

Joe Grummit, who had used it to store, in fairly chaotic fashion, his stocks of paint, turps, wood dye ... and white spirit. When Grummit left the house, which was bought by the council and was due for demolition a matter of days after the fire, he abandoned his equipment. He was off to Ilfracombe for his retirement, and he never wanted to see another can of 'thinners' again in his life.

There was a second reason why the traces of inflammable liquids may not have been quite as suspicious as the police originally assumed. Ignorant of the character of the lodgers at Number 15, they cannot have known that, for the likes of Rubberlegs, white spirit was just part of the normal recreational intake of alcohol. Joe Neary, we were to learn, had been known to turn in desperation to paint stripper – with terrible effects on the lining of his stomach. In equally dire, but more ladylike straits, Mary would choke down some shop-lifted eau-de-Cologne. Grummit's abandoned materials were, in part at least, the group's cocktail cabinet.

Once the police have formed a suspicion, they find it hard to let go of it – a healthy enough attitude, generally speaking, in the police, but also a path along which many dangers lie. Time after time, our experience tells us and bears us out, a miscarriage of justice has its roots in the tenacity with which the police seize upon an initial suspicion – and will not let it go. It happens, usually, when they have a suspect who they are certain, in their own minds, is guilty; from that point on, the investigation ceases to be a neutral enquiry, but is dedicated to collecting proof of the individual's guilt. Evidence which points to innocence is, often in all good faith, discarded as irrelevant. A tunnel vision, a blinkered focus on the fixed idea of a particular conviction, sets in.

I have known a case where the police, presumably anxious to shore up a suspicion, ordered the destruction of a bloodied palm-print found at the scene of a murder, because it didn't match the prints of the suspect. That palm-print could have exonerated the two men who served fourteen years between them for a murder some policemen at least must have suspected they did not commit. Evidence that doesn't 'help' the case is disregarded, and the police may compensate for the absence of more useful, corroborative evidence by planting or inventing it. A confession is blurted out in the back of a police car. An earring, supposedly belonging to the murder victim, inexplicably appears in circumstances linking it with the suspect. This is not simply wickedness by the police; it is a combination, in our experience, of an urgent pressure from public opinion to get results, a very human desire to get facts to fit a prejudice, and a decline in investigative skills – the use of informers and the extraction of confessions have tended to eclipse a tradition of patient and intelligent detection. Meanwhile, the real culprit goes free, because of the refusal of the police to countenance any alternative to the guilt of the men upon whom they had wrongly fastened their unbudgeable suspicions. It's an argument for taking the investigation of crime away from the police, and putting it in the hands of a Scottish-type Procurator-fiscal or a continental magistrate, a *juge d'instruction* – though not an argument I totally subscribe to. (See chapter 6.)

The assumption, then, was that the fire at Number 15 was suspicious. It didn't take the police long to hear – from Joe Neary and Bob Smith – of the previous night's furious row involving Mary Druhan. Druhan was taken in for questioning and accused of the murder. She constantly resisted pressure to admit to her guilt; the tapes of her interview contain the following exchange:

Police: Now Mary . . . it's you who is lying, you who are deceiving yourself.
Druhan: Why should I be blamed in the wrong, I've been blamed in the wrong in the past and I'm not going to be blamed in the wrong this time . . . I don't want to partake in this interview, I've explained what happened to the best of my ability and I'm making no lies up. I'm terribly distressed at what's happened – no, not distressed, I'm going round the twist in my head.

In spite of her passionate denials, Mary Druhan was charged with murder, tried, and convicted.

Mary and her companions led chaotic lives, and this made our re-investigation of the case one of the hardest we had ever undertaken. The commonest problem in journalism is that people –

34

usually for entirely sensible reasons – do not want to speak to you, but at least you know when and where to get to see them. The vagrant community has plenty of excellent reasons for not getting involved with anything remotely involving authority, and firm ways of making this attitude clear; the team's favourite warning-off – preferred because of its vivid originality – came from the man who warned us that if we came a step closer, 'I'll pull your head off and shit down your neck.' Vagrants are also, by definition, mainly of no fixed abode. Most of the people we needed to speak with had no idea where they would be at any particular time; indeed, it would not be an exaggeration to say that, through the fumes of cider and meths, many of the people we met did not know where they were at the time we met them.

An investigation proceeds on two levels, and in two stages. First, there is the reading of all the case papers – everything from the statements of witnesses collected by the police to the judge's final summing up. A preliminary glance at the statements showed us the sort of territory we were about to explore:

Statement of Ronald Besant, unemployed
... Me, Jim the Pole and another Irish chap, I don't know his name ... Mary was attacking Ken with a bottle over a girl. I got hold of Ken and told Mary to fuck off. Mary then left. Mary did not hit Ken with the bottle. I gave Mary a pound to fuck off.

And this – incoherent and self-contradictory within four lines – is a statement *after* it has been tidied up and processed through the police typewriters. It was to prove an accurate forecast of the chaotic social territory we were to explore, once we entered the second phase, and hit the streets.

One of Nina's early field notes (we keep daily records as scrupulously as we can, often recording them on tape as we go) gives a flavour of the problems:

ND Kingston; 23 October; 11.15

At last (fifth visit) I've found Bob Smith – survivor of fire and principal prosec. witness. Passing All Saints when I saw the police bundling a drunk into a van. A skinny man with a Rasta hat was remonstrating and I asked him if he was Smith. Loud and very incoherent conversation, as he refused to remove his Walkman. Two of us screaming at each other in middle of street. Says he can tell me 'the whole story.' Very pissedly maudlin about Mary – 'like a mother to me ... we used to go heisting [shoplifting] together.' Says 'the Irish boys' want Mary kept in for life, as revenge for death of Dick and Kenny, but he thinks she's innocent (odd, coming from principal prosec. witness!) Engaging bullshitter. Slightly worrying that when he returned after buying a packet of fags he had completely forgotten we'd met, and repeated conversation more or less verbatim. Arrange to meet at his place – make contact with landlord, Revd. Ted Belcher. (??)

I won't forget the Reverend Ted Belcher in a hurry, either. Ted has no formal theological background – the title is self-awarded. He is a former children's entertainer and Punch and Judy man, but it must be years since any parent knowingly invited him to their offspring's birthday party. Not that the Revd Ted is anything but a perfect gentleman – it's just that he doesn't seem to have changed his clothes for about ten years. He gave me the impression that as his clothes grew ragged and wore out, he would simply put on another layer. At skin level, presumably, there was merely a residual pattern of threads, which, in turn, would turn to dust and yield to the layer above it. There is some evidence for this surmise, because the Revd Ted is not scrupulous about securing his trouser buttons. His underpants (or at least that layer of his undergarments closest to the surface) resemble an antique, yellowing parchment map, the continents defined in heavier stains. But he is, in other respects, a kindly soul, a father to Bob Smith who he tries, in vain, to turn away from the satanic temptations of the bottle.

No nightmare could do justice to the state of his dwelling. From floor to ceiling, the place is stacked with – well, with everything. The contents of a thousand skips, the unsold remnants of a million jumble sales, are crammed into the two-up, two-down. You fight your way past rusty bicycles, an infinite number of empty egg-boxes, and, eerily, a mountain of dolls and soiled soft toys, confounded with the disembodied pink plastic limbs of shop-window mannequins, like a Grand Guignol charnel house.

The Reverend hacks his way, as if tackling the jungle with a machete, to the stove, where solidified fat stands encrusted an inch thick. He invites me to share a fry-up. For a fleeting moment, I share the sensation of those members of the royal family who, in the attempt to maintain the bonds of the commonwealth, have to drink a brew of herbs masticated and regurgitated by hospitable and respectful tribes. The Revd Ted's poodle methodically and fixedly sought sexual relief on Nina's leg.

Joe Neary, like StarryEyes Bob, the other survivor of the fire and witness against Mary Druhan, lived by himself in a council flat – though he was in permanent danger of eviction for failing to pay his rent. He lived in just one of the three rooms, spending his days sitting on his bed, glazedly watching his black-and-white television with the sound off. The manic smiles of daytime television hosts, the demented scamper of cartoon animals, provided Joe's mute stimulation in the days until the giro came round when the money for drink had run out.

On my first meeting, there was another person in the room; Helen, the ruin of a gentlewoman from Tunbridge Wells – things had gone wrong after her husband walked out on her – lay recovering from a black eye, deep in the anaesthetic balm of drink.

I don't think I ever met Bob Smith sober – and I met him at least ten times – and a conversation with Joe Neary was like a dialogue conducted through double-glazing. What was already becoming clear was the utter unreliability of the two of them, the principal witnesses against Mary Druhan. They would have sounded plausible enough at Mary's trial, of course – the police took the commendable precaution of keeping them as sober as possible, to the extent, we found, of locking Bob Smith up over the luncheon adjournment at Reading Crown Court. That's another, familiar exasperation in the work – the clinical tidiness of evidence as it is produced in court, wearing its Sunday best, when the truth is so much more ragged and bedraggled.

But merely exploring the credibility of the witnesses was not going to be enough. It might help to convince our audience – what we refer to, in shorthand, as the People's Court. But we have, if we are lucky, a second, and more highly critical audience to satisfy – the Court of Appeal. We decided to concentrate on two further aspects of the case – the nature of the fire, and the evidence of motive – that furious, and fatal row in the Kingston Mill pub.

It had always puzzled us, this notion of Mary, drunk, purblind and arthritic, skittling round the house in the dark and stoking up three separate fires. The scenario suited the prosecution of course, in our adversarial system, for it showed that Mary was a calculating, deliberate arsonist; the more seats of fire, the greater the demonstrable malice. Yet our instinctive feeling was that no one, in the chaotic world of these derelict people, could ever manage anything quite so *organized*. Again, it came back to that gap of perception between the courtroom, with its striving for order, simplicity, tidiness, and the random world of the vagrants. Chronic alcoholics can burn down a house in a fit of fury; what they can't do is plan to burn down a house in a set of deliberate actions. The problem is that while most barristers or judges have been a bit tiddly after a Bar dinner, few live their lives in the turbulent and frenzied world of people like StarryEyes, Dancer, or Mary Druhan. Their discipline is to bring order out of chaos; they cannot comprehend that some chaos is ungovernable, unmarshallable, undistillable. For some, chaos is the natural state of living.

Steve Haywood, the producer of the Druhan programme, concentrated on the forensic evidence while Nina spent time on the ground. He consulted experts on the flow of fires, which was an education in itself. Most – ourselves included – have a hazy view that fire spreads rather like an encroaching stain. We were soon to discover the phenomenon of the flashover, where the ambient gases of the atmosphere heat up to the point where a spontaneous explosion of fire occurs. We also discovered the importance of venting – how a fire seeks out a flue, rushing towards it as a stream desperately seeks its own level, how a stairwell can become a blowtorch – the King's Cross Underground fire being the terrible, classic example. Our learning, and, it has to be said, the barbecued images of the scene of crime photographs, led to more than one of us belatedly installing domestic smoke detectors.

We had two good breaks on the fire evidence. One was the result of picking through the statements. Joe Neary, we discovered, admitted to lighting a fire in the first floor kitchen, to make a cup of tea. This was significant for two reasons. First, the place was strewn with litter and rubbish, and any stray spark could have accounted for at least one of the three seats of fire which Mary Druhan supposedly set. Second, the presence of a fire in the kitchen showed that there must have been a chimney, a flue – which would have sucked the fire up the stairs – again, an assault on the theory that Druhan lit three deliberate, malicious, murderous fires.

The second break came from a conversation Nina and I had with StarryEyes Bob Smith – the third of eight separate interviews spread over three months. We had tracked Smith down to Joe's flat (he was always nervous about our seeing Joe alone, for some reason). Joe was in a desperate state, his face one huge scab, having slipped on some ice while drunk and fallen head first onto the concrete outside his flat. It was, by chance, one of Bob's sober days, since he was between giros. We had begun talking about how Bob separated the drunken Druhan from her lover, during the supposed brawl back at Number 15. The field notes of 30 November take up the story:

DJ and ND; p.m. visit to Joe Neary

Bob told us that Mary had lost her bag, had left it downstairs in the hall. Bob went down to look for it. David said: 'but it was quite dark, how did you find your way?' Bob took out a lighter and flicked it. Then he said he hadn't used a lighter – *he'd lit matches to look for the bag.*

As we sat in the car, writing up our notes, the staggering import of that statement hit us; for the first time, the principal prosecution witness, himself an initial suspect, and someone who blamed himself for the fire, was describing how the drunken duo, staggering through a house strewn with litter and combustible materials, picked their way through the darkness by lighting – and presumably discarding – lighted matches. Had that been heard at the trial, the case against Mary Druhan might very probably have collapsed there and then.

Our euphoria was short-lived; what, after all, had we heard but another of Bob Smith's versions of the truth. Bob isn't a liar;

we believe that the eight separate versions he gave us of what happened that night were the truth as he saw it at the time. The fact is that Bob was always an unreliable witness; but the jury heard him, and presumably believed the version which he, that day, produced. There was a disarming, and revealing moment, in our last filmed interview with him, when I asked him about these different versions, 'Look, David,' he said, with the exaggerated emphasis of the drunk, 'I'm alcoholic. I can't remember that night, so I don't know, do I? In other words, I can't tell you the actual truth. OK? Because I can't remember. Got me?'

And yet on Bob Smith's evidence Mary Druhan was convicted of murder.

We discovered that the defence had commissioned a report from Burgoynes, the leading fire investigation specialists. They confirmed our hunch; that the fire could have started innocently, from a discarded cigarette. This rang true; I remember one encounter with Bob Smith when a whole ashtray full of cigarette ends clattered to the carpeted floor. No one took the slightest notice. Any glowing tip could have caught on the detritus in the squat, and then roared upstairs, fuelled by the cans of paint and bottles of white spirit stored by the feckless Mr Grummit, the squat's former landlord.

But if the defence already had this report, why didn't they bring it out at the trial? The answer lies in the very nature of our legal system, which is not so much a search for the truth as a competition between two opposing sides. Although their own report suggested a more innocent cause of the fire, it suited them to adopt the prosecution's story of a demonic Druhan leaping all over the house, starting a succession of fires – *because they didn't think the jury would believe it*. The more ambitious the feats ascribed to Mary Druhan, the defence calculated, the greater the chance that the crippled, half-blind Druhan would be acquitted. As it turned out, that strategy failed.

The British judicial system is not only a competition, but a game played under strict, starched rules; and one of those rules is that if your strategy fails – in this case the suppression of the likely cause of the fire – then you are not allowed a second chance. This meant that, in Druhan's case, the opportunity to suggest the innocent origin of the fire that the defence itself had procured from Burgoynes was lost. We as journalists are not part of the legal process; all we do is try to resuscitate cases when every avenue has been exhausted, by bringing time, money, and a fresh eye to bear; but we know that if we are to get a conviction quashed, we have to operate within the legal mechanisms, and that means playing by the institutional rules. We weren't going to get Mary Druhan free by revealing the truth about the fire. That opportunity had been lost at the original trial.

Where next, then? We went back to the supposed origin of the night's wretched events, the quarrel in the Kingston Mill pub. There is little doubt that Mary, her lover Kenny, and StarryEyes were feeling no pain by the time they turned up at the pub. StarryEyes' own admission to me (made, I remember, as he swung from a lamppost) was that he'd already put away ten pints. Indeed, research revealed that they had been refused admission by the nearby Ram public house before being accommodated by the more hospitable and tolerant Kingston Mill.

It always struck as odd that StarryEyes had never mentioned this supposedly furious row. Where, indeed, had the evidence for it come from? It was, after all, a crucial part of the prosecution's case, establishing a motive for the murder.

The origin of the story lay, as usual, in the mounds of paperwork. A man called Keith Fludgate said he had witnessed the row. He was in the pub at the time. He'd gone there in the company of a man called Mark Haggas, whom he went out of his way to describe as 'sober and respectable'. This was odd, because when we looked up Mark Haggas' statement to the police, to see if it matched his companion's, Haggas said that he had not been in a state to remember a thing about the night in question, but was almost certainly somewhere else, baby-sitting with Patsy Roberts – the supposed 'other woman' in Kenny Roberts' life. We were obviously keen to find Mr Haggas – a word from any sober and respectable witness would be welcome in this nightmare of a case. He proved elusive, but for a perfectly acceptable reason; he was dead. The only clue he could leave us was written on the death certificate we obtained from St Catherine's House; Haggas had died of a drug overdose. Which left us with Fludgate – the man who witnessed Druhan haranguing the wretched Roberts, throwing beer around, slamming her can of drink in his face, and shouting 'I'll kill you, I'll kill you.'

It took us an age to find Mr Fludgate, not least because we

spent a lot of time slogging up to the fifth floor of a dingy block of flats to knock, vainly, on the door of a flat which he had vacated some months earlier. When we traced him – he was living with his mother – he admitted that he had been going through a very hard time, weaning himself off the tranquilliser Ativan. He had been depressed and confused, he told us. He'd also spent some time in jail, possibly, we gathered, as an indirect result of his Ativan dependency. In the frustrating months spent looking for him, we had built up a mental picture of Mr Fludgate, and it was not a flattering one. We were mistaken. He turned out to be a charming and open man, who provided the whole troupe of us, including a four-man camera team, with an overwhelming array of sandwiches and cakes. He spoke openly, awkwardly, candidly. He was quite certain he had been in the pub.

And we, in spite of Mr Fludgate's openness and hospitality, were sure that he had not.

There is no doubt that Keith Fludgate painted a bolder picture of the row than he intended. He admitted that he couldn't really be sure about what had been said, or done. Perhaps he hadn't actually witnessed Mary hitting her lover in the eye. Some of the words in the statement the police had taken were not his, or had gone rather further than he had intended. On camera, he became confused and occasionally incoherent. Anyone can. A television interview – although rarely adversarial – can be a stressful experience, and failure to survive it doesn't make a witness more fallible. But Fludgate's ambivalence was in striking contrast to the apparent assurance with which he had delivered his evidence to the police and the court. Mr Fludgate may be right, wrong, or honestly mistaken – but the fact is that his evidence, the damning evidence that provided the police and the jury with a motive, fell to pieces at the lightest puff of a breath of doubt.

The investigation so far had been a hard slog; an insanitary slog at that, and a frustrating one. It always seemed to be raining on the Monday mornings when I would drive into the slip road next to Kingston station and pick up Nina for another foray into the unpredictable world of the alcoholic vagrant. We had amassed an enormous amount of information pointing to the unreliability of the conviction; but it was unrealistic to expect that we could convey a fraction of our experience within a short television programme. And how could we convey to the neat desks of those at C3, the civil service department charged with assessing miscarriages of justice at the Home Office, the frailty of the evidence which convicted Mary Druhan. The system – understandably – wants facts. All we had was evidence of a miasma. Depression began to edge in upon the team. We could do with a break.

It came, with a routine trip Nina Davies and producer Steve Haywood took to Worthing, to interview the man who had been landlord of the Kingston Mill pub at the time of the fatal row. The two of them returned to the office in a ferment of excitement. The ex-landlord, Paul Welch, had been able to recall that evening well. Indeed, he had kept a special eye on the turbulent threesome, a task made easier by the fact that they were the only customers. A pub landlord is trained to deal with situations such as this. And Paul Welch was ready to swear that there was no shouting, no death threat, none of the 'pandemonium' described by Keith Fludgate, no striking of Kenny Roberts by Mary Druhan. No can of beer had been slammed on the table for the simple reason that Mr Welch would not have allowed customers to bring in their own beer – a fatuously obvious consideration, in hindsight, which had totally passed us by and had also been overlooked by the police, the jury, the judge, and the Court of Appeal, equally unversed in the etiquette of the licensed trade.

Mr Welch was a dream witness, with his calm understatement, careful reminiscence, sensible cardigan and haircut. Yet he had never had the opportunity to tell the court what he told us – all he was asked at the trial was what time the party had arrived. Had he been heard, it is very probable that the case against Mary Druhan, which had always been circumstantial, would have collapsed.

It was becoming clearer every week that this was, indeed, a fragile case which had been 'improved' beyond what it was capable of sustaining. It was not, in this instance, a case of the police lying or falsifying evidence; but once they had lighted upon Mary, they blinkered themselves to evidence that tended to exonerate her, and overemphasized evidence that seemed to point to her guilt. Once again, the usual reason why police inquiries go askew

– less a matter of malice than of narrow-sightedness.

There was another crucial aspect, we discovered, the police had overlooked. On the fatal night, a man called Mark Talbot had parked his car in Canbury Park Road, to have a drink at the Artful Dodger pub on the corner. As he reached the pub, he noticed a puff of smoke issuing from the doorway of Number 15 where, seconds earlier, he had passed a group of vagrants arguing.

'They were pretty well drunk, you know, they were slurring their words and shouting and screaming and swearing. One of them was a man with a bobble hat, another was a woman, white, fortyish, fairly plumpish – the thing I did notice was she had bright red lipstick,' Mr Talbot told us when we met him.

This was important information; we had always suspected that the population of Number 15 was a floating, transient one. There were hints of other people who used the place as their 'drum'. When seriously in drink, Bob Smith would hint darkly that 'the man with bullets' might have something to tell us; we did establish the existence of a man with a leather jacket studded with a bandolier of mock, brass bullets, but we could never trace him. Did this sighting of a woman by Mark Talbot suggest the presence of another, unknown person at the very instant that the fire broke out?

The woman Mark Talbot saw arguing outside the house was not Mary Druhan. We know this because Talbot was present later, as the fire brigade tried to douse the flames, and he saw Mary Druhan who, as we know, did turn up to watch the scene. And he is certain that Mary Druhan, and the woman he saw arguing just before he saw the puff of smoke, were different. At Reading Crown Court, he saw Mary Druhan in the dock. He recognized her as the woman who turned up to watch the blaze. He was also certain that she was not the woman wearing the lipstick and shouting and swearing outside Number 15.

Sadly, in court he was not asked any question which would have exposed that piece of evidence.

There were also some other oddities in the police record of Mark Talbot's account. In the first statement he made, he spoke of a woman 'running' from the scene of the fire. In the second, the word 'hobbling' appears. 'Hobbling' clearly fits the arthritic Mary Druhan better – she was incapable of running. The problem is that Mark Talbot swears he never mentioned the word 'hobbling' to the police. So where did the word come from?

Talbot was also concerned about something which didn't appear in his statement; he reported that one of the male vagrants – Bobble Hat – had shouted at the lipsticked woman who was not Mary Druhan, 'you killed my mates.'

The court never heard that, either.

What, then, remained of a case which left Mary Druhan with a life sentence? Motive and means had evaporated, with the new evidence of the row that never took place, and the discovery that the fire was not started in three places, but spread from a single, possibly innocent source. Everything rested on the flawed and drunken recollection of the survivors, Smith and Neary, one of whom had been the police's original prime suspect, while the other had put as much distance between himself and the blazing house as possible, because, as he told me, 'I didn't want to be accused of anything.' No one seemed to have noticed that the evidence of these two men was mutually contradictory, for instance, Smith said he saw Neary when he was in the house trying to restrain the furious Mary Druhan, but Neary said he'd never set eyes on Smith that night.

We may never get to the truth of what happened that night, and we certainly won't get to it through the pickled reminiscences of Bob, the amiable StarryEyes, and Joe, the taciturn Dancer. What *Trial and Error* had managed to unpick was a shabby piece of second-rate justice, flawed at every turn – from initial police diagnosis of deliberate arson, to the reliance on utterly unreliable witnesses.

Making the programme presented us with an entirely new set of problems. We felt it was vital to Mary's case to show the unreal world she and her accusers inhabited; but the arrival of a camera team among a group of vagrants has the same effect as a thunderclap on a flock of starlings. Our first attempt was to film in Claremont Gardens, at the disused bandstand, rank with urine, where the down-and-outs gather to drink.

People have a right to privacy, and down-and-outs are people, so we didn't want to film them secretly. When I went ahead to ask their permission, half of them made themselves scarce; there were presumably good reasons: policemen they wanted to avoid, families they had abandoned, people they owed money to, lives they wanted to put behind them. Those who remained became a ranting parliament of drunks, debating Mary's innocence or guilt. This, of course, was exactly what we wanted to film, but the moment any of the team came into view with a piece of equipment, we were told that filming was not – yet – on the agenda.

It was, in the end, rather as I imagine David Attenborough and his team set about filming timid or dangerous wild life; time had to be spent getting them used to our presence. Gradually the camera would be introduced, but never switched on. The introduction of sound equipment was, oddly enough, more threatening. People know what a camera is meant to look like, but the big woolly sausage on a pole that is a microphone with a wind-gag is always disconcerting.

And there'd always be someone, at the last moment, just as you'd won their confidence, who would wreck it. Usually, it was Ron. Ron was the only genuinely unlikeable character among the clan of the dispossessed. Even the rest of them, a forgiving and generous group, didn't like Ron. They'd always share their drink and cigarettes, but Ron was simply a sponger. He'd lurch up to me and pull me to one side, pushing his big, bleary face against mine, telling me that he had 'information' if we'd give him the money for it. The rest of the down-and-outs would immediately become suspicious. I'd try to tear myself away from Ron, but he was a powerful man; he'd hold you close, under constant threat of a crisp, sharp head-butt, his alcoholic breath making your eyes water. Once it sank in that we were not an easy touch, Ron made it his business to disrupt any relationship we tried to build with the rest.

Our camera crew were wonderfully tolerant and good-natured, because even dealing with cooperative witnesses could be a trial. Bob Smith would embark on an interview and then break off 'to go round the corner for a widdle' and not surface again for days. Filming in the cramped and unhygienic conditions at the Revd Belcher's they took in good part; I can think of other crews who would have turned the assignment down on health grounds. In a programme like this, the crew serve more than a technical and creative function; they represent a touchstone of common sense to temper our editorial enthusiasm. They'll obviously start off with a considerable scepticism about a case; but gradually they'll form their own opinion on the basis of the evidence put before them. Many times, at the end of an interview, a good soundman has told me he didn't follow the logic of such-and-such a question-and-answer, or has asked how this evidence squares with other witnesses' recollections, pointing out apparent contradictions. He's usually right.

Our responsibilities do not end with transmission of the programme. We have to collate a great dossier of all the evidence we have gathered – far more than we are able, by reason of time or the libel laws – to include in the programme itself or, indeed, this chapter. This bundle then goes to Justice, and is submitted to the Home Office in the hope that its C3 department will judge it worthy of referral back to the Court of Appeal. The Home Office doesn't like doing this, since their Lordships are understandably not best pleased when asked to rejudge their own judgments, but the cases we have dealt with over the years have had a good record of success. We keep our fingers crossed for Mary. It's time she had a bit of luck.

She'd been born in Ireland, but the family had disintegrated under the impact of a ferociously drunkard father. At the first opportunity she'd left and, like so many Irish girls, sought work as an ancillary in the hospital service. In England, she'd met up with another Limerick man, and they'd built a life together. But her husband, too, was a reckless drinker. One night, Mary Druhan woke up to find him dead in the bed beside her. She never recovered. For months, she would lay an extra place for him at supper. Then she began the decline into drink. She lost her council flat, and took to the life of squats.

These people are not aliens; they once had lives, homes, dreams. Pathetic Helen – the woman with the black eye, whom Nina had to tidy up – would tell us of her nice home in Tunbridge Wells, and the husband who beat her up. I'll always remember Gloria, all tousled defiance, waving a cider bottle and saying, 'I wasn't always like this, you know. I used to be in advertising.' And Tiny. 'Where do you sleep?' I asked Tiny. 'In the launderette,' he said. In the tumble drier. And I thought of all the detergent-fresh, damp laundry I had entrusted to Tiny's stained dormitory ...

Six months after the programme, there were two interesting

developments. The Taylor sisters, Michelle and Lisa, had their convictions for murder quashed. While in prison, they had come to know Mary Druhan, and had independently become convinced of her innocence. The sisters dedicated their post-release publicity and interviews to a campaign on behalf of Mary Druhan. Mary, it seemed, had been grateful for the programme, but had been offended by our description of her as 'homeless'. She wanted it known that she did have a place at a bed-and-breakfast hostel. It was her last vestige of pride and we, unwittingly, had trampled on it.

The second development was quite unexpected. We received a telephone call at the Just Television offices. It was from a man who said he knew who had started the Canbury Park Road fire. We went down to meet him. There was a young lad, he told us, who made a habit of laying fires in properties occupied by squatters. He had been responsible for three such conflagrations. In the fourth, said our informant, the lad, who was a glue-sniffer, had died.

Mary Druhan's original solicitors did not cooperate with us. It is the only time I can remember where help was withheld. It is, of course, always awkward for the professionals when we re-investigate a case; implicit in what we do is the assumption that we can find something the defence missed. That assumption is usually right; it would be strange if, with the time and money and people we can invest in a case, and with the basic groundwork already prepared in the course of the trial, we didn't come across new evidence. Most solicitors, once they've overcome their initial suspicions, welcome our interest, even though the case is over and lost, the client off their books.

We've no way of knowing how well Mary was represented, and so her case doesn't help us discover to what extent miscarriages of justice can be the result of shoddy or half-hearted work by the defence. But if Mary wasn't Mary, a drifter, an inebriate Irish woman, would she have stood a better chance of justice? Would a middle-class woman have been convicted on the self-contradictory say-so of two drunks? Did the system fail to go that extra mile in search of the truth because, in the end, no one really cares about people like Mary Druhan?

3

A Mere Entertainment

In 1985, the then Lord Chief Justice thundered against an edition of *Rough Justice* in the Court of Appeal. Lord Lane did not like the crass intrusion of television into the cloistered dignity of the law. On that occasion he did not allow his personal distaste to influence his legal judgement; he quashed the conviction of the man whose appeal he was hearing, on the evidence the vulgar television investigation had unearthed; but he made a point of summoning the producer into the witness box to berate him. Such programmes, he said, were 'a mere entertainment.'

He was half right. These programmes have to be entertaining. It's the tacit deal we make, when we set about doing this work. No one's going – deliberately – to transmit a dull programme. We undertake to provide the channel with an hour's-worth of television which will attract and hold an audience; in fact we usually double the audience for a standard documentary slot, and in exchange the broadcasting channel will supply us with the money to pursue the investigation.

A bonus is that an innocent person may go free.

It is a neat little bargain, and I can think of worse uses for television; what, after all, is the end product of most of the stuff you watch on the flickering rectangle in the corner? But for Lord Lane – and indeed for many canting denizens of the Inns of Court – there is a more insidious by-product of the process; it diminishes public confidence in the administration of justice.

This time Lord Lane isn't just half right; he's scored a bull's-eye. Guilty, a thousand times guilty, we plead with pride. Of course public confidence in the administration of justice should be diminished, because the administration of justice should never

49

presume that it deserves our confidence, any more than government should assume confidence in the administration of our governance. Remember, the lawyers were all tut-tutting about journalism undermining the respect for justice at a time before the scandals of the Birmingham Six, the Maguires, the Guildford Four, and Judith Ward had been acknowledged by the system. Ah yes, the apologists then mumbled, but the 'Irish cases' were in a class of their own; indeed, it was 'Geoffrey's [Lord Lane] tragedy that he had a bit of a blind spot over the Irish cases.'

But the case of Stefan Kiszko wasn't an Irish case. He was a sad and disadvantaged man convicted of a horrible sex murder which he did not commit, and which scientific evidence available at the time of the trial could have proved he did not commit. And what about the systematic lying of the West Midlands Serious Crime Squad, and the cases which – almost a decade on – are finally trickling through the Court of Criminal Appeal and being put right? Those wrongly convicted of the murder of PC Blakelock at Broadwater Farm were not conspicuously Irish. Ah well, the argument continues, but now we have the Police and Criminal Evidence Act, to make sure that police toe the line and treat suspects with care.

But PACE, with its tape-recorded interviews and insistence on access to a solicitor, did not prevent the wrongful conviction of the Cardiff Three. And the police in some forces are already developing crude techniques to make it as difficult as possible for solicitors to attend interviews; solicitors have told us that even when they are allowed access, it's not unknown for them to be shown to a chair which is bolted to the floor in such a way as to deny them a clear view of their clients. A surprising amount of so-called confessions seem now to be occurring in the back of police cars, rather than in the precincts of the police station, where tape-recorders have been installed.

With legislation ending the suspect's right to silence, we can look forward to a new phenomenon. Instead of the so-called 'verbal' – when a policeman would make up an incriminating remark supposedly made by a suspect – we will have what I can only call a 'non-verbal'. That is, the suspect may give a reasonable account of his actions, but the police may suppress it, so that his invented silence can count against him at trial.

The bridge over the River Leen, where the body of Atherton's victim was found. In the days before its discovery, Atherton took friends there to play pooh-sticks. He paddled in the river, and wondered aloud about the possibility of the body being there.

Mark Cleary in a teenage ID photograph taken before the murder for which he was wrongly convicted.

A rare picture of Philip Atherton, who admitted to murdering a ten-year-old boy and seven weeks later tried to share the blame with Mark Cleary.

Mary Druhan on her wedding day. Both her father and husband were hard drinkers; Mary was to end up as an alcoholic vagrant, convicted of a double murder.

Mary Druhan and her two daughters, in the days before her husband died and her life collapsed.

The blackened hall of the squat which Mary Druhan allegedly burnt down. Could paint cans stored under the stairs, and the alcoholic vagrants' chaotic lifestyle, have caused an accidental fire?

A midnight rendezvous with Bob Smith (right), survivor of the fire which killed two of his friends in the Mary Druhan murder case. (*Photo credit: Peter Trievnor, Times Newspapers Ltd.*)

Mary Druhan, after her conviction at Reading Crown Court for the murder of her lover and another vagrant. (*Photo credit: The Surrey Comet.*)

Peter Fell posed for this vainglorious picture – he bought the boxing trophy – thirty days before the murder for which he was convicted. But it proved the basis for an interesting experiment.

We had Fell's hair cut in prison to the same length as he wore it in the boxing trophy picture. . .

Thirty days later we came back – his hair now looks like this. . .

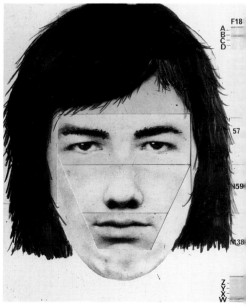

. . . hardly matching the hairstyle of the photofit suspect on Aldershot Common

Custody records like this one of Peter Fell are a vital part of a case investigation. What was discussed during those fifty minutes from 1000 to 1050 when a senior officer visited Peter Fell in the cells?

HAMPSHIRE CONSTABULARY

G12A

RECORD OF VISITS TO PRISONER/DETAINED PERSON

NAME OF PRISONER/DETAINED PERSON	FELL PETER ALAN			CHARGE No	PK 75.14
CHARGED WITH	SUSPICION OF MURDER	OFFICER	DCI LOMG	STATION	FARNBOROUGH

SPECIAL INSTRUCTIONS REGARDING PRISONER/DETAINED PERSON

TIME	DATE	STATION	CELL No	BY WHOM	REMARKS
2210	6/7	FR	4	2004	Asleep on left side
2225	6/7	FR	4	2004	Asleep on left side
2240	6/7	FR	4	2004	Asleep on left side
2310	6/7	FR	4	2004	Asleep on right side
2340	6/7	FR	4	2004	Asleep on right side
2355	6/7	FR	4	1403 / 2004	Asleep on right side
0025	7/7	FR	4	2004	Asleep on right side
0055	7/7	FR	4	2004	Asleep on right side
0125	7/7	FR	4	2004	Asleep on right side
0145	7/7	FR	4	2004	Sink beyond shower
0216	7/7	FR	4	2004	Asleep on front
0245	7/7	FR	4	2004	Asleep on front
0315	7/7	FR	4	2004	Asleep on left side
0345	7/7	FR	4	2004	Asleep on back
0415	7/7	FR	4	2004	Asleep on right side
0445	7/7	FR	4	2004	Asleep on left side
0515	7/7	FR	4	2004	Asleep on left side
0545	7/7	FR	4	2004	Asleep on front
0610	7/7	FR	4	2094	Asleep on front
0625	7/7	FR	4	missing	Awake on front
0650	7/7	FR	4	Over	Asleep / awake
0723	7/7	FR	4	8448	[illegible]

TIME	DATE	STATION	CELL No	BY WHOM	REMARKS
0955	7/7	FR	4	1818	Breakfast offered - cups of tea
0815	7/7	FR	4	1003	Walking about cell
0825	7/7	FR	4	1003	Given cup of tea and light for cigarette
0840	7/7	---	---	[signature]	[signature]
0905	7/7	FR	4	1003	To toilet
0922	7/7	FR	4	1003	Given light for cigarette
0950	7/7	FR	4	1003	Sitting on bench
1000	7/7	FR	4	1003	Visit by D.C.I. Long
1050	7/7	FR	4	1003	Visit ended. Given light for cigarette. Tea
1120	7/7	FR	4	1003	From Police Station with PS Semple and escort
1215	7/7	FR	4	1981	Returned to cell 4
1240	7/7	FR	4	1981	Lying on back awake
1316	7/7	FR	4	1003	To interview room with DCI Long
1450	7/7	FR	4	1003	Return to cell
1455	7/7	FR	4	1003	Cup of tea requested
1458	7/7	FR	4	1003	Cup of tea supplied
1510	7/7	FR	4	1003	Lying on back
1535	7/7	FR	4	1003	[illegible]

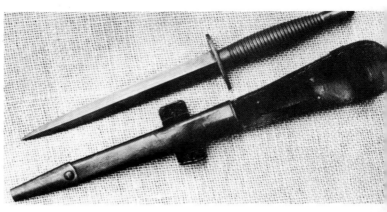

A Fairbairn-Sykes commando knife of the type almost certainly used in the Aldershot Common murders.

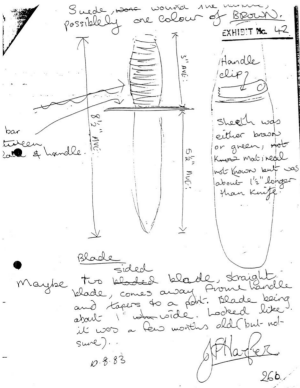

Suede, ~~used~~ wound ~~the~~, possibly one colour of BROWN.

EXHIBIT No. 42

Handle clip?

Sheath was either brown or green, not known material most known but was about 1½" longer than knife.

bar between ~~bar~~ & handle.

3" AVG:

8½" AVG:

5½" AVG:

Blade
sided
Maybe two ~~bladed~~ blade, straight blade, comes away from handle and tapers to a point. Blade being about 1" ~~who~~ wide. Looked like it was a few months old (but not sure).

10.8.83

Harper

26b.

John Harper drew this picture of a knife which, he told police, he had seen in the possession of Peter Fell. He later told us that he'd felt under pressure from the police and had lied.

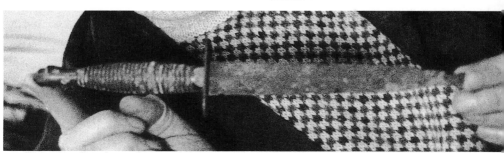

Shortly after broadcast of the Fell investigation a viewer reported finding a commando knife of the type described, buried in woods nearby. (*Photo credit: Clix Photographics.*)

'Omar m'a tuer' – did Madame Marchal ungrammatically name her killer by writing his name in her own blood on this door? (*Photo credit: Rex Features Ltd.*)
Moroccan gardener Omar Raddad leaving court after being found guilty of the murder of Madame Marchal. (*Photo credit: Popperfoto.*)

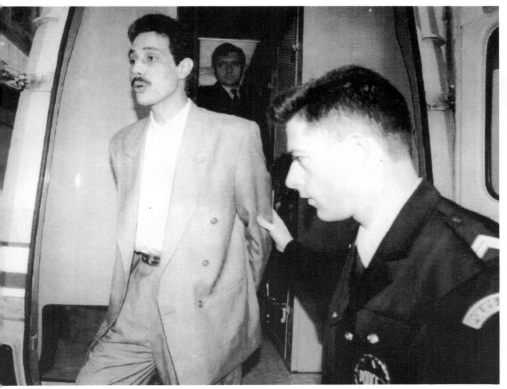

34 Conduit Street, Gloucester, scene of the fatal fight which led to the murder conviction of Gary Mills and Tony Poole.

To achieve the view one witness claimed of the fatal events in the groundfloor flat of 34 Conduit Street, he'd have needed the foresight to bring a ladder. (*Photo credit: Gloucestershire Citizen.*)

And yet the law has a limitless capacity to convince itself first that all is well, and, when confronted with evidence that it is not, to reassure itself that anything that may once have been doubtful has now been put right. I once found myself having a late-night drink in the company of one of the country's most senior Lord Justices of Appeal. We were talking frankly – on my side, I trust, with appropriate respect. Had he, I asked, in all his years, ever had personal experience of justice miscarrying? There was a long pause, so I prompted: 'As a junior barrister, for instance, or even when you became a QC? When you first became a recorder, a judge, a High Court judge, an Appeal judge?' Eventually, 'Yes,' the grand old man replied. 'Once. It was a very long time ago. I was defending this fellow and he got off. And I'm damn sure he was guilty.'

Would a member of any other trade or profession ever believe such a transparent myth? Has no teacher, no physicist, no airline pilot, no greengrocer, no accountant, no journalist, no doctor ever witnessed – let alone been responsible for – just one mistake in the entirety of a professional career? There is, of course, every reason for the terminal complacency of the law. A lawyer, if he is so minded, never really has to leave the collegiate society of his like-minded brethren. In prep school, you cheer for the house; at public school, there is unity against the town oiks beyond the gates; at University, loyalty belongs to the College scarf: when you progress into the Law, sweating over the law books, or in pupillage bound, you still reside within the precincts of a real or perceived quadrangle. You live a life encompassed by assumptions and traditions. And tradition tends not to challenge assumption.

Lawyers will argue that they do not lead such cloistered lives. After all, what other profession deals so regularly with such a socially variegated clientele – burglars, rapists, conmen? But the truth is that members of the bar, with a few honourable exceptions, never truly touch the world of their clients; indeed they are statutorily insulated from contact, needing the services of a solicitor to act as an intermediary. It is still a matter of some surprise to me that you can be on trial for murder, and not see your barrister until the day of the trial itself. It is also a matter of some concern that the first time some barristers get to grips with a case is on the train up from Euston. Journalists bone up on their interviews at the last minute; but nobody's fate depends on our having done our homework properly. Every day the bench grumbles about the decline in standards in one area or another of public life; it seems never to have crossed the mind of the judiciary that they themselves may not be quite as good at their job as their predecessors. The Panglossian complacency remains; Lord Lane, again, said in his valedictory address to a Senior Appeal Court judge that 'if Freddie ever made a mistake, I'm not aware of it.' Freddie almost certainly did, my Lord. But you are right – you wouldn't have been aware of it.

It's an open secret that there have been some dreadful old duds on the bench. But it will remain a secret because it is virtually treasonable to say so – not even an MP can criticize a member of the judiciary in Parliament. The following is a note from my diary; I haven't sanitized it or sobered up the prose for publication, so the rage is rather raw, and maybe the judgements insufficiently tempered. It's about a morning in the Court of Appeal.

It's a bad sign when the presiding Appeal judge, rather than one of his two colleagues, elects to deliver the prepared judgement. Throughout the hearing he's been testy, querulous, interrupting counsel for the Appellant, while seeming to offer more than the usual legal courtesies to the Crown. It doesn't help that he's deaf. But maybe that's just our perception. We are convinced that the man in the dock is innocent, and that we've done enough to persuade the court. After all, we've managed to get the case to the Home Office, through the corridors of the division which deals with these matters, and back for a second appeal against all the political inertia, bureaucratic obstacles, and the reluctance of the legal establishment to re-hear appeals. It would be hard to fall at this last hurdle having come so far. We have a lot bound up in the case of this man. Inevitably, while we hope we kept a proper dispassionate journalistic distance when we were investigating the case, by now we are rooting for our man.

The judge is a tiny, bird-faced septuagenarian, one of whose earlier judgements we have helped successfully to reverse.

For forty minutes he reads. Paragraph by paragraph, point by point, he dismisses every argument put before him over the previous five days. His certainty, his assurance, is kept cast-iron by the knowledge that his decision is final, his power – in his court – absolute.

The man in the dock has been listening intently as he sees his hope of salvation stripped, splinter by splinter, away. But it is only with the final dry pronouncement that the appeal is dismissed that the realization dawns upon him that his last chance has gone. For an instant he is paralysed then struggles to his feet.

'You senile bastard,' he rages at the presiding judge as he and his two colleagues scurry back through the three doors behind their seats, like automata in some Swiss clock; 'you senile bastards, you know I'm innocent.' The prison officers struggle to restrain him. His mother, sitting beside me, shouts: 'Don't, son, don't, it'll only make things worse.' In the stone corridor outside, counsel says to me: 'We just drew the short straw – we were doomed the moment we had that judge.' I tell the mother that we are sorry. We go out by the back door. I'd gone, with the new researcher, to show her at first hand how the Appeal process works, and it would have been good for her to have seen a success. 'Still,' I observe, 'I suppose it's useful to know your enemy.'

A month later I was told that the judge was retiring in a few months' time. So that's all right then.

A lawyer needs more detachment than we can always manage; one of the purposes of the legal system is to drain the passion out of conflict, so that issues are resolved without the participants coming to blows. But we are not lawyers. Nor, I trust, are we the mere entertainers Lord Lane holds in such contempt. We do, after all, get results; innocent people are freed because of the evidence we uncover. We are also, I hope, part of a tradition that rattles the cage of the legal system from the outside – Sir Ludovic Kennedy being the doyen of the craft, the Lord Chief Justice-Botherer.

There are criticisms to be made of what we do; for instance, only a very narrow range of cases fit our brief. It is only worth taking on a case if we can find new evidence to fit the Home Office and Appeal Court criteria – that is, evidence not available at the time of the trial, or some 'other consideration of substance.'

Quite what a consideration of substance is, remains undefined. Working to these criteria means that whole categories of cases disqualify themselves; we don't touch most rape cases, for instance, because usually only two people have been involved, and there is virtually nothing that an investigation can do. There are no new witnesses to find, no new forensic evidence, and the crucial point at issue – usually the degree of consent – has been thoroughly argued in court. We are not in the business of visiting rape victims and asking them if they have had a change of heart since the trial, nor should we be.

Practical considerations dictate other constraints. Even though it might prove the solution to a case, we simply do not have the resources, for instance, to trace everyone who bought a size seven plimsoll from a Plymouth chain store. If we did, we think we could prove a man innocent of the murder he was convicted for. But we do not have the police powers that would be necessary. We have no statutory right to interrogate witnesses or to command the production of evidence. Nor should we have. We also tend not to hare after cases simply because witnesses have decided to change their testimony; they may make good television, but, by definition, the Appeal Court will deem them unreliable. There are, admittedly, areas of miscarriage-of-justice journalism where these niceties are being smudged for the sake of glossy television, and this inevitably devalues the currency and plays into the hands of our judicial critics.

Another valid criticism is that we don't tackle the workaday injustices churned out by the lower courts. It's true that we are going to find it very hard to interest a channel controller in an unfair conviction for shoplifting, even though justice has miscarried just as surely as it has in a murder case, and even though the verdict is a personal disaster for those involved. There is, though, nothing to stop an enterprising reporter on a local paper from wearing out a bit of shoe leather to uncover the necessary evidence that justice has miscarried. We've all got to start somewhere, and, if you care about a wrongful conviction for shoplifting, it's as good a place to start from as anywhere.

Our work is fascinating, and the cases make what every journalist yearns for – great stories. It is – most of the time – extraordinarily enjoyable and satisfying work. But, strangely, it's not really a job for people who are interested in television. We don't make all that much television – maybe three or four programmes a year. What I've noticed in those who do this odd job well is that they are all, to some extent, driven – obsessive, maybe. When the drive, that obsession, is missing, the result shows on the screen merely as a True Crime adventure dolled up with a dash of synthetic moral outrage. A mere entertainment, in other words.

It is the privilege of journalism, and its principal treat, to witness moments of high drama, excitement, triumph and tragedy. It's the special thrill of our sort of investigative journalism to be not just spectators, but participants too.

Ask most of us why we choose to get involved in the specialist area of miscarriage-of-justice journalism, and we will give a number of reasons. The most high-minded of our usual answers is that it puts the resources of television (time, people and money) to good and practical use; after all, many cases fail, and many victims of injustice languish in jail, simply because there wasn't the time, money or wit to do the work that would prove them innocent.

Most of us do it for a simpler motive – because it's so fascinating and, we admit it, exciting. There's the same anticipation of the unknown every time you unlace the pink ribbon from those piles of case papers; somewhere in all this dusty verbiage may lie the key to unlock the secret of a prisoner's innocence, in spite of what your common sense and experience tells you, that this is almost certainly a no-hope case opportunistically pushed forward by a cynical rogue.

Let us suppose, however, that the case survives its first, crucial test and that we make a provisional assessment of it, suggesting that there are possible avenues to explore. That decision is taken on fairly pragmatic criteria. First of all, there must be the possibility of meeting those criteria of 'new evidence not available at the time of the trial, or other considerations of substance.' A consideration of substance can mean anything from the discovery of a polaroid picture of the accused in Bermuda on the same day that he was meant to be blowing the safe of the Clydesdale Bank, to a politic way of saving the system's face when it is quite clear that a judicial error – maybe Freddie's – has been made.

What we can do is to re-excavate the original case, which

means going back to the original witnesses, experts, and, crucially, the scene of the crime. After weeks of studying the papers, a clear image of the geography of the crime has formed. It is, presumably, the same picture which has formed in the mind of the jury. Yet almost always a site visit – an extraordinarily rare event for the jury – presents a radically different perspective. In the case of Mark Cleary, for instance, the murderer had given a graphic account of wheeling his victim's body, on the crossbar of his bike, along a dimly lit lane to the river where he disposed of the body. The lane does, indeed, have few streetlights, but the first thing that strikes you when you actually go there is that it is overlooked by the large, plate-glass windows of the houses which flank the path and spill pools of light from their bright interiors on to what we – and presumably the jury – had assumed was a shadowy path. Suddenly it makes no sense at all, or at least a different sort of sense from that which the court, in its clinical forensic isolation, mistakenly assumed. Again, in the case of Sheila Bowler, discussed in chapter 11, the court did not believe that she became aware of a deflated tyre as she was rounding a particular bend; it's only when you actually visit the bend that you realize that it is the tightest hairpin in southern England – if you had a flat tyre, it's here, above all, that you would be aware of it.

The tingle that accompanies this sort of revelation – with no compromise, of course, to a properly dispassionate view of the case – can also come when you come face to face with witnesses. Again, over the weeks you come to forge a particular perception of a person from the relevant witness statements. But those statements – the 'deps', or depositions which are the core of every case – are filtered through the prism of official procedure and police prose. What you are reading is a photo-fit version of reality. Meet the individual face to face, and preconceptions dissolve; what sounded so firm in typescript reveals itself as diffident, hesitant, unclear; what seemed ambivalent and vague on the official record presents itself, in the flesh, as clear, confident, concerned.

When we do our job properly, there's the ultimate luxury – to see something change as a result of our journalism. It's a bonus granted to few – the reporter who draws the world's attention to a famine, or to the scandal of thalidomide. For us, there's the selfish luxury of having intervened in just one person's life. Lifeboat crews do it every day, of course, and they risk their lives; we risk only the wrath of the police and the scorn of the bench, and we're lucky if we get a result once a year. One recent case concerned two men convicted of murder, whose case we helped to get back to the Appeal Court, this time with a successful outcome.

It's true about prison pallor. The two men were practically ghost-white when they came blinking out of the darkness of the jailer's cell into the bright, airy nave of the secular cathedral which is the Royal Courts of Justice in the Strand. The utter hairlessness of one of the men – he'd gone completely bald during the six years he'd spent in prison – emphasized the almost eggshell whiteness of his complexion. The jailer handed them the bags they'd brought with them from Pentonville, confident that today, at last, justice would be done and they would be free.

Then it was down the steps, out through the arch and into the clatter of camera shutters, a flurry of elbows as cameramen nudged their rivals out of the way: 'Can you look this way, Paul.' 'Over here Wayne . . . *Wayne.*' 'Why aren't you saying anything, Paul? Is it true your solicitor has signed you up exclusively?' 'Wayne?'

We climb into the waiting car, the throng moves with us, but, as we gather speed even the fleetest freelancers abandon the chase. Out in the traffic we recover our anonymity. We have lived with these two men for four years, and never met them. It is difficult to know quite what to say to someone who has just had the Lord Chief Justice quash his conviction and life sentence for killing a woman. Paul – the bald one – retrieves the awkward situation.

'I could murder a lager,' he says. And so we do.

4
Peter Fell

'I Only Wanted to be Somebody'

Two rather strange things happened as we completed the investigation of the case of Peter Fell. A man rang in to say that he'd found the murder weapon, and the police threatened to have us charged with a criminal offence.

We don't come across the police very often, although Holborn Police Station is just at the top of the road, and their officers couldn't have been more polite on the four occasions the premises of Just Television have been burgled. So it was something of a surprise when we heard that the Assistant Chief Constable of Hampshire was on the line. Not an entirely pleasant surprise, as it soon turned out; there was talk of having the team charged with conspiracy to pervert the course of justice.

We knew that our re-investigation of the case of Peter Fell, convicted in 1984 of a double murder, would touch some raw nerves in the constabulary; because we think they got the wrong man, and that even at the time they may have suspected as much.

The senior police-officer said he had statements from people who said that we had offered them money as an inducement to give us interviews, and that we had claimed to be acting on behalf of the police. It is precisely to safeguard ourselves against accusations like that that we make a policy of never acceding to demands to be paid for interviews, and of recording – rather more scrupulously than many police-officers – all that happens on research visits. When it comes to the actual interview, I always begin with a formal 'caution', putting on record that the person I'm talking to is not being paid, not being told what to say, and not doing the interview under pressure. We don't transmit that bit, but if we ever get the case back to the Appeal Court, it's

59

there on the transcript to reassure their Lordships.

The Assistant Chief Constable's threat wasn't the first time the police have used such ham-fisted tactics with us, and in itself the clumsy attempt to bully is not worth talking about; but it raises two of the questions we are most often asked: what actually is our relationship with the police, and how much cooperation we receive from them and other official bodies. It's a sore point. Clearly the very nature of our work challenges the police's conduct of the case. We don't have to go very far into the paperwork before we find corners are being cut. It's not that surprising. Lift the lid on any of the little mafias of the trades or professions and you'll find that things aren't always done by the book. It always amuses us, for instance, that when two or more policemen are present at the scene of a crime or at the interrogation of a suspect or witness, their individual accounts are, to the very word, identical. It's not in itself sinister – why should three policemen waste their time when only one needs to prepare an account, and let the others copy it? The practice only becomes corrosive when it covers an unacceptable tilt in the interpretation, a prejudicial selection of what the witness has said. At the extreme – and much has improved since the introduction of the Police and Criminal Evidence Act – the police would make up what the suspect had said; the mistake in one case I was involved in was that they wrote up a 'contemporaneous' account in notebooks which hadn't even been issued from the stationery stores until several weeks later.

Other corners are regularly cut. The custody record, or Detained Persons Register, logs the treatment of those held in the cells, and, as we'll see, it was to prove important in the case of Peter Fell. A custody officer has a position of the greatest responsibility, and most discharge that duty admirably. But the custody officer is often comparatively junior, and, faced with a senior CID officer investigating the case of one of his charges, the 'woodentop' – as the sharper detectives are wont to refer to their uniformed colleagues – comes under considerable pressure to defer to his superior. As a result, the prisoner may receive visits from Detective Inspectors which go unlogged; he may make requests for food, legal representation, or contact with his family that – even under new legislation specifically designed to prevent this – may go unrecorded and unheeded.

We don't ask the police for their side of the story, for the very good reason that we have their side of the story in front of us already, in the form of the statements they have taken, the transcripts of the interviews they have conducted, and other documentation. What we do ask the police for is all the other evidence which they have accumulated during their investigation, because this is where we usually discover the reason for things going wrong. What the Crown Prosecution Service, the accused's solicitor, and the court get, in the way of the police evidence, is that slice through the entirety of the evidence which points to the guilt of the accused. Everything else is, in legal terms, 'irrelevant'. The defence has an increasing, but not complete, right to ferret through these 'irrelevant' documents, most of which are, to tell the truth, pretty useless; but how many harassed solicitors, on tight legal aid budgets, have the time to read through the mountain of paper?

The mountain, in the case of Peter Fell, was as well-trodden as a Lake District peak in high summer. For as long as I can remember, there have been doubts about the conviction of Peter Fell for the murder of two women in 1982. Back at the BBC's *Rough Justice*, some had tried to unpick the case in 1986, with no success, and we know that others concerned with miscarriages of justice shared doubts about Fell's conviction. Now that we had formed a television company with the express purpose of investigating such concerns, could we make better progress?

Peter Fell was, very literally, the author of his own misfortunes. On 10 May 1982, two women were walking their dogs on Hungry Hill, part of the army tank ranges which fringe Aldershot, home of the British Army. It was that strange spring in 1982, when Argentina laid claim to some half-forgotten islands in the South Atlantic and Britain, to its own bewilderment, found itself on a war footing. Aldershot was fizzing with activity. A squad of would-be commandos was sweating its way through the gruelling endurance test that would qualify the survivors for a para's red beret. Within earshot of the platoon, and a hundred yards from the safety of the main road, the two women were stabbed to death. The weapon was never found – although by a strange

61

coincidence our own researches may literally have unearthed it – but pathologists identified it as a double-edged knife, possibly of the sort used by the army's élite SAS. No other clue was found at the scene of the crime – at least as far as we know; the police fingerprinted an entire housing estate near to Hungry Hill, and we assume that they must have had some suspicious print for comparison, but if they did, it was a piece of evidence they have kept to themselves.

That evening, a young man called Peter Fell staggered out of a local Aldershot pub and telephoned the police – without giving his name. We have seen the official note of that conversation. In it, Fell said he'd met a man in a pub, who had told him that he was the killer, and felt terrible about it. He said that the man lived at 10 York Road, Aldershot. (Peter Fell lived at Number 10.) The police did not come round. So, the next evening, he telephoned again, giving the same story, but this time providing the name Peter – his own.

Nothing happened.

In fact it was almost two weeks before detectives acting on the tip-off came round to Number 10. (Uniformed officers had called earlier, as part of routine house-to-house enquiries, because York Road was reasonably close to Hungry Hill and the murder site.) They asked Fell to account for his whereabouts at the time of the murder, three o'clock. Fell told them that he'd been in the pub until 2.30 p.m., and then he'd walked to the town centre and the pick-up point for the job he had at the time as a door-to-door salesman for a photographic company. He had arrived at 3.30 p.m. There simply wouldn't have been time to commit the murder, go home and change out of bloodied clothes, and reach his three-thirty appointment, and the CID effectively eliminated him; 'Sir,' says the handwritten note of the interviewing officers, 'we are satisfied with Fell.'

A year went by. The police investigation had yielded nothing, except for the suspicious sighting of a young man on Aldershot common at the relevant time. The man, apparently wearing a camouflage jacket, had been spotted by a jogger, a Ministry of Defence policeman called Brian Hackney. The police had also gone to great lengths to interview a lorry driver, a man who had been seen with his head in his hands, weeping, close by the murder scene, but had eliminated him from their enquiries. As for Fell, he had moved to Bournemouth, a town he'd chosen to live in – after getting on the wrong bus one day. He had married, but his pregnant and epileptic wife had gone home to her mother. Fell was out of work, bored, and back on the bottle.

Around the time of the anniversary of the murder, he tottered out to a telephone box, and rang the police again. Bournemouth Police automatically tape 999 calls. This is the transcript of that call:

Fell: Uh, I know who did Bournemouth – uh – the Aldershot murders.
Telephonist: You know the what?
Fell: Aldershot double, double murderer on May tenth, seventy-eight.'

[Fell, in his drunkenness, has got the date wrong by four years.]

Telephonist: May tenth, seventy-eight?
Fell: Yeah, double murderer of two women with two dogs.
Telephonist: I'm not quite with you. You've obviously got something you want to say . . . do you want to say it?
Fell: Yeah.
Telephonist: Go on.
Fell: Uh, the guy talked to me in the pub . . . in the Landsdown, tonight . . .
Telephonist: Yeah.
Fell: (Belch) . . . his name is Mr F., Peter Fell . . . (Belch) . . . Fell, I think.
Telephonist: Yeah.

This time the police were interested, although, it has to be said, it was some days before they paid Fell a visit, and they seemed mainly to be interested in a gas-meter break-in at York Road, the flat where Fell had lodged in Aldershot. Eventually, Peter Fell was driven back to Farnborough police station where he was held for three days. He was interviewed seven times, for a total of nearly ten hours. In spite of his constant requests for a solicitor – and police assurances that they'd look into the matter – he was denied legal representation. He took none of the food he was offered.

It's one of the curiosities of the case that the interviews were tape-recorded, long before the law was changed to make such taping compulsory. It was all done in a fairly rough and ready way – at one stage the principal officer did not seem to have realised that he had failed to switch his machine on – and it gives a revealing insight into the language of police interrogations before tape-recording made them more self-conscious. The conversations were a complete dialogue of the deaf. Why, the police ask Fell, did he make those self-incriminating phone calls? The following is an excerpt from one of the transcripts:

> *DCI Long*:   What did you expect, a police car to come screaming round with flashing lights and all the rest of it to apprehend Peter Fell and take him to the police station, and the next day there it would be in the local press – POLICE SWOOP, DETAIN MAN ON SUSPICION OF MURDER?

That, of course, was exactly what we believe Fell wanted – his moment of transient notoriety. Fell was an inveterate attention seeker. His, we were soon to discover, was a sad and lonely life. His parents split up when he was three, and Peter was brought up by foster-parents. The first couple couldn't keep him, and the second rejected him after ten years. He went into a children's home, where he is still remembered as a lonely child, desperate to draw attention to himself in little ways, for instance, he once admitted breaking a cup which the staff knew he had never been near.

As he grew up, he moved from one institution into another – the Army. But here again he did not really fit in. His insecurity led him to overcompensate, boasting about his macho exploits, cocking a snook at authority in a vain effort to win the respect or friendship of his fellow-squaddies. They simply found him a nuisance. Fell scrawled a weird message: 'FELL WILL DIE IN TWO DAYS' on the barrack wall; you don't have to be much of a psychologist to recognize that as a desperate cry for attention. On two occasions, while on a tour of Germany, he was caught out lying about having been attacked by civilians. There was a touch of the child about him – he was, indeed, still in his teens; while in Germany he would dial a telephone number at random, and shout, 'Achtung! Spitfire!' down the line.

The summit of his army achievement was to complete a course as a pastrycook. But that wasn't the tale Peter Fell told, when he was discharged from the army 'in the interests of the service.' Fell went to a sports equipment shop, and bought a boxing trophy; then he had himself photographed holding it, and bragged that he was an army champion. He also boasted that he had served in the Falklands and Northern Ireland. It was all untrue. In Aldershot, he loved to drink in the local paras pub, as if some of their virile glory would rub off on to him. The clientele tolerated him, but he was generally recognized as a harmless, if pathetic, inadequate. He has since confessed that he telephoned at the time of the Yorkshire Ripper murders, incriminating himself, but we have no proof of that, and the claim itself may simply be another attention-seeking device.

But as far as the police were concerned, as they interviewed Fell, they had at last, after a year's futile investigation, someone who had drawn suspicion upon himself. The police tactic – not unusual in those days – was to confront Fell with a mass of incriminating detail, to convince him of his own guilt. 'Bit by bit, it's building up against you,' they say at one point, 'and the sooner you see clear, my sunshine, the better it will be.'

Fell replies:

> I have not murdered nobody, never have and never will, there's not a lot else I can say. I haven't murdered anyone. I know the phone calls and all that, but there's other things I've done, why I said to my wife and other people I used to box for the army, that's only because I wanted to be somebody, same as the Falklands . . . it was just because I wanted to be someone. I think that's probably why the phone calls were an' all. I'm nobody, never will be and never was, that's the only reason I think I did the phone calls.

The second officer involved, Detective Sergeant Searle, adopts a more confiding tone: 'Peter,' he says, 'I'd like to explain something about human nature. The most difficult thing in the world is for anyone ever to admit they're wrong, no matter when or what circumstances. If you went back to the days of Adam and Eve you've got a point there when people started lying. You do it, forget this job. From the day you started to walk, you lied.'

Few scriptwriters would dare put such a speech in a fictional policeman's mouth.

In fact, the police had got next to no hard evidence against Fell, except for those phone calls which they blunderingly overlooked at the time. Photo-fits of a mystery man on the common had been issued a few weeks after the murders, and they apparently bore an uncanny resemblance to Fell. Eleven people called the police to remark on the similarities; but, again, the police had failed to act on the information. Now, it became part of the supposedly ineluctable weight of evidence against their suspect.

Gradually, Fell began to yield to the police suggestions. You could hear, on the tape, his stumbling, Lancashire whine move from defiance to compliance. At first he said he'd never been on the common, but then he admitted that certain parts of it were, after all, familiar. This was hardly surprising since, in an attempt, as they said, to 'encourage his memory' the police had twice taken him to the scene of the crime. Eventually, at the end of a marathon interview session – the beginning of which incidentally, was unrecorded because of DCI Long's problems with tape technology – Fell stuttered out a partial admission. He had been on the common; he'd met the women, and struck one of them with a stick, because, he said, she reminded him of his hated mother. Reminded by a third officer that death had been caused by stab wounds, Fell said he couldn't remember anything about a knife.

It was a fairly useless confession, and a few minutes later Fell asked to retract it, saying it had all been untrue. The police were exasperated – 'words fail me, Peter'. The jogger who had identified the unidentified man on the common was called in to attend an identity parade, but failed to pick out Fell. So the police let him go.

But three months later Fell was arrested and charged. The police had discovered, from one of Fell's work colleagues, that he had arrived later than usual at work on the fatal day, and that he'd been surprisingly well-dressed. And they had the damning evidence of another lodger at 10 York Road, a man called John Harper. Harper had earlier said that he thought Fell owned a knife; now he was saying that he'd actually seen a double edged knife, of exactly the type we – and presumably the police – believe was used in the murders, tumble out of Peter Fell's kitbag when they were lodging together.

Fell was convicted of murder and sentenced to life imprisonment. At his subsequent appeal, the then Lord Chief Justice, Lord Lane, grumbled that the longer the appeal had gone on, the more convinced he had become of Fell's guilt, which was exactly the sentiment he was to express, four years later, in wrongly rejecting the appeal of the Birmingham Six.

It was a vast case. Throughout, the problem was where to stop. Stephen Phelps, for instance, began to analyse the whereabouts of everyone who had been on the common at the relevant time, duplicating the police effort of the time. But we had to remind ourselves that we are not the police; we do not have police powers – we cannot compel people to talk to us, for instance – nor their resources. Squadrons of officers had set to work – to no very obvious effect – in asking everyone who had been on the common to come forward, in cross-referencing them, and so excluding them from the investigation; just three of us were available to work on the Fell case. We did uncover some fascinating discrepancies in the evidence which seem to have eluded the Hampshire Constabulary, but the sheer scale of the task compelled us to cut our losses and abandon that particular avenue. In retrospect, the exercise would have been as futile as was the police's original strategy; the common is a vast tract of land, and any number of people engaged in innocent, criminal, botanical or adulterous pursuits, might have had their own reasons for failing to come forward. But the problem with this sort of work is that you never know what nugget of information may lie round the next corner, or the next. In fact, months later, and after the programme had been made, one of Phelps' identification analyses was to come in very handy.

For Nina Davies, the Fell case was something of a contrast with her previous researches among the down-and-outs of Kingston. We knew, in most cases, where the relevant people lived, and, for a great deal of the time, the research was conducted on the telephone from the airy third floor of the converted warehouse where Just Television is based. Which brings us back to that question about the help and cooperation we get – or do not get – from various organizations apart from the police.

Not having police powers, we rely on people's goodwill, and, when it comes to individuals, we are constantly refreshed and delighted by their willingness to help. Once or twice in every case we'll come across the odd, truculent don't-want-to-get-involved attitude, but on the whole people are amazingly generous with their time and cooperation. A television team is a cumbersome unit; I remember one interview during the Fell investigation in a front room in Accrington, where the only material possessions on display were a fish-tank, a carpet, and a pot plant. I spilt a cup of generously-offered coffee on the carpet; one leg of the camera tripod somehow crushed the pot plant; the sound man asked for the fish-tank aerator to be turned off for the duration of the interview because of the bubbling noise it made, and I can't swear that we remembered to turn it back on again afterwards. And yet, for all the trouble we represent, once people are convinced of our sincerity and seriousness of purpose, they seem happy to help us.

Organizations are a different matter altogether. In the case of Peter Fell, the actions of Lancashire Social Services and Barclays Bank drove us mad with exasperation. We wanted to talk to a former house-mother at a children's home about Fell's childhood. Clearly, matters of confidentiality were involved and we would need official permission, not least from Fell himself. Fell, unsurprisingly, gave us *carte blanche* to rummage through his life. We knew where the house-mother lived, and that she possibly held important information; we also understood that she was willing to talk to us. We were aware that she would want, and require, permission from her superiors before considering a formal interview. We lost count of the letters we wrote, the telephone calls we made, the sheer waste of days that passed as we tried to cajole a response – any response – out of the bureaucracy.

At one stage we called on a member of our esteemed advisory group, the MP and hero of the Birmingham Six campaign Chris Mullin, to see if we could exert a bit of parliamentary pressure. Chris told us that the etiquette was to get the local MP involved. Unfortunately, that backfired; we had asked for a little gentle pressure to be exerted, but the MP intervened so forcefully that it took us weeks extra to try to smooth ruffled bureaucratic feathers. It was clear, however, that this was an organization dedicated to thinking up reasons why things cannot be done, with the reverse-Micawber philosophy of hanging around waiting for things to turn *down*. It was such a small, uncontroversial thing we were asking – 'what sort of a lad was he?' – and yet the whole inertia of Lancashire Social Services seemed dedicated to obstructing our efforts.

The request dripped along from department to department until it reached the administrative black hole of the Legal Department. It spent a long time there, possibly because, in our experience at least, they seem to knock off from work surprisingly early of an afternoon, especially on Fridays, though I am constrained to say that almost certainly this is a misapprehension on my part, and that our telephone calls simply caught them at times when the staff were too busy to respond to them.

Eventually, we ran out of time. We had already wasted enough. We know the problems of confidentiality that our request might raise; but it was clearly beyond the collective bureaucratic wit of the department to do this simple service for the boy who had once been in their care, and to whom they stood *in loco parentis*. When and if the Court of Appeal quash the conviction of Peter Fell, I hope Lancashire Social Services acquire the institutional capacity to feel ashamed of themselves.

Barclays Bank was slightly more helpful. Fell hadn't been able to remember what he'd been doing on the afternoon of the murders, and it was dogged work by Roy Churcher, a former policeman working for Fell's solicitor, that unearthed his movements at the critical time. Churcher discovered that Fell had cashed a cheque for ten pounds at the Aldershot branch of Barclays. The cheque had gone through the computer at 3.47 p.m. We traced the cashier, who explained that the cheque must have passed through her till between 2.30 and 3.30 p.m. This effectively alibied Fell for the murder, which had happened at three o'clock. We wanted two things – the cashier to repeat this story, and permission to film on Barclays Bank premises.

We did the proper thing and wrote to Barclays Head Office. Eventually, we were summoned to the palatial splendour of the former Royal Mint, where Barclays Bank spends our bank charges on keeping the management in the appropriate style – the reception area is slightly grander than the ballroom of Blenheim Palace. Present at the meeting were the head of security, the head of the legal department, the chief of PR, and someone who seemed to be the head of everything else.

After protracted negotiations, we got permission to film in a branch, and were told that the cashier could talk to us if she so wished. In fact, she later confided to us that they had told her that while they could not prevent her from giving an interview, the bank would prefer her not to. The feeling was, apparently, that for the bank to be associated with a convicted murderer was bad for business. It never seems to have crossed their minds that there might be some corporate sense of duty to help correct a possible – indeed likely – miscarriage of justice. Thankfully, the cashier had the courage and conviction to do what she thought best. In the end, we filmed the interview, with Barclays management hovering nervously on the margins, and we filmed a brief sequence at the Barclays branch where I have my account.

There is no excuse for the intrusive excesses of British journalism, but perhaps there is an explanation in the pig-headed reluctance of British institutions to volunteer the meanest degree of cooperation.

The cashier, Shirley Hewer, sturdily disregarded the bank's advice. 'I'm retiring in a couple of months, anyway,' she said, and told us that she was '100 per cent certain' that she had cashed Fell's cheque at a time that alibied him. But that didn't advance the case very far from our point of view. The bank evidence had already been heard at Fell's trial. Indeed the judge had even invited the jury to accept it and throw out the case against Fell in mid-trial. For reasons which surprised lawyers at the time, the bank alibi was not accepted. We needed new evidence, because that's the only evidence the Appeal Court will accept.

The breakthrough on Peter Fell came through a combination of luck and application. Nina Davies was concentrating on the evidence about the knife. Fell was adamant in correspondence that the only knife he owned at the time was a penknife, with which he opened the cans of cold baked beans which sustained his bachelor life. We were intrigued that his fellow-lodger, John Harper, had changed his mind about whether or not he'd seen Peter Fell with a knife.

For a witness to change his mind, on such a critical issue, rang alarm bells. We became all the more concerned when we investigated Mr Harper's background at the time. We discovered that when he made his second, damning statement, Harper was in a bail hostel, awaiting trial on a number of fairly minor charges. He was, then, clearly in a vulnerable position. Could the police, convinced of Fell's guilt but lacking the evidence to prove it, have found in Harper the convenient final piece of the jigsaw?

We wouldn't know until we ourselves found Harper. And clearly others had been doing that for some time, with no success. We discovered that the birth certificate of every John Harper of the relevant age had been sifted at the St Catherine's House register. Fell's solicitor, the admirable Mike Roberts, another of those unsung heroes, has pursued Fell's case assiduously for ten years. He told us that all his efforts to find Harper had failed.

Nina was about to go on holiday. On her final afternoon, she was leafing through some of the untendered witness statements – the so-called 'irrelevant' papers – when she discovered a vague reference to Harper from a man claiming to know him. Nina's last act, before setting off to Wales, was to go to this man's last known address, near Farnham. It seemed to be a wasted trip. There was no answer. Nina dropped her card through the letter-box, and went off for her summer holidays, not entirely hopeful either that he would respond, or that, ten years on, he would still know of Harper's whereabouts. When she came back to work, she was astonished and delighted to find a reply. Yes, the man said, he had known Harper for a long time; Harper and his own son were good friends. Indeed, following the recent breakdown of John Harper's latest relationship, the two had agreed to share a house.

Gently, Nina won the man's confidence, and finally gleaned the vital address: a small house in a place called Grays, in suburban Essex.

Nina and I set off one evening – the best time to find people in. The train from Liverpool Street dragged its load of weary commuters through the dim estuary-land of London. The lights of Dagenham, twinkling in the murk, provoked wry reminiscences of the glamorous life television had seemed to offer when we chose it as a career. A minicab took us to a drab terrace on the outskirts of town. Dreary as it was, cold as we were, there

71

was still an undeniable frisson of excitement at the prospect of meeting this key, but inconstant witness. Nina knocked on the door. There was no answer. I looked through the letterbox; there was no build-up of junk mail – a good sign – but the coat-hooks in the hall were bare. There was no one at home.

We sat and killed time in Britain's nastiest pub, and we speak with the authority of those who have killed time in a lot of tacky hostelries. Tuesday night, a sign said, was Karaoke night; but this was Thursday. Two regulars sipped truculent halves of anonymous estuarine bitter. Time went by in lead boots. A satellite-television music channel blurted away, but the noise somehow only contrived to make the place seem emptier and more dead. For the first time in thirty years I ordered a Mackeson, reasoning that a drink I did not like would force me to drink it more slowly, thus prolonging my time in the pub. The crisps had a strange, chemical flavour that I have never encountered since. I swear my shoes caught mildew by the time we reckoned the house was worth a second visit. We returned an hour later, but the house was still dark. If we left now, we'd be home by bedtime. It would, however, be more professional to wait another hour. Nina and I looked at each other. We conspired to go home and try again another day. A lot of the work is like that. Waiting, watching, and going home – an evening wasted.

And there are simply some days when you get fed up with pretending to be Woodward and Bernstein, and you fancy an early night tucked up in your own warm bed.

Sometimes, rather more time than necessary gets wasted. I remember the small hours of one particular morning. We were just about the only people in the motorway cafeteria, except for the young couple at the corner table who seemed to be very much bound up with each other and presumably had their own elaborate reason for being there that late. Our own reason, rapidly becoming more threadbare, was that we were there to meet a policeman who said he had important information for us. He'd chosen this particular rendezvous because his colleagues had misbehaved here a few months ago and the management had complained, so there was an informal police boycott of the place. The trouble was he should have been here two hours ago. For the loving couple in the corner, presumably, time had no meaning, but, for us, the moulded plastic seats had grown very hard. It was now two minutes past three. We said we'd give it till three-thirty before giving up.

As we got up to pay for a lot of coffee, the young man at the corner table looked up. 'You the people from the television?' he asked. Yes, we mumbled embarrassedly, adding that he didn't look much like our idea of a policeman. 'Well, if it comes to that,' he replied with a smile, 'you're not exactly my idea of investigative journalists.'

For the next attempt to talk to Harper, Stephen Phelps and Nina took the train to Grays. Once again, John Harper wasn't in, but his flatmate was. John would be back soon, they were told, when he got back from his weekly karate workout. The house – two up, two down – bristled with military trophies. His flatmate went back to his hobby – stripping down a Bren gun. It was that sort of a ménage.

Harper, who was currently in the middle of exams to qualify him as a life insurance salesman, was understandably surprised to have a ten-year-old incident come back to haunt him. Stephen Phelps explained what we were doing, and asked if he could take him through the statements he had made. Harper agreed. He looked at the first statement, in which he denied ever seeing Fell with a knife. Was that the truth? Yes, Harper indicated. Phelps then read him the second statement, in which he told the police that he'd seen a knife fall out of Fell's kitbag. Was that the truth? Harper, his face tight but expressionless, admitted that what he'd said was untrue. There was utter silence in the room. Nina kept her eyes fixed on her notebook, avoiding eye contact with Phelps. After ten years, here was the first crack in the case against Peter Fell.

Getting the admission was one thing; getting it on film another. We had several meetings with John Harper, each time asking about the possibility of a filmed interview. Each time we got a polite request for more time to think about it. At the same time, Harper was anxious to practise his salesmanship techniques on us. We agreed to help him, submitting to the whole patter about the advantages of endowment policies as provision for retirement, as his supervisor assessed his technique. It was an attempt to gain Harper's confidence, but the time came when we felt we had to bring matters to a conclusion. We finally made an appointment to meet him one Monday evening, leaving the open question of whether or not we would bring a film crew with us. We were let in, but Harper was late. Was he trying to avoid us? To make absolutely sure that there could be no accusation of undue pressure, we brought Mike Roberts, Fell's solicitor, with us. Eventually, Harper arrived. His eyes fixed on the television camera which was parked on the sitting room floor as we sipped the cups of instant coffee we had been offered. 'I never said anything about that,' he said, indicating the camera. Slowly we explained our dilemma. We could not indefinitely continue to accept his procrastinations. Was he, or wasn't he going to give us the interview? The choice was his; with any interviewee, it always is.

Harper agreed. At any time over the next hour, as we put up the lights in the front room, he was in danger of reneging on that agreement. But, finally, he sat down in front of the camera. For the next few minutes I had no idea how Harper would respond. He is a supremely fit and strong young man. His language is confident, his conversation is all about action, aggression, assertion. Yet I thought I saw in his eyes a touch of the little-boy-lost. The relationship between the interviewer and the subject is an extraordinarily intimate one, in spite of the artificiality and distraction of a conversation conducted in front of a crew of strangers armed with an arsenal of technical equipment. In any interview, you have to decide the tone of the conversation; it's a matter of instinct as to whether you choose to be confiding and intimate, brisk and businesslike, confrontational, teasing, or whatever. Aggression would have been fatal; a confessional approach would have been alien and awkward. I decided I was dealing with a young man who needed to summon all his reserves of courage to admit to what must have been a long-buried shame. He would respond best, I reckoned, to a firm, adult, but under-standing style of conversation. A father for the lost little boy.

It was, nonetheless, one of the most awkward – though compel-ling – conversations we have ever transmitted. There were aching gaps between question and answer; Harper wasn't tongue-tied; he was just hoping that something, anything, would fill the void, and spare him the pain of articulating his admission. On such

74

occasions, agonizing as they are, the interviewer just has to keep silent and wait for the catharsis of confession. Does that constitute pressure? I suppose it does. Unwarranted pressure? I don't think so, if it's a question of putting on the record something you have already been told.

John Harper said he'd been under pressure from the police to say he'd seen a knife, 'I was a lot younger then,' and had finally told them what he thought they wanted to hear, but what he knew was untrue. Then the police had taken him to a knife shop where he picked out the sort of knife which he assumed the police were looking at. Pathologist Dr Iain West studied the post-mortem pictures for us, and concluded that the likeliest weapon was a Fairbairn Sykes, first designed in 1940 and issued to British commandos. Horrifyingly, anyone can buy one of these killing knives over the counter in any number of shops specializing in militaria – especially common in Aldershot. The Fairbairn Sykes has no innocent function; 'its purpose is to stab, it's a killing knife, it's a strong blade, double-edged, it's easy to extract it from bone if it strikes bone.' Harper knew the weapon well, because he, the essential macho action man, was a member of the Territorial Army.

The admission did not prove Fell's innocence, but it blew a mighty hole in the case that convicted him, and gave us renewed confidence. At the same time, analysis of the taped interviews was yielding some fascinating information. In this awesome case, how many people had actually listened to all nine or ten hours of the recordings? Two women had been horribly killed, families had been destroyed, and a man had spent twelve years in jail. Yet few had deemed it necessary to go back to what had actually convicted Peter Fell. It was to prove a goldmine of information. We discovered, for instance, the origin of the supposed motive for Fell's attack – one of the women had reminded him of his hated mother. This had always puzzled us, because the picture of one of the victims shown to the court was a ten-year-old passport photograph which, anyway, bore no resemblance to Fell's mother. Listening to the tapes, through the hiss and the crackle, we heard Fell trying to explain to his interrogators why he had made those phone calls; he's done a lot of crazy things in his time, he admitted in his thin, clipped Lancashire whine. For instance, when he was

a lad, 'I hit me brother for no reason at all.' DCI Long, a south-
erner, responds: 'You hate your mother?' Fell is baffled. He
corrects the Chief Inspector: 'No, I said I hit me brother.' But
the damage has been done. In the next few seconds, Long returns
to the subject: 'What exactly was your relationship with your
mother . . .?' A simple mishearing has sown the seeds of a fatal
misapprehension.

I took the tapes, all nine hours of them, home, and checked
them against the official transcript. It was a simple, clerical chore,
but it gave me a vital perception of the dynamics of Fell's interrogation. But as far as I could see – apart from the acknowledged
gaps – the transcript was a worthy attempt to make sense of the
distorted static-ridden recording.

It was Stephen Phelps' idea to time the tapes. In a properly
conducted interview, officers state the time at which the interview
begins and ends. Fell's interrogators had been scrupulous in this
respect, so we knew how long each tape ought to last. It was my
fault for not having had the wit to time the tapes myself while I
was listening to them, but my heart sank at the prospect of
listening, in real time, to those wretched tapes again.

I was wrong, and Phelps' instinct was right; nearly all the
interviews came up intriguingly shorter than they should have
been, according to the timings logged by the officers themselves
at the beginning and end of the interviews. There appeared to
be a variation of between three and eight per cent. Fell had
always claimed that the tapes were significantly edited, but we
had not, in truth, taken him very seriously. The tapes, after all,
did conform to the transcript. Had Fell been right all along?

We took our tapes to an expert in York who analyses recordings and appears as an expert witness both for the prosecution
and the defence. We wondered if the apparent discrepancies in
our tapes – which were, after all, only copies, and maybe copies
of copies – might be the result of simple slippage between one
recording machine and another. But the expert's analysis was
that the deviation couldn't be explained away simply by mechan-
ical causes. This was a long way from concrete evidence of deliberate tampering. But Phelps' fascination with the tapes yielded
two other key discoveries. First, he was intrigued by those areas
where, by the police's own admission, the tape had run out or

failed to function. The police statements filled in the gap in the transcripts with their record of what they recalled of the missing conversation.

In the light of our new evidence about timings, this yielded some hilarious results. In one interview, logged as lasting seventy-five minutes, the tape runs out sixteen minutes before the end. The police account of what was said in those sixteen minutes consists of just twenty-five words. The pauses must have been of super-Pinteresque proportions. Sixteen minutes of conversation, conducted at the same pace as the recorded part of the interview, would have covered more than twenty typed A4 pages. Idleness or deception by the officers concerned? Certainly there is an arrogance implicit in the police attitude – the assumption that no one was going to notice this fairly substantial corner being cut.

The deeper we explored the tapes, the more surprises they revealed. No one had thought to question them, because there was, after all, that transcript, which the police had, quite reasonably and properly, incorporated verbatim, like the script of a play, in their own sworn statements. But then we made an astonishing and quite accidental discovery. We were looking at a passage in a police statement, and comparing it with the transcript. Obviously, the transcript and the statement should match each other, word for word. But the police statement incorporates extra material – stage directions, if you like, such as 'the suspect was then shown copies of the photographs' – which doesn't occur in the verbatim transcript because, obviously, those words were not spoken. We discovered that where there were 'stage directions' in the police statement, there were physical gaps in the transcripts – blank, white spaces. The unthinkable began to dawn on us. The police hadn't copied the transcript into their statements, as is usual – it was the other way round; the transcript had been copied from the police statements. For years, the integrity of those police statements had been based on the existence of an apparently independent transcript. Now, we could prove that the transcript guaranteed no such thing.

In these days of word-processors, the discrepancy wouldn't have been noticed. But the documents dated from the time of Xeroxes and correcting fluid.

But the transcript held more surprises in store. We noticed references by Fell to things that had been said 'in the cells' – remarks that were curtly interrupted by the interviewing officers. It became clear to us that the recorded interviews told only half the story. Fell had been visited by officers in the cells, where, of course, the conversations went unrecorded. What could have been said during those encounters?

It was an important question, because at Fell's trial much had turned on whether or not Fell was induced to confess with the promise of a reduced charge – manslaughter – instead of murder, with its mandatory life sentence. The qualification for manslaughter, of course, is that you are not responsible for your actions, and Fell did give the somewhat stagey impression of being temporarily insane when he made his limited admission. 'Everyone was laughing at me . . . the trees were laughing at me . . .' is a fairly B-movie line of confessional dialogue.

At Fell's trial, the judge very sternly told the court that if there was the slightest suspicion that Fell had been offered an inducement to confess, he would stop the trial. Detective Sergeant Searle admitted that an informal conversation about the difference between murder and manslaughter had indeed taken place in the car park of the police station, shortly before Fell was taken to visit the site of the murder. But he insisted that Fell had introduced the topic, and that no deal had been offered.

But the custody record showed us something rather interesting; just before the interview in which Fell made his fatal, if inadequate confession, the record shows that the detective leading the investigation visited him in his cell. Just before trial, DCI Long made a statement to the effect that he'd had an 'informal conversation' with Fell which lasted fifty minutes. His account of that conversation runs to twelve lines; fifty minutes of properly-transcribed dialogue would take up seventy pages. Fell has always maintained that in those fifty minutes he was offered a deal and that, persuaded that the police had enough 'evidence' to have him put away, he opted for the hope of a reduced charge. He said that he naturally brought the matter up shortly afterwards with Detective Sergeant Searle when they were alone together in the station car park. Deprived of a solicitor, he was anxious for any advice. Long, the senior officer, told the court that he had not agreed to Fell's requests for a solicitor because to do so would impede the investigation.

The case against Peter Fell began to look increasingly ragged and rickety. But that, while possibly being enough in law to warrant the quashing of a conviction, didn't prove Fell's innocence. Most police malpractice is the result of officers 'improving' the evidence in a case where they are convinced, often reasonably, that the suspect is guilty. Presumably, there are many quite correct, and ultimately unchallenged convictions thus assisted. In Fell's case, there was, after all, the matter of those self-incriminating telephone calls. Not the action of an innocent man – though hardly, of course, the action of a guilty one. We knew about Fell's pathetic attention seeking, but what was the experts' view?

Nina traced the prison doctor at Winchester and, with Fell's permission and that of the enlightened prison department régime – Lancashire Social Services, please note – we discussed the Fell case. Dr Robin Ilbert is one of the old school, who hides a lifetime's expertise beneath a charming, apparent amateurism. The cell doors clanked again as he let us into the prison hospital wing. I had always imagined prison hospital to be a comparatively soft option, but the hospital cells of Winchester have changed little since Victorian times: cream-painted brickwork, a small window too high to look out of, and a hatch on the door armed with bars at just the right height to aid distressed inmates to hang themselves with their sheets, as they often, in spite of the hospital staff's best endeavours, succeed in doing.

Dr Ilbert remembered in Fell a simple young man who clearly, he said, needed to boost his ego 'by telling whoppers; it seemed to have become a survival mechanism for him.' At the time, Ilbert had been relatively inexperienced as a prison doctor; these days he would have no hesitation in seeking the advice of a forensic psychologist such as the Maudsley Hospital's Dr Gudjonsson, a former Icelandic policeman who had a Damascene conversion when he witnessed at first hand a miscarriage of justice. Gisli Gudjonsson has since developed an international reputation in the assessment of vulnerable testimony.

We did what Dr Ilbert suggested, and showed the Fell case to Dr Gudjonsson and his colleague, Dr James MacKeith. His

79

report, some months later, confirmed what we had, in our amateur way, always believed: Fell was, in 1983 'a psychologically vulnerable person ... I have serious doubts about the reliability of Mr Fell's self-incriminating admissions.'

An alibi at the bank which has never been overturned; a self-confessed perjury about the knife; doubt over both the police practices (they would be totally unlawful these days) and the mental state of Fell – all that was truly left of the case against Fell was his resemblance to the photo-fits issued a month or so after the murders. A number of people rang in to say how uncanny the resemblance was to Fell. But – and it's strange how often the glaringly obvious eludes us – that resemblance must have been to Fell as he was, not at the time of the crime, but as he was a month later.

It's a secret neither the police nor the BBC's *Crimewatch* have ever chosen to share with the public, but photo-fits are, on the whole, worse than useless as an aid to detection. Professor Graham Davies, of Leicester University, is an expert in identification, and he told me that forty-five per cent 'bear little or no resemblance to the suspect who is eventually apprehended ... only five per cent are sufficiently striking to allow the police to make an arrest.' The very first photo-fits were based on features of actual prisoners; and when, in the sixties, male fashion became more unisex, photo-fit experts simply borrowed some female hairstyles and put them in the men's box – so much for the forensic miracle of photo-fits. The inherent problem is that the very technology forces you into being more precise than is warranted by memory – you have to choose one particular set of eyes, or a nose, or a mouth, when all you really remember was the suspect's hair. In fact hair, according to Professor Davies, is the single most reliable feature we can remember.

The photo-fit showed a man with long hair (described, in a statement I will treasure from a former President of the British Institute of Trichology whom we brought in as an expert witness, as 'sort of wodgy'.) Fell's hair was of medium length at the time the photo-fit was issued and people noticed the similarity. But – critically – Fell's hair was short at the time of the murder, and the time of the sighting. We can tell this because we know how long his hair was when he had the infamous photograph taken of him posing as the army boxing champion. So those photo-fits should have served, if anything, to exclude Fell from suspicion.

When we came to make the programme, we discovered more telling details. The suspicious fact that Fell had turned up for work uncharacteristically neat and tidy on the afternoon of the murder, for instance, became a touch less suspicious when we traced his employer at the time. Fell was new to the job – he had only been doing it a couple of days or so – and the boss told us that on the very day before the murder he'd read Fell the riot act about his scruffy appearance, and told him to smarten up. We interviewed a woman who described a terrifying attack by a man who looked exactly like the photo-fit of Fell – at a time when we know Fell was still with the army in Germany.

But there were two possible pieces of the jigsaw which only came to light as a result of the publicity generated by the programme's transmission.

First, a woman regularly employed by the Hampshire Police rang in. She told us she was an artist, who helped the police in rape cases. She had the talents and tact necessary to elicit from victims descriptions of the assailant, and produce an artist's impression. Half-watching the programme, she saw the picture of Fell, 'and the hairs stood up on the back of my neck.' The genuine Fell bore an incredibly strong resemblance to a soldier convicted for rapes at knife-point; assaults which had been perpetrated some four years after Fell had been in prison. That soldier had been apprehended after she had produced drawings of him based on the victims' experience, and he had been found to own a vehicle described in the attacks. Fell may have had the simple misfortune to look like the real murderer.

Another call was from a man whose hobby was treasure-hunting. Thirteen months earlier he'd been out with his metal detector a couple of miles from the site of the murder. His apparatus had picked up an echo. Buried deep was a rusty knife. A Fairbairn Sykes commando knife. We rang up the army to ask if there were any conceivable circumstances in which a soldier might innocently bury such a valuable piece of kit, and were told, unsurprisingly, no.

We handed it over to Fell's solicitor, asking that he pass it on to the police. It could be important evidence. And we don't want to be accused of suppressing evidence, or perverting the course of justice.

We are, at the time of writing, still waiting for the wheels of justice to grind. These things can take several years. Stephen Phelps always reminds me that his daughter was born six days after transmission of the programme we made on the case of the Darvell brothers in Swansea. By the time the two men walked free from the Court of Appeal, she was three-and-a-half. We know that the police are re-investigating the matter. And we haven't heard any more from the Assistant Chief Constable, who may have better and more important things to do.

5
Terry Allen
The Ones that Got Away

I don't know if Terry Allen is guilty of murder. The problem is, neither does he.

Allen's case turned out to be one of the most intriguing – and frustrating – cases we have ever undertaken. Something is very, very wrong with the conviction; on the other hand, if Terry Allen is guilty he deserves to be in prison for a long time.

On the morning of 18 July 1985, on a cheerless and decrepit housing estate near Reading, a neighbour knocked at the door of Anita Kirkwood's flat. There was no reply, only the whimpering of Anita's five-year-old son Damian. Eventually, Damian was persuaded to open the door. In the hallway was the body of his mother. Blood spattered on the walls bore witness to a savage knife attack, although the cause of death was eventually established as asphyxia, brought on by inhalation of stomach contents after strangulation with the cord to the bathroom light. There was a vicious bitemark on one of her breasts. The child, in shock, could volunteer very little information except that someone called 'Peter' had hit his mother.

The body was discovered lying on a pair of knickers. Police suspected a sexual motive, and it didn't take long to establish that Anita Kirkwood had a reputation for entertaining men in her flat. Semen samples indicated that she had had sex with at least one partner in the previous twenty-four hours.

Terry Allen became a suspect by drawing attention to himself in most dramatic style. Just half an hour after Anita's body had been discovered, Willy Crowley went to the lock-up garage he rented to fetch some tools. He had given Allen the key to the garage, so that he could use it to fix up Crowley's white Cortina.

The garage door was slightly ajar, and he heard the muffled sound of a car engine. He ran in, to find Terry Allen slumped in the driver's seat, a cider bottle on his lap, struggling for breath amid the sickening fumes of carbon monoxide, pumped out of the exhaust, along a hosepipe, and into the car through one of its rear windows. The gap in the window was clumsily sealed with a pair of jeans. Crowley smashed the front passenger window with a spanner and turned off the ignition, but he couldn't get the car out of the garage on his own. He ran out to call an ambulance, and then flagged down a passing motorist to help push the car out of the garage. The neighbour frenziedly tugged the car out of the garage to get at the driver's door. Allen was taken to the Royal Berkshire Hospital, suffering from temporary blindness, paralysis and lockjaw. His condition was not helped by the considerable amount of cider he had consumed.

The two events, a murder followed by an attempted suicide, both in the tight little neighbourhood of the same dilapidated council estate, were, for the police at least, too much of a coincidence. It did not take long to establish links between Allen and the dead woman; she had often acted as a baby-sitter for his children. Officers were posted round Allen's hospital bed to monitor his progress and his conversation. A week later he had recovered sufficiently to be charged with the murder of Anita Kirkwood. After caution, he replied: 'Can I say I'm innocent?'

The case against Allen was formidable. It was soon established that he and his common-law wife had had a furious row on the night of the murder. Allen had stormed out, and had been seen near the victim's flat, five minutes' walk away, around the time that neighbours first heard a loud and continuous sequence of screams coming from her flat. Allen seemed to have no alibi for the time of these screams, the twenty minutes or so after half-past ten.

Murder squad detectives swarmed around the flat. Hundreds of swabs, samples, and fingerprints were taken. Police found one particularly damning piece of evidence – a fingerprint on the lavatory cistern. It matched a print taken from Allen while in police custody. Allen had denied ever visiting Anita Kirkwood's flat. The print proved him a liar.

Blood on the jeans which had been stuffed in the window, and on a brown shirt found by the police in the suicide car, matched Anita Kirkwood's. At the post-mortem, Dr Stephen Cordner examined the bitemark on the victim's left breast; it bore the impression of four teeth. An expert forensic odontologist would later testify at Allen's trial that 'the bitemarks on the deceased's breast are consistent with the defendant's dentition.' Allen's teeth are distinctive and irregular. It is difficult to forget them; I keep turning up the plaster cast of them at the back of my desk drawer. Allen made several admissions to the police, shortly after being released into their custody by the hospital. In one, he asks chillingly: 'Was she bitten in half?'

The judge at Allen's trial told the jury that it was 'as cast-iron a case as you are likely to find.' It's difficult to argue with that.

So why wasn't Terry Allen written off as a no-hope case from the very beginning? Why did Steve Haywood nurse a correspondence with Allen over a matter of years? Haywood says it was one of what he calls his 'charity' cases – a small, nagging portfolio of cases which he refuses to sign off. It was, perhaps, something about Allen's pathetic plea that he simply did not know whether he had committed the crime or not. Drink and the car fumes had simply erased all memory. There was also the consideration that anything Allen had told the police, under the mind-altering influence not only of the carbon monoxide fumes, but also of the drugs he was being treated with, had to be profoundly suspect. His mind was a blank tablet; when the horrific facts of the murder were graphically inscribed upon it, he had little option but to accept that what the police were saying was true. But, as he began to recover the use of his brain, and his memory, he started to question the assumptions he had so far accepted.

An intelligent man – he had his IQ measured at 136 at the age of fifteen – Allen has spent his prison years becoming an expert in his own case, and increasingly convincing himself of his own innocence.

It sounded to the amateur psychologists among us as a classic case of denial and paranoia. But the case did have some intriguing aspects to it. For instance, after the discovery of the body, five of Anita Kirkwood's known lovers were arrested, including one whose Christian name was 'Peter' – the name that five-year-old Damian, perhaps in the confusion of his distress, had first volunteered to the police. It became clear that the victim was promiscuous to the extent that she may have had any number of visitors on the night she was killed. We also unearthed, among the documents not used in the trial, suggestions that Allen's common-law wife at the time was bitterly jealous of Anita, after Allen had supposedly spent a night 'on her sofa'.

Strangest of all, as we excavated and cross-referenced the stack of statements which represent the quarry of our investigation, we discovered that the police may well have been within earshot of the murder at the very time the crime was being committed.

Cases which depend on evidence of timing, we find, are fraught with problems. Compile a literal chronology, according to sincerely-sworn statements, and it soon becomes obvious that people are honestly mistaken about the precise times at which key events occurred. All of us tend to measure our journey through the day by the arbitrary milestones of unrelated external events – when the shops shut for early closing, or the familiar bus we just missed. Overwhelmingly, we judge the time that things happen in the evening by reference to the television – 'just before the weather forecast', 'while the commercials were on in *The Crystal Maze.*' In the case of the murder of Anita Kirkwood, 'the ITV news was still on' when one neighbour heard the screaming begin. It went on, according to another 'after ITN had ended.' For another, *Dallas* had just ended, so she could place the scream at half past ten.

It's routine for us, faced with statements like this, not just to get the relevant *TV Times*, but to ask for the log of the television station involved. Programmes do not always run to length, and, as they state in the small print of the listings pages, 'regions vary'. This time, everything was normal: the *News at Ten* ended at 10.30 p.m., regional news, weather, and of commercials took until 10.45 p.m., when *East of Eden* began as scheduled.

We could time the onset of the screaming at between 10.20 and 10.30 p.m. But at least four witnesses who helped pin down the time refer to something else; as they looked out of their windows to see where the noise was coming from, they saw a police car outside. Most of them connected the two events; there must have been a domestic dispute to which the police had been called. In fact, the police had come on entirely separate business;

86

they were delivering one of the residents back to the estate after she had been arrested for shoplifting. But while the residents logged the police arriving during the screaming, the crew of the police car recorded their arrival on the estate at 10.50 p.m., about twenty minutes after the witnesses claimed the cries of anguish ceased. Either the residents or the police, then, were wrong. If, of course, the residents were right, this would leave the police in the embarrassing position of having been present at the scene of a murder – at the very time it was being committed – yet having failed either to detect or prevent it. But the judge at Allen's trial preferred the police's version of the timing.

This had unfortunate repercussions for Allen's alibi – such as it was. Another neighbour, Earl Nickie, said he had seen Allen outside his own flat at half past ten, when many are sure the screaming began, or had already begun. The victim's flat is several minutes away; Allen could not have been in two places at the same time.

But it was the forensic evidence – or rather our re-analysis of it – that was to provide the biggest riddle. Scores of fingerprints were taken inside Anita Kirkwood's flat; but only one was used at Terry Allen's trial. There are two things about this that are odd. First, what about those others? If they had been Allen's, surely the police would have made much of the fact; but if they weren't, whose were they? Why should Allen have been premeditatedly cunning enough to cover his hands, except for one fatal print? Secondly, what actually was recovered from the lavatory cistern? The police sergeant talks about a fingerprint, or a 'fingermark'. He gave it a reference number, exhibit Q – later inexplicably rechristened exhibit CFC1 – and then 'forwarded it by internal post to the Fingerprint Department at the Police HQ, Kidlington.' But when comparisons were made with Allen's, it was the suspect's *palm*-print – exhibit SGH9 – that was used to try to make the match. As the fingerprint specialist records, 'I have compared exhibit CFC1 with exhibit SGH9 and I have no doubt that the impressions were made by the same person.' I'm sure there is a simple explanation, but I would like to know how you can compare a fingerprint with a palm-print. It didn't seem to bother the judge, but then he got it wrong in his summing-up, referring constantly to Allen's palm-print as having been found in the bathroom. We'd also like to know how the reference number came to be changed.

There are some other forensic oddities about the case. The first policeman on the scene of Allen's abortive suicide attempt, records the following objects retrieved from the car: letters, in a see-through bag, an envelope containing a shotgun cartridge and pieces of grass, the bloodstained jeans and a pair of shoes. Later, at the trial he said that he was certain that he would have noticed if there was anything else in the car.

Yet when the other officers – now, of course, aware of the murder – turn up later to take the car away for tests, they find a lot more in the garage; this time there is a bloodstained brown shirt, as well as a belt and underpants stained with blood. On a third visit to the garage, a bloody sock is recovered. The only innocent reason for the piecemeal emergence of evidence – and the likeliest – is sloppy police work. Sloppier still – given that this is a murder enquiry – is that the jeans are variously coded as exhibit MA2 and MA3, but the letters are given exhibit number MA2, and the hosepipe which was connected to the exhaust is also MA3. The identification letters of exhibits, incidentally, is based on the initials of the officer responsible for each one, and it is vital to keep proper records to preserve what's called the 'chain of evidence' and preserve the police from suspicion that they may have tampered with vital clues. One likes to think of forensic evidence as being crisp and clinical. The forensic evidence in the Allen case is a dog's breakfast.

Only the stains on the jeans and shirt can be matched with the victim's blood. Terry Allen's partner always maintained that police had removed the brown shirt from her ironing basket. As for the jeans, there is evidence to suggest that they were removed for a time, from the safe-keeping of the police holding room without apparently being formally signed out. Again, strict police procedures – designed, after all, to protect the police themselves – seem to have been smudged.

And then there was the bitemark. In court, as we know, a forensic odontologist gave his expert opinion that the mark matched Allen's irregular teeth. But it has to be said that forensic odontology – like many apparent areas of expertise – is as much an art, shall we say, as a science. Tissue stretches under the pressure of a bite, especially if the victim is struggling to extricate herself; a three-dimensional object like a breast makes it particularly difficult to gain a clear imprint. There are, it is not surprising to find, very few forensic odontologists in the country, and the same experts are regularly called to the same trials – one for the prosecution, one for the defence. Expert evidence, one cannot stress often enough, is nine times out of ten a matter of opinion. The problem is compounded by our adversarial system, where barristers are competing to get the expert to give black or white answers, when the truth is somewhat grey. Bob Duffield's opinion was that we should submit the bite evidence to a new, digitized system of pattern recognition called maximum entropy deconvolution; if nothing else, it had a fine scientific ring to it.

A brief, and final, word about scientific evidence. One of the most reassuring things about journalism is the discovery that the world is run on a refreshingly human and amateur basis; prime ministers chew their nails, captains of industry can't balance their cheque books, and hospital consultants still don't know how to deal with a virus. In the same way, I can think of a forensic laboratory with a global reputation for the integrity of its scientific work where they keep the samples in the same domestic refrigerator as their lunch-time sandwiches, and where evidence has been known to go missing, or have the vital labels fall off when they become soggy with spilt yoghurt.

When we looked further into the evidence collected at the scene of the murder, we discovered another mystery. In both the dead woman's hands were strands of human hair; hair was also found caught in her watchstrap. It often happens that, in a struggle, a victim's last vain act of defence is to pull at the assailant's hair. But the hair found in Anita Kirkwood's hands and in her watchstrap was not, we discovered, that of Terry Allen. . . .

We were also interested in Terry Allen's interviews, some of which were taken when he was completely disorientated as a result of drugs and poisoning from the car fumes. In the first, a week after the murder, he can't even recall the suicide attempt. Later that day he remembered that he was under suspicion for murdering a neighbour, but he thinks, wrongly, that it is his next-door neighbour until prompted by the police. In another interview he cannot remember anything about Anita Kirkwood's five-year-old son being there, but says: 'How can you go and kill someone with her blinking kid there . . . It don't matter how hard you are, you can't do that. If I was going to kill her I'd kill him as well to get him out of the way.'

We paid several visits to the estate, talking to neighbours, getting a feel of the geography. It was one of the harshest places I have ever visited in a privileged career of covering events in some of the most desperate parts of the earth. The very fabric of the estate breathed resentment and despair. Every piece of public property was trashed, shattered, or, if capable of with-standing destruction, defiled with graffiti. Large loose dogs had begun to hunt in packs. When you knocked at any door, the invariable first response was that so-and-so didn't live there, even though quite evidently they did. The community was united only in implacable distrust and loathing of the local police. The econ-omy seemed to be based entirely on the resale of videotape-recorders of dubious origin. The other source of income was stealing people's cars and setting fire to them, so that their owners could profit from the insurance. Terry Allen did a bit of that. No one I met had a job, or knew anyone else who did. Chain-smoking women held together families of lolling youths and broken, bron-chial, prematurely-aged men. Everyone watched satellite tele-vision. This was a housing estate close to the heart of one of the jewels of the Thatcherite boom, in the high-tech M4 corridor. Here was the underside of that eighties surge for growth. Here was the underclass that was the waste product of the Thatcher revolution.

On one of Bob's visits, he discovered that Anita Kirkwood, the victim, had been the object of a threatening telephone call from a gang of men who threatened 'to come up and do ya.' Anita's sister Marion had taken the call. He also got a firsthand account from Allen's partner of the brown shirt – supposedly found, bloodsoaked, in the car; she was still adamant that the police had called, after Terry Allen's arrest, with a list of clothing that they wanted. She was asked for a brown shirt, and told the officer that it was in her washing basket.

We also know something else about Allen's relations with the police. Earlier on the very evening of the murder, he had gone to the local Roundhead pub for a meeting – a rendezvous with two police-officers. Allen, it turned out, was a police informer. He drove round the neighbourhood with the two detectives, pointing out the addresses of various local criminals. The trio split up at about a quarter to eight.

Suddenly, two of the objects found in the car seem to make sense: the shotgun cartridge mysteriously wrapped around with blades of grass. Grass. The name for a police informer. Had someone discovered Allen's secret, and sent him the traditional warning – a bullet? Was it terror that led Allen to attempt a drunken suicide, rather than the guilt of Anita Kirkwood's murder?

There are so many riddles and irregularities in the case of Terry Allen that I wonder, as I write this, why we took the case no further, after months of research. It looks like a case where some fairly brutal corners have been cut, and where the evidence has been handled in a fairly reckless manner. Who is right about the time of the police's presence at the very time the murder was being committed? Could the hair in the victim's hands be her own, torn out in her death-throes? Was the fingerprint just one of those lucky million-to-one hunches? Did the police just make a botch of the collection, identification, and labelling of the exhibits? Did the child say it was 'Peter' who hit mummy simply because it was the name he knew best?

But is it fair to infer anything more sinister from the mere muddle and confusion of some aspects of police handling of the case? If Allen is innocent, can we seriously believe that the police took Terry Allen's jeans and shirt and dunked them in the blood of a murder victim? According to our own conversations with forensic pathologists, they would have had to get someone to put on the jeans and kneel in the blood, as well as wetting their hands in it and wiping them on the jeans; that's the only way the pattern of the stains could have happened. Policemen do sometimes 'improve' evidence, but there is no reason to believe they would have gone to such disproportionately wicked lengths to guarantee themselves an easier conviction in this sad and sordid affair.

Terry Allen once told us, as we sat in his cell in Maidstone Prison, that he didn't care what we discovered, so long as we could put him out of his misery and let him know whether he killed Anita Kirkwood or not.

Sorry, Terry. We still don't know.

6
Omar Raddad

They Order Things Differently in France

Television is a global phenomenon with a parochial outlook. It is an uphill struggle to get a news editor, still more a channel controller, interested in a foreign story. News values are determined by an unacknowledged graph, the two axes of which are 'severity of incident' and 'distance from west London.' Thus a three-car collision in Shepherd's Bush may make the news, but it takes a very large ferry disaster in Bangladesh to qualify for a place in the bulletin. Yet, in the middle of some tedious domestic documentary, you'll hear the words 'in America they do things differently; we went to San Francisco to discover how.' The reason for this – more often than not – is not to broaden the public's horizons, but to increase the reporters' Air Miles and deepen their tans.

So I feel a certain chagrin in spending a few words on a miscarriage of justice in the South of France.

There are, however, two good reasons. First, at a time when the failures of the British system are coming under intense scrutiny, some lawyers are looking across the Channel to the Napoleonic certainties of French justice. The second reason is that there's no reason to believe that Omar Raddad is guilty of the crime for which he has been sentenced to eighteen years in prison.

It was a blazing Provençal afternoon in the village of Mougins, high in the hills above Nice. Pretty as the old town is, the outskirts are littered with the stylistically unsympathetic villas and ranch-houses of the rich summer visitors. La Chamade is one such summer home, a nondescript pastel house hiding without conspicuous success in this cluttered suburb of Paradise, among the olive groves. Its owner, a widow of sixty-five called Ghislaine Marchal, did manage to keep herself to herself, living quietly off the fortune she had inherited from her late husband's car-accessories firm.

Some time shortly after noon, however, on 23 June 1991, Mme Marchal met a horrible death. She was found barricaded in the villa basement, having suffered multiple stab wounds and a clubbing with a blunt instrument. But she had left one, devastating clue. On the door of the basement she had written – in her own blood – the words 'Omar m'a tuer' ('Omar killed me').

An indictment from beyond the grave is pretty strong evidence, and it did not take the police long to fasten upon the hapless figure of Omar Raddad, Marchal's twenty-nine-year-old part-time Moroccan gardener. A quiet, slight figure, with no history of violence, Raddad's only known vice was a weakness for one-armed bandits; it was assumed that robbery must have been the motive – though why Raddad should kill off a source of employment and income for the sake of at most a fistful of francs was never made clear. There were other mysteries, too. Raddad would have had to make good his escape from the scene of the crime back down the dusty road aboard his moped. But the track is well-populated, by villa owners with time on their hands to cultivate their gardens, and no one saw a man who, on any reckoning, must have been spattered with blood. Again, neighbours testified that an unidentified caller had come to the Marchal household at a time after the supposed murder, and a woman's voice had told him to go away. A strange car with Swiss number plates was reported to have been prowling the area.

Most fascinating of all was that message. Mme Marchal would have had to make an extraordinary effort to lever herself up to scrawl her bloody accusation. Why not write it on the floor, and why, anyway, write such an elaborate sentence? Why not just 'Omar'? Why should someone, who was by definition alive at the time, write that she had been killed? And – horror of horrors to a nation as fastidious in its use of language as France – why should she perpetrate the howler of writing 'tuer' instead of 'tuée'? It's the equivalent of writing 'it be Omar,' not a mistake a well-educated woman like Ghislaine Marchal would have made. Ghislaine Marchal was a crossword addict; was it too fanciful to imagine that she may have been forced to write a false accusation, yet had subtly managed to include a clue that it was untrue?

But this is Maigret territory, and, I'll come clean, it is a detective story to which I have no answers. It wasn't a case we subjected to the full *Trial and Error* scrutiny, although I believe that with the expertise of our team we could indeed have cracked it. No, the importance of the Omar Raddad case – a case as fiercely debated in the cafés and columns of *Le Monde* as the Dreyfus affair some hundred years earlier – is the light it sheds on our own system of justice.

I hesitate to say so, but the case of Omar Raddad makes our battered old system look positively plausible.

Taking the process from the investigation of the crime to the final conviction of Raddad provides several useful points of comparison. For a start, it's a common criticism of the British system that it's the police alone who build a case against a suspect. In France, this process is supervised and directed by a neutral investigative magistrate, a *juge d'instruction*. There is a similar system in Scotland, where an officer called the Procurator-fiscal is in charge of the investigation. The French system, therefore, ought to be comparatively free of the viruses of British police practice – principally the blinkered approach under which an initial suspect is identified, and the case is built against him, neglecting evidence which points to anyone else's guilt.

But the Raddad case was a case study in terminal tunnel vision. 'Once the police had Omar Raddad in their sights, they looked no further,' said one neighbouring lotus-eater. There was little or no investigation of other suspects. The pathologist took no measurements of Mme Marchal which would have established whether in fact she was the author of the bloodstained message. No fingerprints were taken from the victim to match the writing; nor was her handbag checked for the fingerprints of the person who supposedly rifled it. The knife which inflicted the stab wounds was never found; but a piece of timber had also been used to bludgeon the victim, and it was not checked for fingerprints either. The estimation of time of death was even vaguer than cautious pathologists usually allow.

'We don't have a system of justice so much as a system of punishment,' France's best-known criminal lawyer, Maitre

Verges, told me. 'When we have a crime, public opinion understandably calls for the conviction of the guilty. But when you
don't have the guilty man, then we settle for anyone against
whom we have mere suspicion.' It was Verges, a rotund, owl-like
figure, who took on the Raddad case; he has a deep conviction
that even those accused of the vilest crimes deserve the best
defence – and he also has a keen eye for publicity. In this he
resembles some other prominent British QCs. He defended, for
instance, Klaus Barbie, the Gestapo Butcher of Lyons.

The French, of course, is an inquisitorial system, whereas ours
in Britain is an adversarial system. Our system stands accused
(rightly, in my layman's opinion) of being a competition about
guilt rather than a search for the truth. As with any game, a
series of faintly ludicrous rules has evolved and been justified by
custom and practice. British justice, in this respect, is rather like
real tennis, except that real tennis is played out in rather more
sensible clothes.

Wiser people than me, and people whom I admire, like Sir
Ludovic Kennedy and Michael Mansfield QC, believe that an
inquisitorial system is a better guarantee of justice. I used to
think so too, before the case of Omar Raddad. What I had not
understood was that under an inquisitorial system the defence
has no powers to mount its own investigation and find its own
witnesses. I asked Verges, why, for instance, the defence hadn't
conducted its own post-mortem on the victim, as is customary in
Britain. He looked shocked. 'If I did that, I would be accused of
bringing pressure on witnesses!' he exclaimed.

But the real eye-opener came with the discovery that in French
criminal cases the judge actually sits with the jury during their
deliberations (there were also two extra magistrates). The whole
essence of a British trial is that after the forensic experts and
legal professionals have had their say, and the judge has
judiciously summed up the evidence, the matter is left to the
judgement of twelve good people and true. Common sense, in
other words, has its day in court. In every summing up the judge
must make this separation clear – the judge is the judge of the
law, but the jury is the judge of the facts.

With the best will in the world, the majority of judges in any
system will tend towards the prosecution. The reasons for this

are complex. In part, it is because many judges are drawn from the ranks of lawyers who have specialized in prosecution work. There is also the consideration that judges become jaundiced by the daily flood of criminality and depravity that laps around their stockinged feet. Judges in Britain also have foreknowledge of the accused's convictions – which explains why they have sometimes turned their apoplectic contempt on juries who have reached what they consider perverse verdicts. They are also older than average, and while very probably wiser as a result, a certain hardening of the arteries of clemency inevitably sets in.

The idea, then, of a judge joining the jury's deliberations is an extraordinary aberration in a culture as logical as the French claim their own to be. The explanation, I suppose, lies in the historic tension between the revolutionary and conservative tendencies of the Republic. The French Revolution brought in citizen juries, in the name of liberty, equality, and fraternity. But France always feels the need to repress its own anarchic psyche with Bonapartist, centralizing authority. This duality occurs virtually every May, when the young take to the street in a carnival of revolution, and the riot police move in to stop the party getting out of hand. It showed itself in the Commune of 1870, where France scared herself to death, and then turned septic with national self-reproach – a process during which the Sacré Coeur was built as an act of expiation, and Dreyfus was victimized as a semite scapegoat.

It was at another ebb tide of Gallic disgrace that the law was changed to introduce the judge into the jury room. The measure was introduced during the wartime Vichy régime, when the traitorous Marshal Pétain decided to throw in his lot with the Germans. The puppet government, following the penal philosophy of the Nazis, decided that it would be politic to curb the unpredictable freedom of ordinary people to decide the guilt or innocence of their fellow citizens. The French simply did not trust the people – and they still don't. It is, apparently, the one piece of Vichy legislation which was not repealed after the war, when France set about repairing itself – a process in which it has been brilliantly successful except in this one, crucially authoritarian, respect.

Jury secrecy is strictly enforced on both sides of the Channel.

Not for us the freedom of Bernstein and Woodward to knock on the doors of the grand jury panel, to winkle out the *in camera* secrets of Watergate. Try that in Britain, and a judge would send you down for perverting the course of justice. The Lord Chancellor's Department – that creaky old compromise designed to protect us from the perils of a Ministry of Justice – has even systematically frustrated academic research into the workings of the jury, and confidential study of how they conduct their deliberations; the suspicion is that the judges would be embarrassed if they learnt what juries said about them in the privacy of the jury room.

In the Raddad case, however, one juror broke ranks and spoke to the press. There were, he said, insufficient votes for conviction at first – which would mean that Omar Raddad would go free. But the judge, supported by the two magistrates, apparently argued fiercely for conviction; and in the end the jury went along with them. The anonymous juror is now the subject of an intense police manhunt, and, for all we know, his account may not be true.

With or without any judicial pressure, the way the jury reaches its decision looks decidedly odd to Anglo-Saxon eyes. In Britain, the juror has to be convinced 'beyond reasonable doubt'. This conviction clearly has to be based on an objective assessment of the evidence. In France, the criterion is somewhat more elusive – one might almost say ethereal. The French juror needs to attain what's called *conviction intime*. 'It is a magical, almost mystical, some would say sacrosanct concept,' Maurice Peyrot, the veteran court correspondent of *Le Monde* confided to me, as we walked through the marbled cathedral of the Palais de Justice. But *conviction intime* translates brutally as little more than a heartfelt hunch. Intuition, it seems to me, has little part to play in justice. The earthier concept of common sense and reasonable doubt seems safer. Maitre Verges agrees: 'Anything based on *conviction intime* is bound to be subjective, and therefore it is bound to be arbitrary.'

It is a conviction which, in Britain, would automatically go to appeal, but there is no such smooth passage for a French criminal case. Things, heaven knows, are hard enough in Britain, where an appellant has to appear before a judge to seek leave to appeal which, if denied, has to be sought at the appellant's own expense before a panel of three judges. In the old days, at the beginning of this century when the Court of Appeal was first instituted, judges were very reluctant to interfere with the verdicts of juries; they found that they could keep their hands clean by finding the academic excuse of some legal error in procedure or interpretation. But this, it was acknowledged, was a needless handicap to justice, and British judges evolved a criterion of a 'lurking doubt' about a conviction providing cause to quash it. The exact criteria of the court have changed to match the prevailing social and political climate, and the formula now is that there must be 'new evidence not available at the time of the trial' to prevent lawyers running a second defence when their first strategy has failed or 'other consideration of substance' which is pompous Parliament-speak for a sudden realization that a cock-up has occurred. In France, the judiciary are still stuck in the Jurassic period of appeal; they can only reverse a scandalous and clamant miscarriage of justice if there is a legal nit to pick and a riven legal sleeve to unravel.

Just as the sight of a policeman's helmet is somehow reassuring to the voyager returning to Folkestone on the cross-Channel ferry, so, for all its faults, the creaky old British system seemed not such a bad old thing in the light of the French experience. At worst, our system is a series of compromises held together by hypocrisy. And at worst, theirs is a machine for discipline justified by casuistry.

7
Gary Mills and Tony Poole
A Murder by Neglect

One day, we'll get a letter from a vicar, with no previous convictions, wrongly convicted of murder, with an alibi vouched for by a local magistrate and verified by the Lord Lieutenant of the county.

That's the dream; the reality is that most of our mail, sluicing through the office like a rancid tide, comes from the sordid and compromised world of the con man, the hustler, the gangster, the thief. Many miscarriages of justice spring from the understandable frustration of policemen who know very well that so-and-so is a villain, but can't get him bang to rights. So the police yield to the temptation to improve or manufacture evidence, on the grounds that if he's not guilty of this particular crime, he's certainly guilty of other things just as bad. The criminal does not share this rough-hewn penal philosophy; sure, he regards getting caught and convicted as a professional risk, but nothing outrages him more than the injustice of being put away for a crime he did not commit. It is, of course, in legal terms a miscarriage of justice just as much as that suffered by my fanciful vicar; but it's hard to commit yourself and the team to proving the innocence of a rapist who did not commit that particular rape, or of an armed robber who couldn't have held up that particular post office because he was doing the bank around the corner at the time.

Between the vicar and the rapist, as it were, there's a seam of petty offenders who have been convicted for a crime that seems way out of their league. This can mean one of two things; it may be a natural criminal career development, or it may be that there's been a bit of rough-and-ready tidying up – a minor villain is convicted of a major crime, to get him out of the way.

Could that have happened in the case of Gary Mills and Tony Poole? And there were two other good reasons for tidying them away with a life sentence for murder: it diverted attention from the doctors and police officers in whose supposed care the murder victim died. The intriguing fact about this case is that the victim was admitted to hospital with apparently superficial injuries, and after fifteen hours either in casualty or the cells of Gloucester Police Station, the man was dead.

It was a case that was to take us half way round the world, but it began in a scruffy neighbourhood in Gloucester, part of a warren of terraced brick villas which seem somehow out of place in the cathedral city capital of the royals' favoured county. It's as if Coronation Street were unaccountably transported into Inspector Morse's Oxford. Indeed, in the course of our investigation we were to knock on the door of Number 25 Cromwell Street – a house destined, a few months later, to become notorious the world over, as the police discovered the bodies of nine women walled up or buried within its modest precincts. None of us can remember if Frederick West or his wife, who at the time of writing are facing charges of murder, answered the door. They were probably out.

Gloucester is not all tea rooms, cloisters, Laura Ashley, and honey-coloured stone; it has always been a rough old place. It used to be a major inland port; coasters would call and discharge their cargoes onto the docks, for collection by the waiting narrowboats and distribution along the British canal system. Nearby Cheltenham has creamed off much of the quality, while Gloucester is close enough to London – via the M4 or the InterCity – to provide a haven for the capital's criminals when the heat is on.

Conduit Street is part of an urban inner core that's been left too long to rot. A multi-racial neighbourhood fights against the encroachment of drugs and petty crime, typified, in 1989, by the residents of Number 34. One of them, the tenant of the upstairs flat, was Willie Wiltshire, himself a refugee from London's criminal frontline. There was no love lost between Wiltshire and the police; he was wanted in connection with an indecent assault, and was actually suing the Metropolitan Police over a scuffle with some officers, as a result of which he lost a testicle. There were also rumours that Wiltshire was suspected of having grassed up a member of a south London gang. There were good reasons for Willie Wiltshire to lie low awhile in Gloucester, and while he was there, he could teach his country cousins a thing or two about crime.

The ground-floor flat of Number 34 was occupied by Tony Poole, a minor criminal and drugs dealer with a disarmingly rustic Cotswold accent. One evening in January 1989, Poole was listening to loud reggae music with his friend Gary Mills, a former soldier who was also a small-time villain with a reputation as a wild man. With the two white men was a black man called Neville Jukes; he, too, had had his run-ins with the police. They were making their way through bottles of Bacardi and vodka, the ill-gotten gains of an afternoon spent passing dud cheques in the neighbourhood off-licences. They were smoking ganja. The evening was pleasantly relaxed until Wiltshire arrived to join the party.

Wiltshire was already high on at least one score of amphetamines taken earlier that day; he also had five times the breathalyser limit of alcohol in his bloodstream. He was, according to what Neville Jukes later told me, spoiling for a fight. 'He stormed into the room ... he was either on cocaine or angel dust, which makes you feel five, six times stronger than you really are. He was really aggressive ...' First, Wiltshire challenged Jukes to come outside and have a fight. Jukes laughed him off, and the other two, Mills and Poole, joined in the laughter.

This seemed to madden Wiltshire into incandescent rage. He leapt onto Gary Mills, and the two writhed together on the floor. After a minute, as suddenly as the fight had started, it stopped. The storm had passed. The foursome joked, smoked more cannabis together. Then, again without warning, Wiltshire dived across the room at Gary Mills. This time it was more than a mere scuffle. A knife appeared in Wiltshire's hand; Gary tried to fend off the slashing attack, and got his hand ripped open in the process. He dived across the room for a crowbar, secreted behind the settee, and thrashed it through the air in front of him in an effort to keep the maddened Wiltshire at bay. Tony Poole, who had been concentrating on the music and was, it seems likely, in a world more or less of his own up to that point, realized that the situation was getting out of hand and, with Neville Jukes, managed to part the combatants.

Once again, after this second round, the mercurial Wiltshire seemed to calm down. According to Jukes, he said he'd been stupid and he was sorry – they really ought to reserve their aggression for their enemies, and not waste it upon each other. Then, fuelled by whatever frenzy, driven by whatever demons, Wiltshire launched himself once more on to Gary Mills. This time Wiltshire had the crowbar; he was on top of Mills, pushing down hard on his windpipe. Mills managed to get hold of the knife, and, from his disadvantaged position under Wiltshire, managed to stab his legs and buttocks. Eventually Mills, a trained hand-to-hand army combat expert, got the better of Wiltshire, and used the knife to inflict a series of angry jabs.

The house in Conduit Street has been sold, but the new owner, at the time we were in Gloucester, had not got round to doing the place up. He did agree, however, to lend us the keys to the place. There is quite a lot of refurbishment to do. The front room is still spattered with blood; on the wallpaper there are arcs of splashed, brown dots, or smudges caused by blood-soaked clothing brushing against the wall. The scenes of violent crimes are usually disappointingly prosaic. I remember a neat little bedroom in Dover which didn't betray a hint of the terrible killing its walls had supposedly witnessed. The woodland walk where the two women in the Fell case (see chapter 4) met their deaths is as pastorally innocent as ever. But the ground floor of 34 Conduit Street has a chill about it; the very fact that no one has bothered to wipe away the stains has somehow left the crime itself unexorcized. The house, a Gothic Edwardian villa, stands alone, surrounded by wasteland or new developments, as if the neighbourhood itself wants to keep its distance. The cameraman was taking an evening shot, and the dying December sun was streaming through the windows. 'I can't photograph this,' he said, 'it's over the top, Hammer-House-of-Horror stuff; the sunlight makes it look as if it's soaked in blood.'

Wiltshire, bleeding freely, was carried out into the street. It was now just after midnight. Gary Mills shouted for someone to get an ambulance for him, and, with Tony Poole and Neville Jukes, made himself scarce. Wiltshire was taken to the Gloucester Royal Hospital, where he succeeded in alienating most of the medical and nursing staff, and where his wounds were logged as 'superficial'. Staff found and confiscated a small, broken kitchen knife in his sock, not the knife used in the attack, but more probably his drugs knife, the utensil he used for dividing up his angel dust. He had a skull X-ray, but at four in the morning he was discharged from casualty into the hands of the Gloucester Police; he was on the police wanted list because of the suspected indecent assault. After an hour and a half in the dank, Victorian cell, with its spartan green vinyl mattress, Wiltshire was visited by the duty police surgeon.

Dr Chaudhuri says that there's very little that shocks him these days, after what he's seen in his police duties. When I met him, he had just returned from the local railway line to certify that a body found there was dead. 'The head was twenty yards away from the rest of him, they hardly needed a medical opinion,' he laughed. But Dr Chaudhuri was taken aback when he saw the state Wiltshire was in. 'There was blood everywhere,' he said. Wiltshire was shivering in his underpants, confused and restless. He said: 'Don't touch me, I've had it.' Dr Chaudhuri was adamant; Wiltshire should go back to hospital.

Within a few hours, however, Chaudhuri was telephoned by the hospital, 'Thank you for sending us this chap,' said a cheery voice from the accident unit. 'We patched him up and sent him back to the police station.' Chaudhuri was appalled. 'My God, you can't do that!' he expostulated. 'You're taking a terrible chance.' But Chaudhuri deferred to his colleague's judgement.

Later in the day, according to the police account, a sudden crisis arose in Wiltshire's health. He was rushed – for the third time in twelve hours – back to hospital. At half past three, Willie Wiltshire was pronounced dead.

And Gary Mills was wanted for murder.

Mills went round to the police station and made a frank statement. He has never denied being involved in the fight, and he has always accepted that it was he who inflicted the stab wounds. But he insisted that it was a matter of self-defence. 'Look,' he told me darkly on a visit to Gartree Prison, 'the Army taught me how to kill. If I'd wanted to kill Willie nothing would have been easier.'

For a long time, it used to be the programme-makers' policy never to see the subjects of their investigations – the prisoners themselves. We thought there were two big dangers; first, that we would become too personally involved in the people concerned to take a dispassionate view of the evidence. On the other hand, we might be influenced by the fact that we simply didn't like the look of them. There was also the problem that it could place an unfair pressure on the prisoner to lie to us, to improve his case, in his desperation to win our support. And once we find one of our subjects lying to us, all our confidence evaporates.

I was discussing this policy with a barrister, who was surprised. 'The only time I feel I can assess a client's innocence,' she said, 'is when I meet him and can look him in the eyes.' From then on, we began routinely to visit prisoners, and have found it a vital part of the process. It's not just that you can get a lot more done in a face-to-face meeting than you can through the mail, and those familiar blue-lined letters; it's a sharp and vital reminder that what we're doing is more than an intriguing detective story. The moment the door clangs behind you, and that institutional odour of disinfectant, polish and cabbage assaults the nose, you begin to be able to imagine the horror of being locked away for life for a crime you did not commit. I suppose the only thing worse is being tortured to divulge information you don't actually have.

The police charged Mills with murder; it's less easy to understand why they also charged Tony Poole, although those with cynical minds would understand how the evidence of Poole, Mills' principal defence, would lose much of its effect if he, too, was accused as a joint murderer. What, more likely, inspired the police to charge the two of them was the evidence of two people – one inside the ground-floor flat, one outside.

Apart from Wiltshire, Mills, Poole and Jukes, there was another person in the flat that evening. A young drifter called Kimberley Stadden had come round, to buy some drugs from Tony Poole. Tony told her to come back later: he was expecting delivery of a £10 bag of amphetamines. In court, this led to a wonderful misunderstanding; 'a ten pound bag,' asks a barrister, 'that I presume would be ten pounds in weight, m'lud. . . .' Only someone living in a very different world from Tony Poole could entertain the notion of a petty drug dealer lugging round the best part of a stone's weight of speed.

Stadden came back and prepared her injection, dissolving the white granules in a spoon over a candle flame, and drawing the solution up, through a cigarette filter, into her hypodermic syringe. Then she said, the fight erupted around her. Fearful for her fix, she put the needle away and watched, horror-struck, at the scene of carnage. According to her account, Wiltshire was the victim of a vicious and unprovoked attack, startling in its unchecked violence, horrifying in its controlled cruelty. 'Gary hit William over the head a couple of times, and then a blow to the legs and body . . . Then Tony started to stab him in the bum, he did this about five times, saying "who's an arsehole now!" '

This version of events was backed up by a man called Paul White, who happened to be passing. Through a gap in the curtain, he saw the figure of Tony Poole, towering over Wiltshire; 'I saw Tony hitting down towards the floor. I then saw the head and the raised arms of somebody trying to protect themselves and screaming "No, Tony, no!" '

The evidence of Kimberley Stadden and Paul White effectively undermined Mills' plea that he'd acted only in self-defence, and Poole's defence that he had never been involved in the fight at all. At Bristol Guildhall, they were found guilty and sentenced to life. The trial had had its ups and downs; a first trial had to be abandoned, when it was discovered that Dr Chaudhuri was on holiday in India. According to the official court transcript, throughout the second trial Mr Justice Swinton Thomas consistently referred to the good doctor as Dr Tandoori.

Mr Justice Swinton Thomas was also to provide us with a major headache when it came to the filming. We were shooting reconstructions in the old crown court at Oxford of various courtroom exchanges, when we decided to check that the actor playing the judge was wearing the right robes. We called the legal outfitters Ede and Ravenscroft, to ask what a Crown Court judge on the western circuit would wear. Apparently, the rig changes with the seasons, but one thing was clear, the Father Christmas outfit we had ordered – the red robes trimmed with the white fur of the High Court – was not the authentic regalia; we should have kitted him out in a fetching purple number.

Panic. Here we were, with a day's hire of a courtroom, stocked with expensive actors and a camera crew, with a judge dressed in the wrong clothes. It would make us the laughing stock of, well, of Mr Justice Swinton Thomas, I suppose, because no one else would notice. But we do like to get things right. And, on reflection, several other people would notice – their Lordships of the Court of Appeal, if it ever came to that. Frantic phone calls and feverish motorcyclists flashed between Oxford and London, until we got the requisite outfit. Someone always notices if you get a detail wrong; a recent *Panorama* programme contained the O-level journalistic gaffe of portraying a judge's gavel – it's only in America that judges avail themselves of little wooden hammers. The feature film *In the Name of the Father*, concerning the conviction of the Birmingham Six, begins with a clanger – the solicitor, Gareth Peirce, drives to work with a barrister's wig on the car seat beside her – and gets worse; solicitors do not address the Court of Appeal, where there are three judges not one; barristers do not ask to approach the bench; there are no gavels; and the Maguire Seven were not convicted in the same trial as the Birmingham Six. This shouldn't matter – the film-makers' intention is to make a broader point – but somehow it seems silly not to get such simple things right.

But, who are we to talk? A few weeks later, we just thought we had better check the matter once again. To our consternation, we discovered that the judge had, within months of the trial, been elevated to the High Court. But that was only in the Family Division of the law; would that entitle him to wear his Father Christmas outfit while presiding over a sordid criminal matter? We made endless calls to the Lord Chancellor's Department, only to find that we had been right the first time. Although the judge had no words to speak, and was effectively little more than part of the scenery, we re-shot the entire sequence.

So perhaps we shouldn't be too hard on Mr Justice Swinton Thomas for getting Dr Chaudhuri's name wrong.

We had thought long and hard about taking on the case. Mills and Poole were not the kind of people you'd instinctively choose to be your children's godparents – although in fact Mills has 'got religion' in jail, and we always found the pair of them courteous and quietly spoken. There was also the problem that the BBC's *Rough Justice* had been looking at the case, and we do not trespass on each other's territory. The BBC, after sitting on the case for several months, had only managed to send a researcher up to Gloucester for one day. But our hands were tied until Mills and Poole themselves took the BBC off the case and asked us to look into the matter.

As ever, Steve Haywood, producer of this edition of *Trial and Error* and the man with the responsibility of assessing and processing the casework, told the men that we could offer them no guarantees, and that they should not get their hopes up. The only thing we undertake to do is to take seriously every case that comes our way. Each case, however hopeless, represents somebody's fate, and we have a duty to give it serious consideration.

From the very start, from the very first opening of the files, the case didn't seem to add up. Why, for instance, did the court pay so much heed to the junkie, Kimberley Stadden, while the evidence of Neville Jukes, the other neutral observer of the fight in the room that night, had not been called?

Our suspicions deepened when Bob Duffield, researching the case, rang in from Gloucester. He'd done the single most important thing in any investigation – he'd gone to the scene of the crime. We had always assumed that a ground-floor flat would be just that – so that Paul White could easily have looked in through that convenient gap in the curtains from his vantage point on the pavement outside. But, as Bob had found, the ground floor at Number 34 isn't at street level; you get access to the house up a flight of stairs. For Paul White to have seen anything of what was going on on the floor, he'd have needed the foresight to bring a stepladder along with him.

It was a promising start. We began to investigate Paul White. He, too, was a petty villain. Around the time of the Conduit Street murder, he was involved in a burglary at an Italian restaurant called Fabio's; he was also accused of setting fire to the place. We traced White to a town in East Anglia, but, for the moment, decided to concentrate our researches in Gloucester, among White's associates.

White, we were told, was a weak-minded, whining young man who would always take the line of least resistance. In the hours after the murder, he had excitedly told friends the news that *Tony Poole* had been murdered, confusing the supposed perpetrator of the crime with the victim. He told other friends that he'd made up the story of seeing the attack take place because the police had leant on him – he did have, after all, the Fabio's charge hanging over him.

Another of White's associates, a criminal called Andrew Neal, told us that White could not have seen what he swore to seeing in court. White, he said, had been round at his house that night. He was deeply drunk before he arrived, and, eight or twelve cans of lager hadn't made things any better. White wanted to borrow Neal's car, and nip round to Conduit Street to buy some drugs from Tony Poole. Neal said White was in no state to drive, but at ten o'clock took him round to Number 34 anyway. Poole, however, was still waiting for his supply, and the two of them went back to Neal's house. Just after midnight, they returned to find Conduit Street alive with flashing blue lights and the wail of sirens. It was not the sort of situation that two villains, intent on buying illegal substances, were likely to forget or ignore. They had clearly arrived after the attack, after Gary Mills had called for the ambulance. It was, said Neal, patently untrue for White to claim he'd been there in time to witness anything of any assault.

Even with a stepladder. Even through the chink in the curtains. In any event, there was no such chink. The scene-of-crime photographs, used in evidence at the trial, show that the curtains were drawn. Tight.

So what about the other witness, Kimberley Stadden? Sue Walker was the other researcher involved in this case, and when she dies you will find the name of Kimberley Stadden engraved on her heart. Sue spent months searching for Stadden. We knew just two things about her from the police statements – her name, and date of birth. The first thing Sue discovered was that these two facts appeared to be mutually incompatible; no Kimberley Jane Stadden had been born in the entire decade of the sixties. Sue checked the registers for England and Wales, the separate Scottish and Northern Irish records, and even the Republic of Eire. No luck.

It is not easy to get lost. There are usually friends who know where to find you, or a chain of forwarding addresses to follow. Officialdom – as anyone who has tried to avoid payment of a parking ticket will know – has its ways of catching up with you. But Kimberley Jane Stadden seemed to have disappeared; exasperatingly, faded away. In vain Sue pumped the computer with its lists of Telecom-subscribing Staddens the length and breadth of the country. In vain she tried the lateral attempt to look for Staddons rather than Staddens. In vain she tramped the streets of Bournemouth, the scene of the last reported sighting of Kimberley Stadden.

At one stage Sue came tantalizingly close. Through friends of friends of Stadden, she went to an address, only to discover that Stadden had just left, leaving behind her, in her haste, her driving licence and national insurance card, as well as a few debts to her rather rueful hostess. Eventually – and there are some professional secrets we have to keep to ourselves – we traced her to an address on a Swindon housing estate.

We knew that if we approached her openly, Stadden would take flight again. We planned a discreet stake-out of the address, but the lie of the land made it impossible to park, unobtrusively, anywhere near. We thought of other, ever wilder schemes to flush her out without arousing her suspicions – a bogus letter from a lawyer, for instance, telling her she'd come into an inheritance. Eventually, we hit on the scheme of having Steve Haywood knock on her door with a special delivery letter she had to sign for. It would give Haywood the chance to get a look at her and confirm that it was the same woman.

We mocked up an identity card for Steve in the name of a fictitious courier company, and prepared some official-looking letterheads. The idea was to enclose a postal order for £12.78 in respect of a supposed underpayment of benefit – Steve would be working for a notionally privatized department of rebate deliveries. To confuse things further, the payee would be a Mr Keith Stadden, so that the real Kimberley Stadden would assume there had been a succession of clerical errors. That, at any rate, was the plan. To make things look more authentic, the *Trial and Error* team equipped the 'mailman' with a stack of similar envelopes; that way, we hoped, Kimberley Stadden would not feel singled out.

We were rather pleased with our plan. Unfortunately, it didn't work. The flat turned out to be just an accommodation address. All our forgery had been in vain. In fact Steve got a lot of leads simply by the old-fashioned technique of talking to the neighbours.

Harassment? Intrusion? Invasion of privacy? By my book,

harassment is continuing to try to see or talk to someone after they have heard what you have got to say, and declined an invitation to discuss it further. Intrusion is when, without breaking the law, you've used your native wit to get access to a place or a person and steal articles, possessions, or private information – pinching a letter, or a photograph off the mantelpiece. As for invasion of privacy, I'm afraid that by definition investigative journalism invades people's privacy. Most people who have been involved in a criminal case have good, or bad, reasons for not wanting it raked over again. We understand that; we also understand that embarrassment or discomfort have to be weighed against the scandal of a wrongful conviction. All we can do is to try to cause as little unnecessary pain as possible.

While the search for Stadden continued, we were investigating the matter of the third witness to that night's events, Neville Jukes. He had actually been in the room, and had tried to separate the combatants. And yet, we discovered, he had not given evidence. Why?

The answer lay in a scruffy interference with justice by a senior police-officer. Just before the committal proceedings – the stage at which the evidence is rehearsed before a magistrate in order to establish that there is a case to answer – there was a telephone conversation between Detective Inspector Gladding of Gloucester CID and Neville Jukes, which Jukes, at his mother's insistence, took the precaution of recording. In the conversation, Gladding clearly warned Jukes not to turn up at court. Jukes protested that he didn't want to see his friends get sent to jail when his evidence could save them; Gladding replied: 'It's for them to go to jail – or for you to go to jail.' Gladding reminded Jukes that he hadn't paid his fines for various previous offences, 'So if I see you, I've got to arrest you. . . . I'll talk to you another time. *Don't turn up at court.*'

Jukes heeded the warning-off, and so his account of what happened in the fight – an account which vindicated Mills and Poole – was not heard. This severely compromised the defence – and it was all because of the rules of the legal game under which the administration of justice is conducted.

Jukes, we are fairly certain, made two statements to the police. He says he was himself threatened with a murder charge. One of those statements supported Mills and Poole, but neither we, nor anyone else, knows what he may have felt induced to say in the other. The truth could have come out at the committal proceedings, a sort of dress rehearsal of the evidence before the trial proper. If Jukes hadn't been warned off attending the committal, and had given evidence, he would have been questioned by the prosecution and the defence, so everything he'd said to the police, whichever side it helped, would have come out. Then, when the case moved to the Crown Court, the defence would know whether Jukes was a vulnerable witness – in other words, whether his support of Mills and Poole could be torn to shreds by the revelation of other things he might have told the police in order, as he put it, 'to get them off my back.'

Because Jukes had been warned off, this opportunity to discover whether he was an asset or a liability to the defence case was lost. The defence asked to see the statements – a judge even asked to see them – but the police did not divulge them. So at the full trial, Jukes was never called to give evidence. Legal technicalities, the risk of the unknown, and a policeman's interference had seen to that.

It doesn't exactly square up to the notion of justice. But everything about this case felt tainted, tarnished, compromised. The witnesses themselves were a crew of addicts, thieves or liars; the victim, too, was a villain, the police – if Gladding's recorded conversation is anything to go by – seem to have taken a fairly flexible view of the proprieties; and now the trial process was revealed as compromised also.

The evidence, after all, was reduced to that of Paul White (who we believe lied) and Kimberley Stadden; and, if we were having difficulties running her to ground, we were, in the process, discovering some interesting things about Ms Stadden. For instance, she didn't exactly beat a hasty retreat from those involved in the fight; she walked home with them, and let Mills use her telephone. She wasn't, it seemed, a casual visitor to Number 34; she knew Tony Poole. She went thieving with Tony Poole. In fact the very vodka the party was consuming had been bought by Kimberley Stadden and Tony Poole that afternoon, using dud cheques backed up by stolen credit cards. The police, it transpired, knew about this, but Kimberley Stadden had understood that no charges would be brought against her, if she gave evidence against Mills and Poole. And Kimberley Stadden had been visited by a carload of Wiltshire's friends and associates before the trial.

We discovered seventeen major contradictions in the three accounts she gave of the fight at the committal proceedings, the first aborted trial, and the final hearing. That's quite apart from the scores of minor discrepancies you'd expect from a witness to such a distressing and confusing incident. These included fairly significant matters, such as whether she had, or hadn't, seen Tony Poole with a knife.

Sue eventually found Kimberley Stadden, through the usual combination of intuition, hard work, good luck and farcical coincidence. Through the electoral roll, she had discovered the name of the tenant of the flat where we had vainly delivered the bogus letter. He had moved, but Sue knew where he was now living. He, surely, must know Stadden's whereabouts, if he had been prepared to allow her to use his flat as a 'drop' for mail. Sue staked out his house, parking unobtrusively in a slip road opposite. It was a two-day vigil before she saw a man make his way to the house. She knocked on the door and introduced herself. The man was clearly uncomfortable, and claimed that he didn't know where Stadden was now living. The situation was saved by another member of the household, a fourteen-year-old schoolboy. He was thrilled to meet 'someone from the telly' and asked what it was about. 'Oh yes, we know Kimmy Stadden, don't we?' he piped up, to the man's obvious flustered consternation. He retreated to the back kitchen and, a few moments later, Sue heard a voice sing out, 'D'you want to talk to her now – I've got her on the telephone.'

Sue followed a set of complicated instructions to an isolated farmhouse. She admits to being terrified as she drove, in pitch darkness, down the seemingly endless track. As she stopped the car, a large, shaven-headed man was caught in her headlights. The farmhouse was, apparently, a sort of commune, organized by a woman who was Stadden's protector and companion.

Stadden, shrewdly defiant, came into the farmhouse kitchen and asked Sue two things: how she had found her, and how much would she pay. Sue said she couldn't answer the first question, and as for money, that was out of the question. 'If you insist on money and that information,' she said, 'you'd better ask me to leave.' After a six-month search, it was quite a gamble to take at the very moment of success, but it succeeded.

Stadden – in spite of threats to complain to the Chief Constable of Gloucester – eventually agreed to come to London and be interviewed. We prefer our interviews to be conducted openly, rather than the gimmicky and morally ambivalent process of secret filming. It's harder, but we think it matters. We'd rather persuade than steal. She admitted that she was 'surprised' not to have been charged for her crimes, and that her evidence contradicted itself. Her explanation was that 'all this happened a very long time ago' – but of course her statements and her court testimony were made at the time, so that explanation loses a bit of its force. She had clearly been frightened – maybe that explained the sixty-odd times her address had changed since the events at Number 34; but was she frightened of Mills and Poole, or of the Wiltshire clan? Had she committed herself so deeply to the version of events which suited the police that she didn't dare step back from it? Stadden maintained with her familiar defiance; however muddled and confused her testimony: 'Yes, I admit it's got a lot of holes in it, but contradictory or not, whether they had provocation or not, it was over the top; it's unfortunate that they're on a murder charge, but at that point in time I believed they were guilty.'

We had gone as far as we could on the evidence available and, indeed, on the evidence not available, like Neville Jukes'; it was time to advance the case in other ways. For Mills' claim of self-defence to have any validity, we had to explain why Wiltshire had so many wounds. We went to an expert in toxicology at the National Poisons Unit, and asked him to assess, from the post-mortem levels of drug traces, how much of each Wiltshire would have had at the time of the fight. Dr John Henry's assessment was that the level of amphetamines would have had two very significant effects on Wiltshire; first, the combination with alcohol could lead to spontaneous, uncontrolled, paranoid violence – exactly the scenario Jukes had described to us. Second, the anaesthetic effect of large doses of amphetamine would have made him impervious to pain; this would explain why Wiltshire kept on coming, and was not deterred by the wounds he was receiving.

115

The whole focus of the investigation had switched to those wounds. The strange thing was that, on his first admission to hospital, only a few, 'superficial' wounds had been logged and sutured. When he came back – having spent an hour and a half in the police cells – they recorded many more wounds than had been listed the first time, including, for instance, a broken leg, and a very visible wound on his nose. Either the hospital had failed to note these wounds, or he had – unthinkably – acquired them in police custody.

The whole thrust of the prosecution case was that whatever happened after the fight was irrelevant; the moment Wiltshire received his wounds, the Crown argued, he was done for. Expert witnesses explained that the gravity of his injuries meant that fat and potassium were released into his bloodstream, eventually resulting in death. This argument, of course, meant that the issues of hospital care and treatment in custody need not arise.

'Bullshit!' said Dr Donald Trunkey of Oregon State University Hospital when he read the expert witnesses' assessment. Bob Duffield and I had flown to Portland, Oregon, to meet Don Trunkey because he is the expert's expert when it comes to casualty treatment. We had talked to top professionals in Britain who were appalled at the treatment Wiltshire received, but professional etiquette prevented them from saying so in public. If we couldn't get the best opinion in Britain, then, what about the best opinion in the world – they are not necessarily the same. Everyone told us that Don Trunkey was our man. It was just rather a nuisance that Oregon was on the other side of the world. Coincidentally, Bob Duffield tracked him down to Glasgow, where he was giving a lecture, and flew up with the bulky dossier of medical notes. Dr Trunkey promised to read them on his thirteen-hour flight back home.

Bob and I flew out to hear the great man's verdict. It was staggeringly clear and forthright; Wiltshire hadn't died of any complex release of fat and potassium; the man had died of simple medical neglect. The wounds he received were 'absolutely not' fatal. Simple, basic care would have saved his life. A consultant's sworn opinion that death could not have been prevented by any form of treatment at hospital was, according to Don Trunkey, 'balderdash, absolute balderdash; this man was salvageable when he was brought into hospital. He received inadequate care, unsupervised care, inappropriate care.' The hospital hadn't sewn him up adequately, nor had they replaced what Don Trunkey estimated was the forty per cent of his blood volume that had been lost. His discharge into police custody was 'totally unacceptable, negligent care.' The apparent high levels of fat and potassium had occurred, said Trunkey, as a result of Wiltshire's terminal agony; they weren't the immediate and fatal result of the stabbing. At any time in the twelve hours since the fight, Willie Wiltshire's life could have been saved.

We flew back with the evidence that there should never have been a murder charge against Mills and Poole at all – because there should never have been a death. Nothing of this had been heard at the trial. There had been virtually no challenge to 'expert' opinion that was, quite simply, wrong.

But Willie Wiltshire's last hours weren't only spent in the care – or lack of it – of the Gloucester Royal Hospital; they were also spent in the care – or lack of it – of the Gloucester Police. And that was the next area the team began to investigate.

For several days, Bob Duffield retired behind a stack of documents, armed with a ruler, sellotape and scissors. At times like this, it's as well not to interrupt him and ask him what he's doing. It's obvious he doesn't want to be distracted. Eventually he produced a vast chart; he had plotted some thirty-eight police statements, breaking them down chronologically. We could now see where every policeman had been – or said he had been – at every stage of Wiltshire's confinement, and what their view was of the condition of the man in their care.

The chart showed a remarkable, self-corroborating schedule of police statements; all supported a perfectly plausible, coherent account of Wiltshire being an uncooperative inmate, 'shamming' his distress, but being properly and professionally attended and supervised. At around midday, Wiltshire suddenly took a turn for the worse; the police registered the crisis, and called at once for an ambulance. But there was one policeman's statement, buried in the material not used at the trial, which did not chime with the others. That statement suggested that the police only registered the gravity of Wiltshire's condition when it was too late, and then only because his solicitor had turned up, and had to be taken down to the cells.

We asked the solicitor, Paul Griffen, for his recollections of that day. A quiet, mild-mannered man, he was still shocked by the memory of what he saw when he was taken to the cells: 'I was amazed ... there was blood – I can't say there was blood everywhere, but there was blood on the walls, blood on the blanket, blood on the floor ...' Wiltshire seemed to be asleep, and a detective constable tried to wake him up. Griffen continued: 'His eyes then opened, but they sort of rolled around in his head ... and that's when things got into a bit of a panic ...' Officers tried to pound some life back into Wiltshire by chest massage and mouth-to-mouth resuscitation, but the only response was the terrifying and terminal sound of what Mr Griffen described as Wiltshire's death-rattle.

So here were two versions of the attention Wiltshire received in custody where, although he was officially declared dead in hospital, he almost certainly died. In the first, a comprehensive and interlocking series of statements presents a picture of a situation professionally and carefully monitored. The second, based on a 'rogue' police statement and the solicitor's recollections – never heard, incidentally, in court – presents a picture of the police being unaware of Wiltshire's state until the arrival of the solicitor exposed the terminal gravity of his condition.

That was a discrepancy mirrored by another, intriguing difference. The solicitor's arrival at the police station was logged – by the police – at 12.18 p.m. But the solicitor himself said he had arrived at 12.10. Eight minutes' difference might seem a trivial detail – until we established that the call for the ambulance too, was timed at 12.18. If the police were to maintain that they had the situation well in hand before the solicitor arrived, it would obviously be more convenient if the solicitor arrived later rather than earlier. Was this, then, the explanation for the discrepancy between the police's timing and the solicitor's recollection?

The team trawled through the low life of Gloucester – to track down other prisoners who had been in the cells of Gloucester Police Station that night. Each of them provided a piece of the jigsaw; one had heard 'a lot of moaning and groaning', another was moved to protest, but 'I was told to shut up, the hatch on my cell door was slammed down, and I was told to mind my own business.' 'I heard a policeman say "shut up, don't be a baby." ' 'I don't see how the police could have had any doubt at all that he was in need of help.' Some had been picked up as drunks, some were professional thieves, and their reliability could be blasted away by the greenest barrister on his first day in court. It was, nevertheless, a disturbing and coherent account, but why should we suspect a police concoction, yet uncritically accept an account compiled from such morally unfragrant sources?

The answer, as so often, lay in the paperwork. We sought help from a neutral expert, a former police sergeant in the Metropolitan Police, who specializes in the interpretation of custody records – the Detained Persons Register. His view was that the document represented 'one of the worst neglects of duty' he had ever seen. Worse than that, the Gloucester Police were acting unlawfully in detaining Wiltshire; they had originally held him because the police in London wanted him for questioning in connection with an indecent assault, but in the small hours New Scotland Yard had telexed through to Gloucester that they were no longer interested in Wiltshire. From that point on, the police had no legal right to keep Wiltshire in the cells. They did make a feeble attempt to justify holding him on account of a kitchen knife discovered in his sock at hospital – probably the little knife Wiltshire used in connection with his drug habit – but possession of a knife is not a reason in law to keep a man detained in custody.

Willie Wiltshire died after receiving inadequate care at hospital, and after being wrongfully held in the cells. Even if we accepted the compromised evidence of Kimberley Stadden and Andrew Neal, even if we reject the muzzled evidence of Neville Jukes, even if we reject Gary Mills' claim of self-defence – the fact is that Willie Wiltshire should not have died. Responsibility for his death lies with the system designed to protect him – the police and the doctors – just as much as with those who may, or may not, have inflicted an unprovoked attack on him.

So much suspicion understandably surrounded the case that the Police Complaints Authority itself investigated the matter. This is, for all its claims to independence, effectively an investigation of the police by the police. To make matters worse, their report is secret; all we know is that it runs to twenty-six volumes of evidence and – as I was unattributably assured – it was one of the most exhaustive investigations the PCA had ever undertaken.

Bullshit, to borrow a phrase from the good Dr Donald Trunkey.

In the course of our own investigation we routinely asked the people we spoke to about the Police Complaints Authority investigation. Key players told us that they had either not been spoken to, or had been interviewed in a perfunctory manner. One prosecution witness said 'they just asked me if I still stuck to my story.' The actions of DCI Gladding, who had sworn in court that he had never warned Neville Jukes off attending court, were described as 'a genuine mistake.'

The Police Complaints Authority is the public's only defence against the misdeeds of the police force. This mixture of complacency, secrecy, and – to judge from our own researches – indolent and sloppy coppering, ought to make all of us worried. If this was indeed one of the PCA's most exhaustive investigations, it makes you wonder about the quality of the others it has conducted.

Support for this view comes from an unlikely source – Gloucester's Conservative MP, Douglas French. In spite of the fact that Mills and Poole do not represent his natural constituency, French describes the PCA report as a 'whitewash.' Since making the comment on *Trial and Error*, the Chief Constable of Gloucester has protested and asked for a private discussion so that he can explain matters to the MP. Douglas French has very properly decided that too much of this case has been conducted in, let us say, an informal manner, and has insisted that if there is to be any conversation, it should be in the open.

There is something about this case I have felt before, in other, small, self-contained towns and cities. An informal 'freemasonry' of the local professionals develops over the years, a way of rubbing along together, cutting the odd corner, turning the occasional blind eye, ensuring that the boat remains conveniently unrocked. The relationship is like an old and much-loved piece of clothing, which gets increasingly shabby and unhygienic. The holes in it are patched over with the threads of complicit chumminess. I can hear the gin-and-tonic conversations even now – 'when it comes down to it, old boy, they're a couple of ne'er-do-wells who are better off behind bars anyway ... you don't catch villains by doing things by the book, y'know ...'

Filming presented us with the usual crop of absurdities and frustrations. From a film unit's point of view, the distressing thing about the criminal classes is not their moral shortcomings but their sheer unreliability. We picked up Neville Jukes, for instance, one morning, to drive him to a place where we could interview him. On the way, he suddenly asked if he could 'drop something off' round the corner. The convoy – the researcher's car, production car and crew wagon – scrunched to a halt. Five minutes passed. Then ten minutes. After quarter of an hour Steve Haywood grew edgy. Had we been stood up? Twenty minutes. At this rate we wouldn't make the next interview on time, and the whole carefully planned schedule would (as usual) collapse. After half an hour, Neville Jukes sauntered back, a cheeky smile on his face, but with nothing in the way of explanation. All I can say is that Neville has a lot of girlfriends in Gloucester.

Like the famous epitaph of the Raj, 'Here lies a man who tried to hurry the East', when you're dealing with the underworld you have to deal at its pace, respect its priorities. A knock on the door, for instance, does not lead automatically to the door being opened; because a knock on the door could be the police, the bailiff, the man from the electricity board. You can usually tell when someone's in, but not answering; as you knock, you keep your eyes firmly on the windows, to spot the telltale flutter of the curtain; by night, people may be prepared to forego electric light – but a dim, mauve flicker shows they cannot resist their fix of *Emmerdale* or *Eastenders*.

A film unit is not a discreet animal, especially at night, when arc-lights flood the streets and, like moths to the candle, we attract all the drunks and local cowboys for miles around. Television can be an arrogant guest, imposing its own demands when, in truth, we rely on the goodwill of those on whose neighbourhood we have trespassed. But Gloucester drew heavily on our reserves of tact and diplomacy. Every hard man in the city seemed to have lurched up to the camera, to challenge our presence. On more than one occasion these encounters demonstrated our sense of priority. Producer Steve Haywood would put himself between the would-be assailant and the cameraman; the cameraman would put himself between the loudmouth and his own £45,000 camera. Usually good manners work the trick, though not in the case of one neighbourhood tough. 'This is Gloucester, remember,' he said menacingly, and as he left us, pulled the floodlight down

121

from its pedestal and brought it crashing, in a shower of sparks and shards of glass, to the ground.

We're always very conscious of the police when we are filming. Usually they know perfectly well what we are up to. If they didn't one would be very worried about their local intelligence. Sometimes they make a point of cruising slowly by, but more usually they keep out of the way. Gloucester provided the exception. We had it in mind to film a shot to cover the part of the narrative when Wiltshire was brought out onto the street, after the fight, as Mills called for an ambulance. The problem with this sort of documentary is that a lot of the main characters are missing – they tend to be dead or in jail. So this was to be a subtle, oblique, stylized shot of the kerb, black and shiny in a midnight rainstorm, with a trickle of blood running across it, with the reflection of a blue flashing light (you'll have to believe me, it wasn't as crass and vulgar as it sounds). The problem was the blood. Jill, the supremely competent production assistant, had brought a full range of gore – powdered, liquid, diluted. Unfortunately, the shot just would not work. Time after time, take after take, we tried in vain to get just the right balance of blood and blue light.

It was then that the police arrived. Their torches lit up a forlorn crew, soaked to the skin with rain and spattered with suspicious red blotches. We were asked what we were doing. On these occasions there's no point in fibbing, although a certain economy is diplomatic; we explained that we were making a documentary about a murder. Whose murder? Willie Wiltshire's, we explained. 'My God,' said the officer, exploding with mirth, 'you've made enough mess of the street; what are you going to do when you come to the scene in the cells!'

As ever, transmission of the programme stirred up new evidence from this silted, stagnant pond. We had always been puzzled why the police had hung on to Willie Wiltshire for so long. We assumed that it was because they wanted, quite reasonably, to screw out of him further evidence about the Gloucester drug scene. That certainly would be a plausible, if charitable, explanation. It was only later that we learnt that police searching Number 34 Conduit Street had found the fruits of a burglary – an expensive coat and some video equipment. The burglary was from the home of a woman closely related to a Gloucester police officer. Could this consideration have affected the police's apparent determination to hang on to Willie Wiltshire? Could this have blunted their concern for his well-being?

There is no guarantee that there will be answers to these and a hundred other questions raised by our investigation. I can already see it all spiralling down the black hole of bureaucracy; the Home Office will find that the PCA has already reviewed the case, and so no action need be taken, in spite of the fact that the PCA investigation is itself a cause for concern. An appeal has been lodged, but will their Lordships have access to the PCA report? It's almost certain that the appellants won't be allowed sight of it, so will they be fighting with one hand tied behind their back? Will the Court be at all interested in the fact that Wiltshire died when better care could have saved him – or, delighting in parsing the small print of *nova causa interveniens*, will they follow *R v. Smith* or *R v. Jordan*? It's the arbitrary nature of our system that sometimes so appals; we think of it as a majestic, passionless automaton, when in truth its foundations are as fickle as the men and women who work for it, be they police, lawyers, civil servants, or ministers of state. Barristers representing some of our cases at appeal have told me matter-of-factly that they are confident of winning – unless 'we get [so-and-so] on the bench, in which case we haven't a chance.' It is just bad luck. It's not just the judges; cases can be won or lost, whatever their merits, because of the bumbling indolence of the particular barrister. I've met members of the profession who dazzle with their brainpower, but I've met others, to say no more, who do not. For all the efforts, the arguments, the evidence, justice remains the ideal – but the law remains a lottery.

8
'M.'

The Ones that Got Away

I won't tell you M.'s real name. He is in hell already, he will spend very many more years there, and anything I do to identify him is only going to make things worse – though it is hard to imagine how. M. is in prison for life for murdering his baby brother. There's another charge, of sexual assault, that lies on the file. The trial judge said he was 'a cruel and unfeeling young man.'

I don't think he killed his brother. I think his father did. So do most of his family. But what I think doesn't make much difference, if I haven't got the evidence to back it up. It still remains a live case for us – we haven't given up. I suppose I'm really including M.'s case out of a sense of frustration, and in the hope that someone will read it who can succeed where I have so far failed.

M. was sixteen when his brother died. Born in Pakistan, he was one of a first-generation family of immigrants. By all accounts – including his own – it was a traditional and repressed home life.

'I was brought up very strictly,' he has written. 'My father is a very strict Muslim, and relations with the opposite sex were taboo. If there was any kissing in the film on television he would get up and switch it off, that's how bad he was about it. Although he prayed five times a day he was a right bastard to the family, and still is. He just takes everything out on the family. I was a very shy person and could not start a relationship with a girl. Naturally I had the desire but was not able to fulfil it.'

M. says, naively, that he must have been 'over-sexed' in that he used to masturbate 'a lot when looking at pictures in a pornographic magazine . . . and fantasizing having intercourse with the girl in the picture . . .' Not that M. had much time for such diversions; his mother was a chronic invalid, spending a lot of time in hospital, and, with father away at work, M., as the eldest of five, had the responsibility of looking after his younger sisters and baby brother. Another reason for his mother's absences was her ill-treatment at the hands of her husband; at one stage she went back to Pakistan – only to make a humiliating return to England because her family could not afford to support her.

For whatever reasons, the baby brother failed to thrive. Twice, in 1978, he was seen tumbling down the front steps of the terrace house where the family lived. Both times, on admission to hospital, he was found to be suffering from much more severe injuries – including multiple fractures and bruising. On the second occasion – horrifyingly – the examining doctor remarked that the child had injuries which he had never seen 'outside the sphere of professional boxing.' There was also evidence of anal bruising. The child was kept alive on a ventilator, then allowed to die.

M. was asked to come to the police station the same day. He was interviewed three times. On the second and third occasion he was interviewed under caution, and in the presence of adults – his father and two social workers. But by then it was too late; because on the first occasion, without being cautioned and alone, he had – it seemed – virtually confessed.

There are two versions of what happened before the adults arrived. One of them, at least, must be untrue. For all I know, both are. There was no taping of evidence at that particular police station – or indeed anywhere in Britain – in 1978. All I can do is set out extracts from both accounts:

The police account

Q: It's vital to know just what happened to the baby. You were in charge of it, so surely you must know something?

A: Maybe it was the wrestling . . . on Wednesday afternoon I wrestled with the baby on the floor.

Q: Were you rough with him?

A: No, not really, I don't think I was.

Q: If the wrestling part is responsible for the bruises, you must have been rough, so were you rough or not? It would take a lot of shaking to injure the brain, that's according to the doctors.

126

The police statement then says:

> M. paused and remained silent for quite a while and then continued
> as follows:
>
> A: I remember now throwing baby on to the couch and he bounced
> and banged his head.
> Q: I don't think we have got through to you yet – baby's brain
> injury is not a result of a bang but a good shaking up. Did you
> shake him up when you were wrestling with him?
> A: I might have.
> Q: That sort of reply just won't do – either you did or you didn't,
> which is it? ... Look, I think we both have a feeling something
> is wrong ...

When the news of the baby's death was broken, according to the
police statement, M. showed no emotion. He continued to deny
anything more than brotherly rough-and-tumble, though admitted 'clapping' the baby's head between his hands. He was asked
if he wanted to wait until his father arrived, but indicated that
he did not. The police are clearly not satisfied with the horseplay
explanation, especially with regard to the baby's anal bruising.

> Q: The other thing that could have caused internal bruising is of
> course interference.
> A: I don't understand.
> Q: Then I'll tell you, poking something up baby's bottom could
> have caused it.
> A: What do you mean?
> Q: A finger, an object, even your penis.
> A: Oh no, not that.

The record states: 'at this stage he became very agitated and
uneasy.' M.'s father had by now arrived, and M. was left alone
with just one policeman.

> A: Father will be angry now, I am ashamed.
> Q: Why, what have you done?
> A: You know, wanking; well, I wank and then put it on the baby's
> bottom ...

Then M.'s father is brought in for the confrontation.

Q: Tell your father what you have done to baby.
A: I've hit him. I lost my temper.
Q: What about kicking?
A: Yes, I kick him as well.
Q: And the other thing.
A: I do that on his bottom.

Two social workers then witnessed the final part of the interrogation. Their joint statements are remarkable for their innocence. 'I had the impression that the police wanted us there because they wanted it done properly,' one of them stated. 'M. took a little bit of prompting from the officers saying things like "do you remember what you told us happened next?" It was carried out in a first-class manner by the police . . . they took him through the whole of his story before his statement was taken down. The details of the sexual offences took some getting out of him. If he said something different to what he had previously told the officers, then they reminded him of what he had said before. The police officers would say "you could say so-and-so", or "you might put so-and-so." '

Much of the conversation above is reproduced in M.'s account. But there are significant additions. There is a third policeman present, a bully of a man whom M. refers to as Man C.:

M.'s account

Man C: Tell me what happened?
A: I have told these officers what happened.
Man C: It doesn't matter if you have told them or not, you f—ing tell me. . . . If you want to play games, you black bastard, we will play games . . . Perhaps I can remind you, you black twat; on Wednesday something happened and you lost your temper and hurt that child.
A: I did not.
Man C: Don't give me that rubbish again you f—ing black c—

M. says he made up the whole explanation about 'wrestling' with the child to appease Man C., who was being physically as well as verbally threatening. At this stage the baby is still alive.

128

Man C: I don't care if you have done anything to your brother or not, but we are going to have you for it if he dies. We are going to put it on you so good that no one on this f—ing earth is going to believe you, not even your parents . . .

According to the police's statement, M. demonstrates how he slapped the baby between his two hands. M.'s report puts it rather differently:

Man C: I'll show you how it all happened. All those bruises were caused like this – you slapped your brother like this (he was slapping my jawbone slowly, then he started to hit harder). Now I want to hear from your f—ing mouth that you kicked him and slapped him or else we'll both be standing here all night, until you say that you did it . . .
Then Man C. got hold of the back of my head and punched me in the stomach . . .

In M.'s account, it's a classic hard-man, soft-man routine, with Man B. offering the gentle alternatives.

Man B: You know when they say 'I want to make a deal with you' in some films?
A: What do you actually mean?
Man B: What I mean is, tomorrow morning at ten o'clock you will have to go to court. If you plead guilty we won't tell your father about the sexual assault on your brother. We will write a good report for you. We'll say you have been a truthful boy and you haven't been in trouble with the police before, and you'll get only three months D.C.
A: What's D.C.?
Man B: D.C. stands for detention centre where they send boys like you.
Man C: If you plead not guilty you haven't a chance, anyway, because the doctors are on our side and so are the social workers you'll see later . . .

I don't know which of the two accounts is the more accurate. M. certainly wasn't taking notes, though he would have good reason to remember what was said. Some may be disturbed that I even

presume to give each version equal status: but we have learnt a
lot since the seventies about what went on in interview rooms.
On the other hand, the prisons are full of people claiming that
false admissions were beaten or bargained out of them.

M. was sentenced to be detained at Her Majesty's Pleasure. It
has pleased Her Majesty so far to keep him locked up for sixteen
years. He would be out by now, of course, were it not for his
refusal to accept his guilt.

Justice, too, is concerned that M. may be the victim of a miscarriage of justice – a victim, too, of a strict social and ethical system
which made it impossible for him to accuse his father of the
crime. Their former legal officer, Peter Ashman, conducted a long
and patient correspondence with him. But getting the requisite
breakthrough in the case still eludes us.

I have no doubt that M. did indulge in a fumbling, adolescent
sexual act with the young boy. He himself describes it, in a
painfully awkward letter; he was masturbating, he writes, when
his baby brother tried to get under the blanket with him. The
child 'snuggled under with his back towards me.' Contact – the
first contact ever with another's flesh – precipitated M.'s orgasm.
He continues:

> After ejaculation I felt the feeling of anticlimax and only then I
> realised what an atrocious act I had committed; and I felt great
> compassion for my brother then and I felt very hurt from inside.
> So I hugged my brother and I began to cry; my tears fell on my
> brother's back and my hands and I said 'I am sorry for doing this
> to you, little brother.' I cannot reverse what I have done, no matter
> how much I cry, repent and anguish.

M. confessed what he had done to his family. It cannot have been
an easy thing to do, but it also had a fatal effect on M.'s defence.

To raise even a figurative hand against a father is one of the
gravest sins in the Islamic calendar. M. could hardly accuse his
father when he had himself admitted to something as equally
abhorrent, the abuse of a defenceless child. But that, M. has
always maintained, is the truth of the matter – his father had
dealt the baby the fatal blows.

On the night before the baby was taken to hospital M. writes:

I was lying on the bed and my door was ajar. My father went into the room, I think he hit my brother S. first, the usual, a sharp slap square on the lips, or on the head. Then he went and hit my sisters. Then he went to [the baby's] room and began to beat him. My brother was screaming and crying. We were all frozen with fright. I could see him slapping my brother on the face and head. I heard a sort of 'thud, thud' noise, it sounded like punches. He went on for about, I am not sure, twenty-five seconds or even forty-five seconds.

Next day, the baby's evident distress was noticed, and he was taken to hospital. M.'s father went to the hospital.

About half an hour after arriving home my father asked me to sit down to have a talk. He said to me: 'Son, you are only sixteen and if you said to the police that you had lost your temper you would not get much time.' He gave me numerous other reasons which made sense then, such as his reputation in the family would be ruined, he had to be home because he was the breadwinner, and a load of other rubbish. I agreed, because it made sense to me then. I took my father's word but things did not turn out as he made me believe.

On the day of the trial M. writes: 'I was hoping that having to swear to tell the truth on the Koran would compel my father to admit to what he had done. But he did not.'

M., in spite of his anger, is surprisingly understanding about why his father hurt them all so much. 'He was under too much pressure. My mother was in hospital, he had to do a lot, he was working six days out of a week, when he came home from work he had to cook for us all and go and visit my mother in hospital. I wasn't well. He had to do most of the washing, cleaning and tidying the mess made during the day by my brothers and sisters.'

The father had a history of unpredictable bouts of violence against the children. He had spent several periods in mental institutions. M.'s mother was faced with a terrible choice; after the trial should she implicate her husband, who would almost certainly turn upon her and, given her son's confession, would be unlikely to be convicted? Or should she let her son, the self-

131

confessed defiler of her youngest child, suffer the consequences of what she suspected were the all-too-familiar acts of her husband?

She now realizes she took the wrong decision in standing by her husband. She writes:

> His behaviour changes from fair to good and very bad; he becomes paranoid aggressive, restless, touchy, very excited when watching boxing or wrestling on television, when he is violent towards my children . . . He still hits the children, he is only reserved in the seriousness of ill-treatment because my children threaten to tell the police what he did to [the baby]. My husband says that next time he will take care of all of us. I wish to make clear that I have no doubt that my husband was responsible for my son's death. I am convinced because many a time he had said when he had lost his temper that he would put the rest of us where he put his other two sons. When I came from the hospital my children told me that Daddy had beaten [the baby]. Although he often hit and beat the children, that incident was unusual in a way that it had a profound effect on my children, they told me in a very shocked and frightened way . . .

The father, it seems, admitted to M.'s uncle that he had murdered the child. But he was terrified that such an admission would have him sent back to the mental hospital where, he said, he was subjected to electric-shock treatment. The uncle then took the father to M.'s solicitor, to get the confession on record. But the solicitor had to explain that an independent interpreter was necessary. By the time someone with the necessary skills had been lined up, the father had changed his mind. It is debatable, anyway, if such a confession would cut much ice. The father, as we know, is mentally unstable. And the courts are sceptical about these late conversions. There is an element of racial stereotyping in the case, as well: more than once we heard the allegation that there were financial reasons behind the campaign to shift the burden of guilt. M.'s father is now too old to work – it would make economic sense to swap him for his healthy, potentially breadwinning, son.

We may be faced with the desperate irony that a man is in prison following a crime he committed as a sixteen-year-old – but not the crime of which he was convicted. The charge of buggery was put to one side, yet the prejudice that accompanied that confession – and of course the trial judge would have been well aware of it – has swept him towards conviction of the crime of murder which he very probably did not commit.

I cannot think of any reason, besides M.'s innocence, why he should continue to imprison himself – for that, effectively, is what he is doing by continuing to protest his innocence. And there's a special dimension to M.'s imprisonment. I began this chapter by describing his life as hell. For people convicted of sex offences, prison provides a very special form of torment. In prison, no one is lower than a 'nonce'. Sex offenders are regularly beaten up, slashed, kicked. Even when they choose Rule 43, voluntary segregation, their food is, to put it delicately, interfered with by the time it reaches the cell. M. has steadfastly refused to accept his status as a 'nonce' or to go on to Rule 43.

And he is paying the price for his principles:

Because of what I am in here for, and what I am supposed to be in for, the prison officers snarl at me and give me dirty looks (in a way I don't blame them at all). The reminder of what I have done is constant. Whenever I am standing at the dinner queue or the canteen queue or anywhere in the prison, inmates standing there always say 'he's the one who shagged his little brother, he's the one who f—ed his brother to death'. I have been spat at, called a brotherf—er, childf—r, a beast, an animal; I have had hot water thrown on me with sugar in it [a sort of home-made prison napalm, DJ]. I have the scar there to show you what it does to you. I have had bust lips and bust nose so many times that I lost count in the first year inside. Save all the punches and kicks I have had from inmates. Do you really know how it feels to be treated like this day by day, week by week, month by month and year by year? If I did not come inside an animal I will surely get out like one, one day.

When he went into prison, M. was a shy and pleasant young man, perhaps a little too anxious to please. He is now a changed person. He has worked assiduously to gain qualifications he's unlikely ever to be able to use. And he's become hard. He fights back. I quote from a recent letter:

A couple of inmates came into my cell and asked if I knew what bacon tasted like. I said no. They pinned me down and tried to force a rasher into my mouth. But I stabbed one of them with a sharpened pencil, and bit the other one's ear. Another wanted me to sell him my watch, and when I refused tried to take it off me. I threw salt in his eyes, and kicked him all over the floor while he was down there with his hands on his eyes. I discovered chilli powder would be more effective.

And it leaves the family as prisoners, too. Despairing at the parole board's refusal to grant her son freedom on licence, his mother writes:

Who is the parole board? Does it know what it feels like to have two sons taken away from me? Does it know how it feels to leave a son who is sobbing, miserable, and often close to tears behind in prison? Do they know what it feels to have the guilty sitting in the house and the not guilty in prison? I only care about the truth and justice of which I have seen little from the people of this nation.

The case remains on our conscience and on our files.

9

Matthew Richardson/Maxine Ryks

The Ones that Got Away
by Stephen Phelps, Nina Davies and David Jessel

Among the prisoners waiting in the visitors' room at HM Prison Nottingham, Matthew Richardson was easily identifiable. Like many in the stuffy room, he had pushed up his regulation uniform shirt to reveal Hell's Angels' tattoos on his hairy forearms, but he was the only inmate wearing Edna-Everage-style glasses, glittering earrings and bottle-black hair worn in a smart-but-casual 'flick-up' coiffure.

Richardson is the only 'female' inmate in Nottingham Prison, but he has a greater forensic claim to fame; he was the first man in English legal history to stand trial twice for the same murder – and be convicted twice. With two trials and an appeal, Richardson can't claim to have been short-changed by the legal system; except that he still claims to be innocent of the murder for which he is serving a life sentence.

The facts of the case would challenge the patience of even the most fanatical devotee of crime fiction. The victim was a Brighton prostitute of some maturity and experience. Margaret Bolingbroke was in fact sixty-five years old; for five years she had enjoyed the privilege of a senior citizen's bus pass. The convicted man is fighting a battle not only to clear his name, but to receive an NHS sex-change operation to complete his transition to femininity. The crucial piece of evidence comes from another prostitute in Peacehaven, with whom Richardson was having sex at or around the time of the murder. And the crucial evidence in favour of Richardson's innocence lies in the fact that the victim was seen by at least a dozen witnesses some twelve hours after the time that, according to the pathologist, she was dead. If we added that the case also hinged on the nature of the cucumber sandwiches found in the victim's stomach, perhaps we'd be stretching your credibility too far . . . but that, too, is true.

Margaret Bolingbroke, like the Marine Square flat on the Brighton seafront in which she lived, was a woman of faded grandeur. The entrance to her flat was down a steep flight of stairs and into the basement area. The front door opened straight into the living-room. Friends came in the back, through the tradesman's entrance, but this was the way in for Margaret Bolingbroke's clients. Occasionally she would answer the door to a new client who, not anticipating such a level of maturity, would retreat sharply up the front steps, making his excuses and leaving. Margaret Bolingbroke had a steady clientele, offering, apparently, a curious mix of 'relief' massage and straight sex with tea and sympathy. She seemed to belong to an earlier, and perhaps mythical, age of prostitution, when the trade was a therapeutic branch of the social services. Indeed, as a former geriatric nurse, she often still wore a starched white nurse's uniform. She was a methodical worker; at the trial, the court heard how the towels laid on the bed before going to work on her customers were colour-coded – white for guests, maroon for friends. She had, in the past, maintained other, larger premises, and had taught her art to many an aspiring young hooker, most of whom kept in touch with this likeable, middle-aged lady.

The only vice Margaret Bolingbroke would admit to was a passion for gambling. Her social life revolved round a regular weekend spin of the roulette wheel at Sergeant Yorke's casino, close to the railway station. She also enjoyed a regular lunch break with John Sansom who worked close by, and used to arrive at the back door with sandwiches and cake; Mr Sansom was a former client, in whom sexual appetite had matured into friendship. According to the prosecution, he was the last person to see her alive when he shared his lunch with her on Friday, 7 February 1986.

In a perfect example of the curious things that go on in the bewigged and solemn atmosphere of a murder trial, an enormous amount of time was spent trying to identify the filling of those sandwiches. That's because the contents of Mrs Bolingbroke's stomach are at the centre of one of the most vexed areas of murder investigation – the time of death. The prosecution claimed that Margaret Bolingbroke died just an hour or so after eating Mr Sansom's sandwiches. But if this were so, how can the presence in her stomach of a sizeable chunk of red meat – which the Home Office forensic expert described as the sort you'd find in a casserole – be explained? That meat, the only recognizable object in the usual 'brown slurry' extracted at the post-mortem, suggests that she ate another meal.

And if she ate another meal before she died, there would not have been time for Matthew Richardson to kill her.

The weekend of 7–9th February was the coldest of the year. After they'd finished their sandwiches, Mr Sansom left about half past two by the back door, thereby escaping the notice of Rosie Gerrard-Wright, a Sussex University student swotting for her exams in the window overlooking the front entrance to Mrs Bolingbroke's flat. The *ennui* of revision was often relieved by the comings, though of course not the discreet back-door goings, of Mrs Bolingbroke's clients.

One hundred minutes later, at ten minutes past four, Matthew Richardson walked into the local police station. He had deep scratches on his face. He also had a cock-and-bull story that he had been mugged by two balaclavaed men who had stolen the proceeds of his recently cashed unemployment cheque. The police photographed his injuries, took a statement, escorted him to casualty – and promptly forgot all about him.

At the time Richardson presented himself at the police station, there was nothing to suggest that he was a killer, because it was two days before the body of Margaret Bolingbroke was found.

If she did die on the Friday afternoon, the body lay, undiscovered, in her flat for almost two days. It was wedged between a wall and a single bed. The windows were all shut, and the gas heater continued to churn out the heat in a loyal but unnecessary attempt to keep the flat warm for its occupant. Inside the flat, all would have been quiet apart from the occasional ringing of the telephone – calls from clients, and from friends who were beginning to get worried about her absence. The steps outside the flat, as Rosie Gerrard-Wright would later testify, were busy with visits of eager, but soon-to-be-disappointed customers.

It was her son-in-law who eventually called the police. Mrs Bolingbroke's daughter had made several unsuccessful attempts to call her mother over the weekend, and she asked her husband to go over to Marine Square and see if there was anything wrong. He was able to get to the back door, and peer through the windows of the flat. He could see that all was not well.

The ambulanceman who came remembered being hit by a wall of heat when the back door was broken down. He estimated the temperature at 75 degrees Fahrenheit. Police found the body where she had died; she had been beaten, prodded several times in the chest with a knife, and then killed by a large stab wound to the side of the neck. There were signs that she had put up a spirited defence.

No one connected the bedraggled figure of Richardson – who had gone to the police station two days earlier, with the murder until nearly two months later. And even then, the connection was made largely because Richardson himself pointed it out.

The Sussex Police threw huge amounts of time and manpower into the inquiry. Several suspects were questioned, including a local restaurant owner called Ashdal Hoque. He said that he knew Mrs Bolingbroke socially – certainly not professionally – and had no involvement with her murder. The police did not believe Mr Hoque, one of them challenging him at one point with the assertion: 'I always understood that Pakistanis were a proud, honest race of warriors and cricketers, and here you are blatantly lying to us.' Hoque successfully sued Sussex Constabulary for wrongful arrest.

By late March the trail was cold. A new tack was needed. They began a systematic trawl of all known prostitutes in an attempt to turn up information about violent clients. Mrs Bolingbroke's own regulars must have got a nasty shock when their telephone calls, arranging appointments for muscular relief, were answered by a burly policeman asking them to help with their inquiries. It was not long before the police struck lucky with Jane Collins, a tall, deep-voiced hooker working from an unprepossessing block of flats among the prim, retirement bungalows of Peacehaven, some eight miles from Brighton.

Ms Collins had a clever method of weeding out the merely prurient timewasters. She advertised her telephone number in shop windows, and when clients rang she would direct them to a particular telephone box on the front at Peacehaven. They then had to phone again, and quote the number of the phone box to her. Then, and only then, having established earnest of their sexual intent, she would tell them where they should come to.

On Friday, 7 February, the day Margaret Bolingbroke died, Matthew Richardson had done exactly that.

The trick Jane Collins turned that day disturbed her deeply. Prostitutes are not often surprised by the peculiarities of their clients, but there was something unforgettable about this one. Some time in the early afternoon – Jane Collins was to offer three different times – this client had sex with her, while her 'boyfriend' waited in the kitchen. The client first asked for oral sex, and Ms Collins obliged, for a £20 fee. Then the client requested a £45 upgrade to full sex. Richardson later admitted that he spent the bulk of his dole money on half an hour with this hooker; he would later go to the police station with his claim of having been robbed, in the hope that a gullible and sympathetic DHSS clerk would make good his loss.

As Richardson prepared to leave, Jane Collins saw something out of the corner of her eye which made her freeze. As she was dressing, she saw him retrieve a knife from underneath her pillow. She kept calm, but when he left, she told her boyfriend, who ran outside to try, unsuccessfully, to catch the client. Jane Collins made a note of the incident in her diary – in an entry which was later to become a key exhibit at trial. She wrote 'Marlboro Country/Personnel – Pillow Panic.' Marlboro Country referred to the red-and-white, promotional Marlboro cigarette jacket which Richardson owned.

This was to prove a vital clue. Staff at a nearby leisure centre remembered a man in a similar jacket asking to use the telephone that Friday afternoon. He was wearing a distinctive red-and-white jacket. And when the police put the idea of Marlboro Man to Rosie Gerrard-White, she too remembered a man with such a jacket calling at Bolingbroke's flat.

On 4 April, the police went to meet Richardson. It was only when they saw that he still had fresh weals across his cheeks and forehead that they realised that he was the same person who had come to them with the farcical mugging story the very afternoon of Bolingbroke's death. Richardson, for his part, assumed that the police were conscientiously following up his complaint about the 'robbery', but instead he was taken to Brighton Police Station for questioning in connection with the murder of Margaret Bolingbroke.

The police, however, had a problem. Jane Collins said that Richardson was having sex with her at three in the afternoon. If this was the case, how could he have travelled – by public transport, with his now depleted finances – to Brighton, murdered the prostitute, and then presented himself at the police station just over an hour later? Ironically, the very witness who linked Richardson with the murder now provided an alibi for him. The police paid two further visits to Ms Collins to sort out the problem; one of the police-action slips logging the progress of the investigation, states 'tighten up timings.' Ms Collins did tighten them up in further statements in which she changed her original timetable in a way which gave Richardson more time to get to Brighton.

Eventually Richardson told the police that he was responsible for Mrs Bolingbroke's murder. He confessed that he had gone on from Jane Collins' flat to Margaret Bolingbroke for another bout of commercial sex. When he had failed to get an erection, Margaret Bolingbroke had laughed and he 'saw red'. Various parts of the confession are clearly wrong, but perhaps such discrepancies can be explained by the red mist colouring Richardson's perceptions. Margaret Bolingbroke did have blood under her fingernails – but it was not Richardson's. By the time of his trial, however, Richardson had come up with a different version of events. He had gone to Mrs Bolingbroke, with a friend called 'Pete', intending to rob her. Things got out of hand, and Pete viciously attacked the woman. When Richardson attempted to intervene and save Mrs Bolingbroke, he suffered scratches to his face. His solicitors failed to trace Pete. The jury were unconvinced, and found him guilty.

Six weeks into his sentence, Richardson retracted the 'Pete' version of events, and claimed that he had never been to Margaret Bolingbroke's flat. When barrister David Martin-Sperry took on the appeal that was lodged, however, he discovered some intriguing evidence. There were statements from several witnesses who had seen Mrs Bolingbroke enjoying a game of roulette at Sergeant Yorke's casino on the evening of the Friday when she was supposed to have been killed. This evidence had not been featured in Richardson's trial because it simply did not fit with his first, fatuous, 'Pete did it' defence. At the appeal, Martin-Sperry's persuasive charm raised sufficient doubt on the prosecution evidence that Bolingbroke had died on the Friday afternoon that the court granted Richardson a retrial.

At the second trial, there were two further witnesses who claimed to have seen Mrs Bolingbroke alive after 4 p.m. on that Friday afternoon. She had been recognized late in the afternoon by a client, a prison officer who was understandably sensitive about revealing that he enjoyed Mrs Bolingbroke's services. Another witness said he saw her outside her flat the Saturday morning following her supposed death. But the arguments which had persuaded the Court of Appeal failed to convince the jury – and a remarkably interventionist judge – and Richardson was convicted once again.

The case was a mess, and there was enough doubt about it to arouse *Trial and Error*'s interest. We began by tracing a woman who was convinced of Richardson's innocence, a friend of his called Sue Jones. Sue had picked up a local Brighton paper to see a photograph of Richardson as the man charged with the Brighton prostitute murder. She recognized him as 'Rick', a former colleague when they had both worked, some years earlier, for British Rail. Sue could not reconcile her memories of Rick with the monstrous crime Richardson had been charged with.

Stephen Phelps and Nina Davies met Sue Jones on Brighton Station. A shapeless Laura Ashley dress ballooned over her cruelly thin frame, festooned with a heavy crucifix. Throughout the day, as the team timed the relevant distances and visited all the relevant locations, she talked compulsively about 'Rick.'

At the end of the day, she invited Stephen and Nina into the Hayward's Heath flat which she shared with her ex-husband in spite of their recent divorce. A catalyst for the breakdown of their marriage had been Sue's dramatic conversion to Christianity, and her husband's sudden, simultaneous and whole-hearted adoption of the Marxist-Leninist cause. The two philosophies coexisted uneasily together, noticeably in the lavatory, where an 'I am the Light of the World' poster jostled with a Che Guevara poster, and in the living-room where Patience Strong nestled uncomfortably next to *Das Kapital*.

Sue showed the team several photograph albums, with pictures of Rick and several prison friends in drag for a theatrical event. There was a collection of pictures of other men whose cause she had adopted. Most of them had been convicted of revolting sex crimes. She talked about them with a level of affection extraordinary even in such a forgiving Christian. 'Here's Brian the rapist – nasty job with a serrated knife, but he's a pussy-cat really... This is one of Eric before he was sent to Grendon [psychiatric prison], convicted of five rapes, but he's such a darling to me...'

With some relief, we returned to London. There, we consulted the eminent pathologist Dr Iain West. He is married, as we discovered, to Vesna Djurovic, the pathologist in the Bowler case (see chapter 11). The world of forensic pathology is a small one. Perhaps it's just as well. Dr West examined photographs of Richardson's facial scarring, and concluded that, while some of the marks could have been self-inflicted, the majority were not.

There comes a point in a case when you have to decide how much you are prepared to invest in it. We could spend the rest of our lives on the Richardson case, and never solve the conundrum. Who scratched Richardson? If it was Margaret Bolingbroke, how come it happened hours, possibly a day, before she died? Do the mysterious lump of meat and the casino sightings confirm a later time of death, in which case, why does Richardson present himself with his wounds at the police station? What is the truth about the timing of the Peacehaven prostitute? Who is the mysterious 'Rick' in Margaret Bolingbroke's appointments diary for December? Is it worth looking for 'Pete'? It would help a great deal if Richardson had not spun such a web of admitted lies.

In the end, we decided that we could prove the case a legal miscarriage – but that's a job for the lawyers. Deep down, we felt we could never prove, to our personal satisfaction, that Matthew Richardson, or Maxine Ryks as we should more properly call him, did not kill Margaret Bolingbroke. But the case still enlivens lunches in the basement of Ciao Bella, the Italian restaurant in nearby Lamb's Conduit Street which is Just Television's local canteen. We talk of rigor mortis, transsexual intercourse, and undigested lumps of meat long into the afternoon, until we notice,

to our surprise, that we are the only people left in the
restaurant . . .

10
Paul Blackburn

Work in Progress

[Too much of this book is written from my perspective – and, although I try to get involved as early as possible in a case, much of the work is done before a case reaches me. So I've asked Bob Duffield, our research consultant, to write this chapter on the intriguing case of Paul Blackburn. DJ]

I suppose it was just a matter of time before I found myself immersed in a Manchester-based story. This work has taken me virtually everywhere else in Britain. The re-investigation of Mark Cleary's conviction, for instance, had taken me back to Nottingham, where in a previous life I had posed and postured about the place as a long-haired undergraduate. And then, rather unexpectedly, I'd been off to Gloucester on behalf of Gary Mills and Tony Poole (see chapter 7); I was in the middle of an intense bout of research in Glasgow on behalf of Thomas Campbell and Joseph Steele, convicted of the biggest mass murder in Scottish history during the course of the infamous Ice Cream wars. But then we discovered that the BBC Community Programmes Unit were on the case, and it seemed fatuous to be in competition, so I decided to put the Scottish research on hold and headed down to Manchester.

Ever since coming to Just Television in September 1992 I had been waiting for a Manchester case. I don't know the place as well as I would like to, but I think I have a feel for that vibrant and confident city and for its people, thanks to a few close Mancunian friends. I had also spent a frenetic couple of months working there on a live consumer programme for Granada Television. With the Gloucester case completed and the Glasgow one

145

on hold, I had been fishing around for a new case. There was little that was promising in the correspondence, the daily trickle of cases that make it along the prison grapevine to our offices. But Stephen Phelps had been tipped off by Cleary's barrister, David Martin-Sperry, that there might be some mileage in the Brannan and Murphy case. The two men had been sentenced to life imprisonment for the murder of a gangster in a dingy Manchester nightclub. Unfortunately, they had gone to the club armed with a knife and an axe – but there was compelling evidence that the victim had pulled a gun on them first and that it was a case of self-defence; if this could be proved, then Brannan and Murphy would have been wrongly convicted.

I was delegated to head off to Manchester and meet Brannan's solicitor. Many of us have different ways of tackling a case, but to me meeting the solicitor and getting hold of a full set of case papers is the essential first step. While I was in the area, I could also take the opportunity to go to Liverpool to meet Eddie Gilfoyle's family. He too was serving life, for the murder of his wife Paula, by hanging her in the garage. The jury were convinced by evidence that suggested Gilfoyle – involved in some sort of social work training – had induced his wife to take part in a 'suicide experiment', to the extent of writing out a suicide note, to help him in his studies. The case remains Britain's only recorded case of a conviction for murder by hanging.

To round off the trip – and get the best value out of my northern tour – I was due to meet Steve Haywood at Wakefield Prison. We had VO's – the official prison department visiting orders – to see Gilfoyle and, while we were about it, a man called Blackburn.

That's how Paul Blackburn came into my life. It's somehow fitting that he should have been an afterthought – his whole life seems to have been somewhat accidental.

The elements that day conspired against me. I set off from Manchester to cross the Pennines on the M62 to Leeds. As I left, the city was being battered by a terrible storm – alarms were shrilling all around from shaken premises and rocking cars. Fire engines skidded round the greasy and glistening street corners. Managing to steer the hire car clear of most of the flying objects, I reached the comparative haven of the motorway. As the road

The hall of Number 34 Conduit Street. Willie Wiltshire was wounded in the front room (see bloodstain by door to right). He left his blood on the floor and chair as he was helped to an ambulance.

Gary Mills and Tony Poole. Harder men than this choirboy picture suggests – but are they guilty of murder?

Sheila Bowler, on right of picture.

Florence Jackson. Was 89-year-old Aunt Flo drowned by Sheila Bowler?

Aunt Flo was said to have been pushed in from the lower level of the stone platforms on the banks of the River Brede. Her body was found floating at the point in the distance (right) where the river bends.

The green Audi whose tyre Sheila Bowler supposedly deflated, to fake a breakdown after drowning her husband's elderly aunt. Interestingly, the tyre lost pressure while being driven by the police themselves.

From the hairpin bend on the A259 (left) to the pumping station (top right) is more than a quarter of a mile. Could Aunt Flo have walked there unaided, or did Sheila Bowler drive her to her death?

We chose Nick Barnett as our regular cameraman for his photographic skill and his versatility in tight situations.

Friends of Sheila Bowler discuss the case as unselfconsciously as the mechanics of television allow. Producer Stephen Phelps (far left) watches the monitor.

We had to end this session of night filming at 5.30, when dawn inconveniently broke.

Sir Ludovic Kennedy, doyen of the craft, and chairman of Just Television's advisory board. (*Photo credit: Rex Features Ltd.*)

Steve Haywood.

Bob Duffield whose research unravelled the case of Mark Cleary. Nina Davies had a rough research baptism among the down-and-outs of the Druhan case.

Olwyn Silvester.

The staff of Just Television.

David Jessel.

Stephen Phelps.

ue Walker, who led the
esearch into the case of
heila Bowler.

The central support team of Just Television – Laura
Carter and Emma Coghlan

Outside the Court of Appeal, seconds into freedom after ten years'
wrongful imprisonment. Mark Cleary (centre) is flanked by Bob Duffield
(left), with Olwyn Silvester and David Jessel. (*Photo credit: Nottingham
Evening Post.*)

Victory celebrations back at Just Television's Emerald Street office after
Mark Cleary's successful appeal. L to R – barrister David Martin-Sperry,
Steve Haywood, David Jessel, Mark's solicitor Ron Birkett, Mark Cleary,
and Stephen Phelps. (*Photo credit: Nottingham Evening Post.*)

climbed into the mountains, however, huge lumps of cotton wool came bowling out of the sky, and before I knew it the carriageway was blocked. I was stranded in a queue of parked vehicles that stretched, for all I knew, all the way to Leeds.

As ever, I was brilliantly prepared – no road map in the car, and a very distant memory of fifth-form geography. I had just assumed that I would follow the blue motorway signs to Wakefield. I managed to crawl off at the next junction, and sought directions on the mobile phone from the unflappable Emma back at base. I had almost given up hope of making HM Prison, Wakefield, expecting at any moment to join the growing number of cars abandoned in drifts on the side of the road. But thanks to the improvised drive-by-wire system with Emma at the helm, I managed to reach the M1 and then Wakefield about forty-five minutes before visiting time was up.

Things weren't going to get any easier. Steve, who I was to meet, had one VO to meet Gilfoyle, and I had one to meet Blackburn. The idea was that we'd each chat with our prisoner and swap over at half-time, thus making the most of our visit. As luck and mismanagement would have it, I had driven through the arctic snows with Steve's VO, while he had mistakenly got mine. Over the telephone we agreed that Steve should pretend to be me and that, if I ever arrived, I would impersonate him. And we'd just have to hope that prisons are sloppier about their admissions policy than they are about keeping their visitors inside.

Luckily, that seemed to be the case. I spotted Steve across the visiting hall, chatting with Blackburn. He seemed surprised that I had made it at all. I sat down for a few minutes with them, while I waited for the system to winkle Eddie Gilfoyle out of his cell. So it was that I came face to face with the man whose destiny was to haunt me for months.

Blackburn is a thin, pale man with bright-blue eyes and an unruly mess of wavy hair. He greeted me with a firm handshake and a cheeky smile; he struck me as the sort of man who survives the prison régime by challenging it with calculating insolence. I had already read a lot of Blackburn's letters from prison. They touched upon fragments of evidence, his past, his family, and so on – but the overall impression was one of outrage sprinkled with facetious remarks, mostly jokes against himself, each one punctuated with a smiley-face drawing to make sure that the reader got the joke. Here was Smiley Face himself. Anyone can lie, and appearances are deceptive, but I must say I warmed to Paul Blackburn from the outset. I can remember thinking – if you're banged up for an eternity because of a crime you did not commit, a sense of humour, or certainly of the ridiculous, is probably quite useful.

Blackburn passed another subtle test on first meeting. He didn't bang on about his innocence. In our game, it is very easy for prisoners to fall into the trap of protesting too much. Innocence is for juries to decide. What I'm interested in is the quality of the evidence which convicts someone, and the prospect of discovering new evidence. In the course of that discovery, I will form my own conclusions about the question of guilt. Having said that, what will keep me going, on cold inhospitable doorsteps, and grim no-hot-food-after-nine hotels, is the conviction that justice has miscarried. I find it less easy to go the extra mile, or two hundred miles, for a rogue who has been stitched up for the inappropriate robbery – as David Jessel says, the man who is done for the Clydesdale bank, when he has the perfectly reasonable alibi that he was doing the local Barclays at the time.

What terrible deed must Paul Blackburn have done at the age of fourteen – to keep him in prison still at the age of thirty? What enormity, committed by a child, can have induced the state to keep him confined six years longer than the average murderer? There are two answers to that; the first is because his supposed crime was a vile one – the attempted murder and buggery of a nine-year-old boy.

The second reason why he was not freed years ago is that he denies doing it.

The case goes all the way back to June 1978. I had never taken on such an old case; this re-investigation would have more in common with an archaeological dig than normal detective work. The fossil evidence was clear about one thing – Paul Blackburn was one of those people who, in another age, would have been described as 'born to hang'. By the age of fourteen, Paul was in trouble – lots of trouble. He had several convictions for assault, burglary and arson. He had burned down part of his school. For this offence, local magistrates issued an interim secure care order confining Blackburn at Red Bank Approved School.

Early in 1978, Paul's father drowned in the Manchester Ship Canal. Drunk, he had fallen off the gangplank of his barge. Paul's brothers and sisters received the news with delight and relief. Fred, an older brother, crept into the bedroom and said: 'You'll never believe this – but, thank God, Dad's dead.' For years they had had to endure their father's drunken thrashings, and his brutalization of their mother. Now, that shadow at least had passed. And there was more good news: secure care orders are reviewed on an annual basis, and Paul was expecting to be released from Red Bank shortly after his fifteenth birthday in the summer of the same year. Paul was allowed to come home to attend his father's funeral, but he didn't show up, making out that he had 'caught the wrong bus.' Social work reports show that he did not grieve for his father, and that he had major problems relating to adults, and in particular men.

My researches quickly revealed that Blackburn's social worker at the time reckoned that his time at the approved school 'did not touch' Paul. He merely saw it as something to survive. The school régime was based on 'behaviour modification' – jargon for the old carrot-and-stick approach to the reform of juvenile delinquents. On the old, character-building public school model, the inmates lived in 'houses', each one split into a number of dormitories and supervised by a housemaster or housemother. Everything, every petty privilege, had to be earned through the allocation of 'points' for good behaviour. Too few points, and you would lose your home-leave weekend.

If only Paul Blackburn had managed to behave himself a little less, he would not be in prison today. For it was on one such hard-won home leave that the crime was committed which horrified Warrington and put Blackburn in the frame.

It was a Sunday, 25 June, and a nine-year-old lad from nearby Sankey Keys left home for an afternoon's fishing. He took his rod, its stand, and a bag of sandwiches to join his uncle at a local pond called Geoff's Pit. I retraced the journey; these days it's a pleasantly manicured municipal area called Sankey Park, but in 1978 it was a rough trek across open countryside. The grass, I was told, came up to your waist; you could be playing soccer one moment in the street, and then hop over the fence and be in Indian country.

The boy never reached Geoff's Pit. When he hadn't returned home by nine in the evening, his parents called the police. Teams of volunteers scoured the area until dark. Hundreds gathered at first light the next day to continue the trawl. Police divers were brought in to investigate the depths of the Sankey canal – where, incidentally, the missing boy's brother had drowned a few years earlier. By late evening, the boy was still missing. Police were beginning to suspect that he had been abducted away from the area.

But at nine in the evening on the following day, Billy Manuel and his son, close neighbours of the missing boy's family, found themselves near to Seven Arches – an impressive Victorian railway bridge over the Sankey Canal. The Manuels had refused to give up the search. They were rummaging through a disused, roofless sewage works near the bridge – a honeycomb of brick cells with interlocking walls of varying heights. From one such cell they heard a muffled noise. Billy quickly tore away a pile of bricks which was weighing down a square piece of boarding at the bottom of the cell. Underneath the board was the body of a boy – totally naked, barely conscious but mercifully, still alive. He had been lying in the pit for some twenty-eight hours waiting to be rescued, unable to move because of the brick-weighted coffin lid above him.

At the hospital, the doctors found he was suffering from hypothermia, a number of cuts and bruises, and a badly broken little finger. It was also apparent that there had been an indecent sexual assault. The boy was clearly the victim of a loathsome attack, and the police-search exercise instantly became a manhunt for the assailant. Squads of extra officers were drafted in, and the local media gladly cooperated in publishing appeals for information. Someone out there must have known, or seen, the assailant – it would only be a matter of time before the 'red-haired thug' was caught and brought to justice.

That indeed was one of the key characteristics the victim was able to report to the police – that his attacker had shoulder-length, curly ginger hair. He was aged between sixteen and eighteen and was wearing a green parka jacket with a fur-lined hood.

He wore blue jeans and Doc Martens boots. The boy also told the police that the man had stabbed him with a pocket-knife. But in spite of large headlines in the local and national press, the trail went cold.

The police strategy was a devastatingly simple one. They interviewed every ginger-haired young man in an ever-expanding radius from the scene of the crime. Within weeks, literally thousands of red-headed boys had been spoken to. Warrington Police Station was clogged with queues of carrot-topped lads brought in for elimination purposes.

The problem with this approach was that the police fell victim to it. By using the media to heighten awareness of the 'red-haired thug' they had created public pressure to apprehend this ogre; and this, in turn, brought pressure on them to lean on any ginger-haired youth who couldn't adequately account for his movements on 25 June.

This method certainly produced results. Within a few weeks the police obtained a full and detailed confession from the admitted assailant. In fact, within weeks they had obtained no fewer than three such confessions.

None of them were from Paul Blackburn.

There are times when the work consists in poring over endless documents and files, analysing witness statements, cross-checking custody records – but sometimes you have to sit back and use your sheer imagination. I had to think myself into the mind of a fourteen-year-old boy on a boring Sunday afternoon. How much grasp would I have of the timetable of an afternoon's 'mucking about'? How well would I have been able to account for my actions? There were certain landmarks in Paul's aimless day of home leave. He'd got up late on the Sunday, and strolled over to visit his oldest brother Harry. At the house, he ran into a friend called Tony Chadwick, and the two decided to go out and shoot with brother Harry's air rifle. Over the next few hours, various luckless birds and old tin cans were on the receiving end of the rifle, and the pellets made satisfying noises as they hit the waters of the old canal. But, before long, the interest faded, and hunger began to grow. They split up. Paul walked home, fixed himself a can of soup, and then – he told police – strolled out to the shops just a few hundred yards away. He hung around, smoking, in a shop doorway, before wandering back home to see if there was anything on television. Yes, I think most of us have had adolescent afternoons like that.

Paul could fix the time that he got back home with reference to what he saw on the television (this, it seems, is how the entire population defines its day – 'just after *News at Ten*', 'half-way through *Neighbours*'). At 4.30 p.m. on Sunday 25 June, when the poor boy was being assaulted, BBC1 was playing *Willy Wonka and the Chocolate Factory* – an innocent, childish extravaganza which was to dominate the eventual trial and conviction of Paul Blackburn.

Why did police light upon Paul Blackburn? He was interviewed a total of four times. For the first two, he was seen by a couple of lowly police-officers at Red Bank, where Paul, in the presence of a housemaster called Jim Dillon, had given a surly and skeletal account of his day. But then – and this is where a detailed chronology yields such fascinating insights – came brother Fred's false confession. The police quickly rejected it. Indeed, the fool's gold of three such confessions had been rejected. It was now nearly a month since the manhunt had been launched.

The third interview was conducted by the two senior officers involved in the case. Strangely, no record was taken of any interview this time. But they returned exactly a week later, and, in the presence of senior housemaster Fred McVitie, subjected him to a formal interrogation. By now, it must have become clear to Paul that he was the principal suspect. He stuck to his account of the day's events; but the more he protested, the clearer it became that he had no independently verifiable alibi for the critical time between four and five o'clock when, the police calculated, the attack on the boy had taken place.

The only point of reference Blackburn could produce was the time at which he had got home; *Willy Wonka* was on, he said and it was 'the bit where the dwarves were singing a song in the cave, and the boat was just about to go into the tunnel.' This remembered fragment of film was to sink Paul Blackburn. Spooling back the video, the police calculated that these images must have appeared no sooner than 4.45 p.m. – so Paul was without an alibi up to that time. What's more, he had been in the area,

wearing a parka. Worse, Blackburn seemed to be changing details
of his account between statements, as if he was trying to squirm
his way out of his inevitable guilt. All this strongly indicated a
guilty mind. It was only a matter of time before Blackburn broke
– or so it must have seemed to the police.

The senior detectives now pulled an ace to trump Blackburn's
supposed lies. Two years earlier, when Blackburn was just eleven
years old, he had admitted assaulting four younger lads along
with another youth. The case had rested on file as an unpleasant
episode of childish bullying – two of the little boys had been
forced to strip, and Blackburn had pricked their genitals with a
pin. Warrington CID now went back to the victims, and obtained
evidence which cast a heavy shadow over Blackburn's psycho-
sexual make-up. The boys added new features to their evidence,
including simulated buggery and fellatio. And their new statements were unequivocal; it was the ginger-haired older lad who
had initiated the torments – Paul Blackburn.

Confronted with this evidence, at 11.40 on 21 July, Blackburn
broke down and confessed to attempted murder and buggery.
The officers took his confession in his own handwriting. Within
days he had retracted it, saying that it was extracted as a result
of a continuous barrage of threats, shouting and abuse. He would
also claim that the 'special knowledge' of the attack contained in
the confession had been spoonfed to him by the interviewing
officers.

So why should Paul Blackburn's case cause me to give up so
many nights of my life to tossing and turning in the overheated
bedrooms of this lousy, pretentious Manchester hotel? Mind you,
I wouldn't stay anywhere else except this overweight, over-
dressed, overpriced tart of a hotel, reminiscent of a *fin-de-siècle*
Parisian brothel. I fell in love with the Britannia while working
on Granada's *Out of Order* programme five years ago. At the
end of a foot-slogging day around the lost estates of Warrington,
Irlam, Eccles, Peel Green and Bolton, the Britannia offers a
warm embrace like a blousy and slightly inebriated aunt. The
club in the basement, slightly encumbered for six days of the
week by its name 'Saturdays', beats on relentlessly until 2 a.m. –
I swear you can hear it from the fourth floor – and on Tuesdays
the lager is given away at a pound a pint. Nothing much has

changed at the Britannia in five years – not even the midweek disc jockey. Social anthropologists [of which Bob was one, in a former postgraduate existence. DJ] will tell you that the essential purpose of ritual is to suspend the passing of time – to evoke a perfect world where things never age. It's a tricky illusion to pull off, and usually requires loud music, intoxicants and frenetic dancing to suspend the collective disbelief. Saturdays is such a timeless place, even on Tuesday night – a crossroads where sporadic flocks of hen-partying girls collide with lads on the razz, and businessmen up for a conference pair off with a couple of single mums who have managed to get last-minute baby-sitters, to flicker in the strobe-lit darkness.

But to answer my own question – why haven't I written off Paul Blackburn as a sad but dangerous young man who continues to protest his innocence because he cannot confront the enormity of his disgrace? A man, as they say, who is heavily in denial? The answer is that I do not believe he should have been convicted, and I am haunted by the fear that he is innocent.

Let's take that confession statement for a start. This is a confession made by a boy who has just passed his fifteenth birthday. Blackburn was interrogated for five hours by the two senior officers. He's a streetwise kid, but he is without doubt under considerable pressure – why else should a tough lad break down in tears, as it is acknowledged that he did? Why wasn't he allowed a solicitor, or his mother, present? A senior housemaster was present to oversee the interrogation, but might not Blackburn have seen Fred McVitie as an authority figure, rather than a protector? Mr McVitie had almost total control over Blackburn's life – he had the power to punish, discipline, and withhold privileges. As Red Bank's senior housemaster he was almost universally feared. My own researches among former members of the staff suggested a figure very much 'of the old school'.

In the contemporaneous notes recorded by the police, McVitie at one point said to Blackburn: 'It's up, Paul, the officers only want the truth.' This would surely be taken to imply 'the game's up', or 'stop lying'. But in court this was said to be an incomplete note and that Mr McVitie had said: 'It's up to you, Paul, the officers only want the truth.'

There is a difference.

The remarkable thing about the Blackburn case is how little paperwork survives. Instead of my usual submersion in the endless files, I was forced to concentrate on the bare essentials of a mere two hundred pieces of paper. This made me scrutinize the confession itself all the more carefully. It's a strange document for an inarticulate, sullen, ill-educated lad to have written. It suggests a strangely powerful and precise vocabulary. The word 'ejaculated' is used, and spelled correctly – would a fifteen-year-old have talked in such clinical terms? Blackburn wrote that he had attacked his victim 'in a frenzy' – a good, vivid phrase, but hardly part of a normal teenager's everyday usage. ('Sorry I kicked the dog, Mum, but I was in a frenzy . . .'?)

Yet everything hung on that confession – admissions which would certainly be thrown out as evidence today. These days, it's part of the law that there should be an 'appropriate adult' present, and that interviews should be carefully and unoppressively conducted – although, typically, there is no legal definition of oppression. The care taken in the interviewing of the children convicted of murdering the toddler Jamie Bulger shows how attitudes have changed – too late for Paul Blackburn.

Another thing that didn't help Blackburn was the fact that he'd had his hair cut – twice – after the attack, and on dates which tallied with the publication in the press of artist's impressions of the attacker. But as I tracked down former staff members, a benign explanation for the haircuts began to emerge. Red Bank, as a highly disciplined régime, did not allow boys to wear their hair over their collar. There were two routes to acceptable hair length – the 'gentle' cut administered by the housemother, or the 'brutal' cut for which you were sent to the barber. Boys being boys, fashion being fashion, and the seventies being what they were, everyone was desperate to keep their hair as long as possible, while avoiding the disciplinary scalping.

On the day before the murder, I discovered, while Paul was at Red Bank's Open Day, a passing housemaster had noticed Paul's hair and said: 'We're going to have to deal with that hair, Paul . . .' Luckily, it being Saturday, there was no one available to cut it, and Paul was able to go on home leave with his hair fashionably bedraggled. But on his return, remembering the scissors of Damocles hanging over his head, he took the opportunity of a trim –

155

his last hope of avoiding the barber's butchery. But Paul was far from happy with the result – and went to another member of staff for a more acceptable modification. Wasn't a mixture of vanity and savvy just as likely an explanation as the sinister one – that he was trying to make himself look different from the description of the assailant?

Come to that, how well did Blackburn match the description of the attacker, anyway? This was a crime carried out in an area frequented by people walking their dogs, by ramblers and fishermen, on a sunny Sunday afternoon. Yet the only person on file who actually saw and described the attacker was the victim himself. Was this really credible? Outdoor crimes in daylight, such as the Wimbledon Common murder, usually spawn a plethora of witnesses. The police had boasted in court of having taken more than two thousand statements, and having interviewed three thousand people. Where was all this material? The slim ring binder in front of me was clearly a mere abstract of the available evidence – yet it was the evidence that had convicted Blackburn. Having worked on the Cleary case, I knew only too well of the evidential land mines that lurk in evidence which the police, and the defence, deem not to be relevant.

So there was only one description of the attacker: long, curly ginger hair, aged 17–21, 5'7" to 5'10" in height, white speckled shirt, green parka, blue jeans, Doc Martens, deep Manchester accent, and carrying a white-handled pocket knife.

Blackburn was fourteen. But let's now look at what the victim said to the police: 'I know boys of just fifteen who are as big as [the attacker].' But checking the chronology, I found that this was a statement taken by the police after Blackburn, who had just turned fifteen, was arrested. It does seem a strange opinion to offer, unless the police are anxious to cement their suspicions.

Blackburn didn't have red hair, or ginger hair. It was blond. Interestingly, a subsequent statement from the victim amends the gingerness – which had so dominated the publicity surrounding the manhunt – to 'light ginger'. His parka was brown. He did not have a speckled white shirt, but wore instead a blue sweatshirt with a large logo of an American university. Yes, he wore jeans and Doc Martens – the national dress of teenagers. And the knife? In his confession to the police, Blackburn admitted using a large Indian knife with a carved wooden handle to assault the youth – but it was an ornamental item, whose blade would have buckled before puncturing the skin. Normally, one would accept that in the desperate circumstances of an attack, the victim is not coolly engaged in issues of comparative knife design; but in this case, the victim said he had been virtually mesmerized by the knife. He had observed his attacker 'open' it – but Blackburn's knife was not the sort that could be closed.

Wrong age, wrong clothes, questionable hair, wrong knife. Not bad for a start. But deeply frustrating. Most of the papers are lodged with various government departments – some of whom, absurdly, have been claiming that they are covered by the thirty-year-rule. There's not a lot more that I can do until I have some more evidence to get my teeth into. And for that to happen, I'm subject to the timetable of bureaucrats who may not feel the same urgency about a possible miscarriage of justice as I do.

But I have already found some tantalizing leads. Weeks before Blackburn was in the frame, a lorry driver from the Newcastle area who had seen the artist's impression in the *Manchester Evening News*, immediately came forward with a vital lead. On that very Sunday afternoon he had picked up a hitchhiker in Manchester who fitted the description – long, curly hair, green parka, aged around eighteen, with a deep, strong local accent. The youth claimed to be a slaughterman on his way to Tiverton in Devon. The driver had dropped him off in Great Sankey at around three in the afternoon, near the scene of the attack. Was this man ever found, or even pursued? Perhaps the answer lies in some dusty bundle of papers, deep in a forgotten cupboard of a government department.

Something else worries me. The police religiously preserved the scene of the crime and took a number of forensic samples, including swabs likely to contain semen from the attacker. Somehow – and what bad luck for all concerned – all the crucial exhibits somehow disappeared at the forensic science laboratories before trial. They were apparently thrown away by mistake – exhibits that might have proved once and for all the non-involvement of Paul Blackburn in this horrible crime.

It's a cock-up too far; was this shoddy, panicky investigation by the police desperate to find any local youth with the opportunity to commit the crime? Something else is already ringing alarm bells. The discovery of Paul Blackburn's sexual bullying at the age of eleven clearly confirmed police suspicions. But on one of my field trips I tracked down one of the lads who had been the victim of that bullying in 1976. He's now twenty-five, and I showed him the statement he had made to the Warrington police in 1978.

He told me that he still remembered the incident clearly, but it wasn't Blackburn, but his accomplice who instigated the bullying. 'The guy who was ordering us about had dark hair – I know him, and he still lives here in Irlam. The other one, the one with the blond hair, he was guarding me, stopping me running off sort of thing – that must have been Blackburn, although I didn't know him at the time.' This does not chime with the version the police took away when they, with Blackburn already under suspicion, went to investigate this former attack – they had Paul as the instigator.

It's one of the great bonuses of this work that you run into remarkable people who you'd never meet under any other circumstances. There are people on the Bestwood estate, during the Cleary investigation, who I am now proud and happy to count among my friends. Investigating Blackburn, I met another remarkable person. A probation volunteer called Norma Green and her husband effectively adopted Paul's younger brother, John. John got into trouble himself, and Norma found herself visiting two Blackburn brothers. Now that John is out and going straight, Norma remains as Paul's lifeline. Her investment in him has been incalculable – thousands of pounds spent trekking around the country, visiting the many prisons where Paul has been moved. She usually writes a letter a day. And yet Norma herself is quite seriously ill. She regularly has to visit hospital for special injections which marginally mitigate her agony. Like medieval scholars, I do not know how many angels can dance on the head of a pin, but I do know there is one living in Peel Green, Manchester.

Norma has a million stories about Paul: about his fight to survive, his paintings, his moods, his anger, his scars from countless run-ins with warders and inmates alike, his periods of solitary in various punishment blocks and the withdrawal of privileges.

Paul has refused to take sexual counselling, even though it might speed his early release – if you can call release after sixteen years early. He simply says he doesn't need sexual counselling, because he is not a sex offender.

In fact the path he has chosen is nothing less than an assault course through Hell. Child sex offenders – as in the case of 'M' (see chapter 8) – are universally despised by inmates and officers alike. Yet Blackburn has always refused the sanctuary of Rule 43, which segregates the despised 'nonces' from the 'normal' prison population. He has told me that he will only walk out of prison as an innocent man.

Work in Progress, this chapter is headed. I hope it won't join the sad pile of reject cases. There is something deeply wrong with this case. It is a casual conviction, reached on evidence which no court today would tolerate. If we could get his case back to the Appeal Court, I believe it would genuinely shock their Lordships. It may well be that we have enough now to prompt an official re-investigation of the case. But we need a little bit more. We need to get hold of the rest of those papers. I am convinced that somewhere, among them, lies the key that can unlock Paul Blackburn from the prison to which he was sent so long ago, and in which he is now effectively confining himself.

I won't give this one up.

11
Sheila Bowler

Murder in Toytown

The case of Sheila Bowler took us straight into Murder-at-the-Vicarage territory. Nothing could have been in greater contrast to the seediness of, for example, the case of Mills and Poole than the lace-curtains, tea-shops, cobblestones and gossip of Winchelsea and Rye in East Sussex; a murder in toytown.

Except I'm not sure it was a murder. In fact, it is one of the strangest aspects of one of the most bizarre cases we have ever investigated that a woman was convicted of murder on no evidence whatsoever.

The mystery began on a fine summer's evening in 1992. Mrs Bowler, a formidable, somewhat forbidding, and recently-widowed woman of sixty-two, had just finished teaching at Battle Abbey School. She was a freelance piano-teacher, and the school was one of those where she taught. Pausing only to telephone her son Simon, she set off for the Greyfriars Residential Home in the coastal village of Winchelsea. The town, perched on a mound from which the sea has long retreated, is proud of its historic status as one of the Cinque Ports; and local wisdom, with all the unhesitating arrogance of proud parochialism, has it that its street layout – parallel roads intersected at right-angles – provided the inspiration for the urban planner of New York. Winchelsea's mellow brick and white-timbered cottages make it picture-postcard pretty. A Neighbourhood Watch sticker peeps from every window, and one suspects that any felon apprehended in possession of his burglarizing tools would face a summary gibbeting outside the town gate. It seems, however, a depressingly lifeless community; doubtless it has its own busy economy of committee meetings and village-green vendettas, but, to the visitor at least, the place looks suspiciously like a commuter community, a neighbourhood degraded into a dormitory, in contrast to the bohemian vivacity of Rye, just two miles down the road.

Greyfriars was a noble pile on the edge of town. Sheila Bowler's aunt, Florence Jackson, had been resident at Greyfriars only a matter of months, judged incapable, at eighty-nine, of looking after herself. For years, she and her sister Lil had coped on their own in a small flat in Rye, and were known as local characters, trotting up the cobbles to Simon the Pieman's coffee shop for breakfast every morning. But Aunt Lil had died a few months earlier, and Mrs Bowler, on one of her regular visits to her aunt, had found Flo one day lying in a pool of vomited blood, the result of an undiagnosed intestinal illness; it was clear that Aunt Flo could no longer look after herself, and, under some protest and after receiving assurances that this needn't necessarily be a permanent arrangement, she had allowed herself to be taken into care at the home.

Mrs Jackson was in fact the aunt of Mrs Bowler's late husband, but she was known to all the family as Aunt Flo, and, to avoid cumbersome reference to aunts-in-law and nieces-in-law we'll leave them as aunt and niece. Just after eight one evening, Mrs Bowler tucked Aunt Flo into the front passenger seat of her ageing, but well-tended green metallic Audi, to take her home for two days. The plan, according to Sheila Bowler, was to assess whether or not she could be looked after at Fairmeadow, the Bowler family's pleasant, modern detached house on the outskirts of Rye. Mr Bowler, in one of a series of family tragedies which included Aunt Lil's death and Aunt Flo's illness, had died earlier that year, after unexpected complications following routine surgery. Sheila Bowler's children, Simon and Jane, had left home – he to work as a civil servant, she to pursue a promising career in music. Fairmeadow was too large for just one person; and there would be the advantage that if Aunt Flo could be cared for at home, she would avoid the weekly £250 haemorrhage of nursing-home fees.

Thirteen hours after waving goodbye to the staff at Greyfriars, Aunt Flo was found dead in the River Brede, where it runs through the marsh pastureland at the bottom of Winchelsea Hill. She had been reported missing at midnight. At one in the morning a police helicopter had been scrambled. In spite of having only a limited area to search, it drew a blank. The eye-in-the-sky, we were later told, had a sophisticated thermal-imaging system to detect the body-heat of anything below; we were also told that the helicopter used not a sophisticated satellite system but the *AA Road Atlas* to navigate by. Next morning, though, the crew had better fortune. Just six hundred yards away from where Mrs Bowler had abandoned her car they found the body of Aunt Flo.

Much of what happened during those thirteen hours is not in dispute; but the motives of each and every action are fatally ambiguous. For a start, Mrs Bowler did not drive her aunt straight home to her pleasant detached house on the outskirts of nearby Rye. She set off in the opposite direction towards the seaside town of Bexhill, saying she wanted to pick up a protein supplement from a supplier and family friend. It was, we later discovered, an errand on behalf of another elderly lady whom Mrs Bowler had taken under her wing. When she called at the house in Bexhill, however, leaving her aunt in the car with the radio to keep her company, she was told that the supply had not arrived. 'Never mind,' she said. 'I'll be passing this way tomorrow.'

There are two explanations for the detour. The first is that Sheila Bowler, a woman forever dashing around who made her plans on the spur of the moment – even Aunt Flo's outing was arranged at the last moment – thought it worth combining an errand with a pleasant summer's evening ride. Aunt Flo had been cloistered in Greyfriars, and she would appreciate the liberation of a trip in the familiar and friendly car.

The other, and less charitable, explanation is that Sheila Bowler wanted to use up the hours of daylight and dusk, so that she could tip her aunt into the river under cover of darkness.

There are also two explanations about what happened next. On the way back from Bexhill, as the Audi was sweeping along the straight road bisecting the plump orchards and sheep-dotted pastures of this idyllic corner of East Sussex, Mrs Bowler was aware that the car was handling badly. She noticed it as she drove along Icklesham straight, but kept on for another couple of miles, until she got to Winchelsea. At Winchelsea, the A259 skirts the town, and then plunges steeply down to the bottom of the inland cliff on which it stands, resolving itself in a sharp hairpin bend.

The gradient and the abrupt change of direction put an intolerable strain on the wheel and, some sixty yards beyond the bend, Mrs Bowler parked her car on the kerbside. Finding that the front nearside tyre was badly deflated, she made her aunt comfortable in the passenger seat, tried, unsuccessfully, to find some music on the car radio, and set off, at a brisk pace, in search of help from a row of roadside cottages a quarter of a mile or so distant. Ringing the doorbell of Number 4, she discovered that she vaguely knew one of the residents of Tanyard Cottages, a local barber, Mr Soan. Explaining her predicament, she used Mr Soan's telephone to call the Britannia Recovery Service, to which she subscribed. She was connected at 10.21 p.m. After gratefully accepting a glass of orange squash, Mrs Bowler, accompanied by Mr and Mrs Soan, then walked back to the car. It was Mrs Bowler who was the first to realize that her aunt was missing.

That's Mrs Bowler's story. It is everyone's nightmare; most of us have, against our judgement, but due to circumstances beyond our control, left our children or those dependent on us for 'just a few minutes'. Every minute seems an hour, as we fret at our separation; the relief when, on our return, the house has not burnt down, and the children have not electrocuted themselves, is palpable, and we vow never to take such a risk again. But there was no relief for Sheila Bowler. A ragged search party set out – soon to be joined by the police and the man sent by Britannia Recovery. But Mrs Bowler told them not to range too far – her aunt could hardly move without her zimmer frame; and the zimmer was back at the nursing home.

There could be, again, a more sinister explanation; as it became conveniently dark, Mrs Bowler drove her aunt down to the bottom of Winchelsea Hill, and instead of following the hairpin bend round to Rye, she turned left at the smaller road at the apex of the bend. The road, called Station Road because it eventually leads to the picturesque Railway Children station just outside Winchelsea, is a well-used local short cut to Udimore and, eventually, the main London road. Station Road passes a caravan site on the right, a couple of houses a little further up on the left, crosses the River Brede, and then winds in a big curve to the left. Shortly before another kink to the right, there is a small, squat brick building. It houses an enormous Archimedes screw,

164

and at unpredictable times of the day and night the screw revolves, pulling water up from one of the drainage ditches and into the River Brede.

The pumping station has an area of concrete hard-standing, and it is easy to drive in, off Station Road, and park a car behind it. Local romantics know it well as a discreet and convenient venue. But Sheila Bowler – according to the version of that night's events which ultimately convicted her – wanted to exploit the convenience and discretion of the place for a darker reason. She parked the car, escorted her confused old aunt to the bank of the River Brede, and pushed her over the edge. She would have been able to see the lights of Winchelsea twinkling on the hill dead ahead of her, some four hundred yards across the fields, and the headlights of cars sweeping down the hill. But, so long as no one came down Station Road, she would be safe under cover of darkness.

Then she drove back up Station Road. Reaching the hairpin of the A259, she turned left, towards Rye, but then – and this, of course, is still the murderous explanation of the night's events – she pulled into the kerb after ten to fifteen yards or so. She got out of the car and, checking to see that no one was passing, crouched by the front nearside tyre, and let it down. Then she set off, ostensibly to seek help, but in fact to recruit the unwitting and innocent Mr and Mrs Soan into a calculated charade. The whole night's events had been coldly planned; Mrs Bowler had not even prepared a bed, or laid in food, for her guest back at Fairmeadow. What would be the point in making a meal, or taking sheets out of the airing cupboard, for someone who – you knew – would not be coming home?

Two versions, then, of the night's events. Everyone in the area subscribes vehemently to one version or the other. Each person we met was convinced either that Mrs Bowler was a wicked murderess, or a woman with a heart of gold who had become the victim of a tragic misfortune. Each conviction is held passionately, angrily.

It doesn't seem to matter that there is literally no evidence either way. There is nothing upon which to base a passionate conviction of Sheila Bowler's innocence. Nor of her guilt. But that doesn't seem to stop people clinging, furiously, to their views.

Toytown always was a place for passionate prejudice.

It was this that made it such a frustrating case. We need a degree of evidence, because we then have something to investigate. But with the Bowler case, there was nothing; what evidence there was, as we shall see, was totally discredited in court. We needed to find a new dimension to the case.

In fact, our preliminary investigation almost immediately revealed matters which the court, and the gossips, were unaware of. Sue Walker, the researcher who originally went to Sussex, met a redoubtable octogenarian who volunteered interesting information on the state of the tyre. A few weeks earlier Sheila Bowler had driven her – in what she described as a typical act of charitable friendship – to Hastings. She remembers the day well, because she had to buy a hat for a wedding. On the way back, the old lady said how much she missed the sea views she used to enjoy when she lived on the coast. Mrs Bowler immediately swung the car off the main road, and down the narrow lanes to the local lighthouse, where they stopped to enjoy the view. As they left, however, Mrs Bowler complained about the way the car was handling. 'It absolutely sticks in my mind,' the old lady told us, 'because I had this naughty thought; oh dear, if we crash, I won't be able to wear my lovely new hat.'

But even that cuts both ways; it could suggest that Mrs Bowler was studiedly laying the groundwork for her cunning plan, relying on the old lady to come forward with her corroboration. Indeed, practically every aspect of the Bowler case is capable of two interpretations. Take that somewhat heartless injunction not to bother looking too far for the missing eighty-nine-year-old. Well, Mrs Bowler was a bit like that; a heart of gold, everyone would say, but one of that brittle breed of uniquely English, no-nonsense, unsentimental matrons who are the bossy backbone of every village committee. Mrs Bowler is the kind of mother who might say of her son's broken collar bone that it would jolly well teach him to keep his feet in the stirrups; the kind of woman who tells you that she doesn't suffer fools gladly – leaving you with the firm impression that when it comes to fools, she regards you as a prime specimen of the species. Such women provoke simultaneously contrary reactions; and, as even her friends told us, Mrs Bowler was a wonderful woman, but your heart tended

166

to sink as you saw her looming towards you in the High Street at Rye.

Other features of the case are sinister or redeeming, according to prejudice. Mrs Bowler was said to have told Greyfriars staff that her aunt wouldn't need a zimmer frame. Well, of course she wouldn't if Mrs Bowler planned to murder her; but, on the other hand, Aunt Flo had recently fractured her wrist, and was wearing a cast, so she couldn't have used a zimmer even if she had wanted to. Again, the point about her not having a bed ready upstairs – was that because she knew Aunt Flo would not be coming home that night? If so, for a calculating killer it seems somewhat remiss to leave such a blatant statement of intent. A more prosaic reason – and the one that Mrs Bowler impatiently gave me in a 'what-sort-of-idiot-are-you' tone of voice – is that she did not know whether or not Aunt Flo could manage the stairs at Fairmeadow. If she could, she'd make a bed up upstairs, and if not, she would have made up a couple of beds on the ground floor, to be close to the old lady.

In the absence of evidence, and with the circumstantial detail open to such widely varying interpretation, everything depended on the attitude of those investigating the affair. Detective Sergeant Linda Booth was with Mrs Bowler on the next day, Thursday, when the news was broken. 'She seemed really quite jovial, full of the joys of spring,' DS Booth reported to the incident room. Particularly suspicious was the fact that Bowler, instead of collapsing in the requisite flood of tears, had begun capably to bake a batch of biscuits. 'But Sheila's not like that!' one of her friends exclaimed. 'She'd never cry in front of strangers – particularly not the *police*.'

The Bowler case was unique in our experience, in that it was the first time that we had access to the police side of the story. Since the major miscarriage-of-justice scandals of the eighties, the Crown has been compelled to take more seriously its duty to disclose any relevant information to the defence. Among this stack of paperwork, in the Bowler case, were the duty logs of the Sussex Police, and their internal briefings on the progress of the case. It has long been our belief that most miscarriages of justice arise not from malice but from the onset of a fatal preconception, which accentuates any information tending to support it, while blinkering officers from anything that tends to challenge it. With the police logs we could see how the prejudice set in from the very first hours.

At five past two in the morning, for example, the sergeant at the operations room spoke to a senior figure at the Greyfriars home. The log reports: 'She expressed great concern about the circumstances of the disappearance, and was scathing of Mrs Bowler. Although she didn't openly accuse Mrs Bowler of doing harm to her Auntie, she left me in no doubt that she thought it a distinct possibility.' It seems inconceivable that such an observation would not have been passed on to the woman detective sergeant who went to see Mrs Bowler next day, and it must have coloured her perception of the person already emerging as prime suspect. Indeed, DS Booth reports to the incident room with a breathlessness that disregards the usual canons of syntax: 'Mrs Bowler appeared very sprightly and jovial having just learnt that she had been informed of the death of Mrs Florence Jackson, however, she showed no signs of distress.' During the course of the (uncautioned) conversation, 'She kept jumping up to tend to the workmen and various other excuses and albeit answered my questions appeared reluctant to do so . . . she expressed that she was extremely tired and felt that she'd really been inconvenienced enough by the police over the matter.' WDS Booth's suspicions are further aroused when it appears that Mrs Bowler has not got much in the way of food ready for her Aunt's visit – and 'she also remarked that she was finding it extremely difficult making ends meet on a widow's pension . . .' The conversation ends when 'she virtually ushered myself and some fello [sic] officers who were taking a statement from her son out of the house, saying that she needed to go and get a meal and could assist us no further that evening . . . *'She was evasive, and had a number of phone conversations with her daughter'* who *'was surprised at her mother's resilience; at which point Mrs Bowler explained that life must go on.'*

It's easy to picture the taut relationship that developed, almost from the outset, between these two obviously tough-minded women, the policewoman and the haughty suspect. One suspects that Mrs Bowler is the sort of person who would have preferred the police to use the tradesmen's entrance. When Mrs Bowler produced the boots she was wearing the night before, and said she had 'rubbed them up', suspicions deepened further still. Later, Mrs Bowler would produce a second pair of shoes – these, too, 'rubbed up' – saying she'd been mistaken about the first pair she produced; she also said, according to WDS Booth, that this was the first time the car had misbehaved (again, she was later to modify her story). When, a few days later, she said she had been down Station Road on the very day that Aunt Flo disappeared, the police interpreted this as Mrs Bowler desperately covering herself against the possibility that incriminating tyre tracks had been found. (None were.)

Back at the incident room, meanwhile, the case was taking shape. A slipper had been found near a pumping station on the River Brede, apparently pinpointing the murder site (the case had very rapidly been categorized as a murder). Bruising had been noticed, in the form of 'grip marks', round Aunt Flo's upper arm. A pathologist would later testify that abrasions on Aunt Flo's head were 'encouragement blows'. Authority had been gained to examine the bank account statements both of Mrs Bowler and her aunt. It was established that Greyfriars was owed £3,589 in overdue payments for Aunt Flo's care. Aunt Flo's will would shortly be examined.

A week later came a significant, and damning statement from a woman who had passed the parked Audi that night. Judith Pearson said she was driving round the hairpin bend at 9.40 p.m., and saw a woman walking away from the car towards the cottages; this must have been Mrs Bowler. But the important thing was that Mrs Pearson did not see anyone in the car. If she was right, this would be proof of Sheila Bowler's cynical pretence of seeking help for a car she had herself disabled, having earlier disposed of its passenger.

A briefing from Detective Superintendent Foster reviews the situation a fortnight after the death of Aunt Flo. A critical experiment had been carried out to see if it was possible for Aunt Flo to shuffle the distance from the breakdown scene to the pumping station. A woman of similar weight was charged with walking the distance wearing new slippers, and the soles of those slippers were compared with the sole of the slipper recovered from the bank shortly after Aunt Flo's body was found. 'A recap of the available evidence was carried out and we still do not have evidence to suggest that Mrs Jackson was in Mrs Bowler's car after the alleged puncture ... In fact we have statements which lead us to believe she was not in the car. In view of the implaus-able [sic] accounts given by Mrs Butler [sic] together with these statements which tend to conflict with her account and her chang-ing of the original stories to DS Booth, we must suspect Mrs Bowler of involvement in Mrs Jackson's death. As such, Mrs Bowler will be arrested on suspicion of murder today and interviewed.'

We've read our fair share of police interviews; Mrs Bowler's are, in their way, the strangest. Her solicitor, Russell Parkes, had advised his client to say nothing. This was eminently reasonable, given that Parkes had actually overheard a knot of policemen discussing Aunt Flo's fate a few days after the fatal night and saying that 'they had a body' for the murder, that it was now just a matter of getting the proof. Mrs Bowler's garrulous nature – she struck us, from what we knew, as a very much blurt-now, think-later type – made it even more sensible to recommend his client to say nothing. It was particularly apt given the extra-ordinary devices resorted to by the interviewing officers. Every technique in the interrogator's arsenal was brought to bear.

Andrew Sanders, at Oxford University's Department of Crimi-nology, has identified a number of inquisitional tricks of the trade. The Bowler interviews illustrate them all. There's the Battering Ram approach: 'You're not defending yourself, you're not main-taining your innocence,' says DS Booth at the outset; she then accuses Mrs Bowler of being 'a liar – there's no other nicer word that I can use.' Then there's the A Thousand Scientists Can't be Wrong approach. Mrs Bowler is confronted with the evidence of the scientist who has examined that tyre: 'Mrs Bowler, this man is an expert in this field; he's a forensic scientist ... there's nothing wrong with that tyre; you let that tyre down.' Then there's the Sympathetic Psychology approach: 'Was Aunt Flo that much a source of irritance to you? Did you feel bitter that she was still alive and in reasonable good health ... Your husband had recently died. Did you feel some bitterness towards her?' Next comes the Normalization Tactic – the suggestion that murder is a quite understandable temptation: 'After all, she was ninety wasn't she – she'd had a good life. So did it really matter if she died? Perhaps it didn't. Perhaps we shouldn't be caring anyway ... perhaps you didn't mean it to happen?' There's the Soft–Hard approach: 'You're an intelligent woman, Mrs Bowler' wheedles DS Booth, confronting the suspect with the logic of the case against her; and then her colleague DS Renno chips in brutally a few seconds later: 'You knew [your aunt] was face down in the drink, didn't you?' Heavy Irony makes an appearance: 'Lo and behold, yes, when you get back to the car she's not there, but then of course you would have been aware of that because she wasn't in the car when you left it, was she?' There's the Overwhelming Evidence argument: 'Are all these people telling us the truth, or are you the only one that's told us the truth and everybody else is telling lies?' The police even – presumably as a shock tactic – show her photographs taken of her aunt's body.

To all of this, Sheila Bowler resolutely responds: 'No comment.' 'So you're making no comment because you're guilty of this offence?' suggests DS Booth. 'Are you finding it difficult to face up to reality ... is it something you feel embarrassed about ... do you find the fact that we are sitting here accusing you of murder an uncomfortable situation?' And, later: 'Are you really this cold, callous woman that we're hearing from people?' There are four of these interviews, together totalling two hours and eight minutes. Given that Mrs Bowler only says 'no comment', there must be the best part of two hours of this barrage.

This interview, clumsy, hectoring, insidious, and apparently dedicated to proving an assumption rather than entertaining the possibility of innocence, was tape-recorded, in the full knowledge that it could be heard in court. One shudders to think of how interviews were conducted before taping was introduced. Had Mrs Bowler confessed, and had she been convicted on the basis of that confession, I am sure that the Court of Appeal would have quashed the conviction because of the not-so-subtly oppressive way in which it was conducted. Sanders himself, whom we commissioned to cast a dispassionate academic eye over the interviews, reports: 'The interviews reveal a remarkable single-mindedness – the police are not really after the facts, not really after the truth, what they're after is a confession ... what they're trying to do here is to take a short cut and get the evidence through interrogating her.'

But Mrs Bowler did not confess. Why then was she convicted? The defence were confident, throughout, that the case would fall.

The trial took place at Hove Crown Court. Halfway through, after the Crown had put the evidence against her, the defence stood up and asked the judge to stop the trial and let Sheila Bowler go. The defence's 'respectful submission' was entered at the conclusion of the Crown case. With deft and drastic forensic surgery, Nicholas Purnell QC sliced away the evidence such as it was; Purnell preferred to call it 'a theory which effectively is wrapped in a straitjacket upon the minds of those investigating the case and a blinker upon those who present the case'. The prosecution had rested on three pillars, he said. (Read these speeches often enough, and you soon find that the world of advocacy divides between those for whom cases either rest on 'pillars' or 'planks'; some barristers are planksmen – Purnell is for pillars.)

First, there was the question of the sighting of an empty car, with Bowler striding away from it. Judith Pearson had said that she 'couldn't be sure' whether she would have seen a passenger in the car. There was a second witness, a Mr Beckett, but he, too, admitted that he 'was not sure' – so that evidence collapsed. We were later to confirm the frailty of this evidence. We parked the same Audi on the bend exactly two years later, and, travelling past in another car at precisely the same time, videoed what would have been apparent. We hired an actress of exactly the same age and build as Aunt Flo and put her in the passenger seat. We discovered that the head restraints of the Audi would have made it impossible for anyone to tell whether or not anyone was in the passenger seat. We also noticed, with some amusement, that a police television programme called *Crime Monthly* had also reconstructed the experiment. Quite inexplicably, whereas we had used the very motor car involved in the night's events, with permission of the Bowler family, the model of Audi that *Crime Monthly* used did not have solid headrests, but merely a moulded frame. One would really have hoped that a programme being made with the cooperation of the Sussex Police would have paid more attention to such an important detail. But one is often disappointed. Besides, common sense suggests that you would recognize a car as being 'empty' with reference to the driver's seat, not the passenger's. All things considered, pillar one lay in pretty spectacular ruins.

Pillar two supported the theory of how Mrs Bowler had perpetrated the murder. The pathologist, Michael Heath, had first maintained that Aunt Flo had been pushed from the top of the bank. It was only when he was invited to go down to the River Brede that he realised that the theory could not be sustained. The banking is incredibly steep – I myself, though even my best friends would not see me as a metaphorical gazelle, found it hard to maintain a footing on the slope. More importantly, though, there is a ledge made out of stones, bound together in blocks by stiff wire netting – a construction known as 'gabions'. If Mrs Bowler had pushed Aunt Flo from the top of the bank, Aunt Flo would have crashed against the hard ledge – and there were no such injuries. The jury actually went to the site of the supposed murder – a rare, imaginative and often crucial move in a murder trial.

It was obviously a salutary experience for Dr Heath, who had to revise his original theory. The pathologist had to improvise a new scenario; this time Bowler had to lead Aunt Flo down the precipitous slope, along the top of the ledge, down two more feet of steep slope to water level, before tipping her in. The jury had to work hard to contain their laughter at what was a self-evidently absurd scenario. No one could have coaxed a frail woman – who, after all, as everyone agreed, was virtually immobile – down a slope which would have challenged an athletic teenager. Heath tried to recover his position in the witness box, saying that his mother of eighty could have bounded up the slope in a couple of steps. Purnell asked him, witheringly, if he was trying to be funny. The judge, evidently sceptical himself, asked Heath if his theory was predicated on Aunt Flo going voluntarily to her death, and described the scenario as outlined by the hapless pathologist as 'rather improbable'.

We were, it has to be said, astonished by the state of the pathological evidence; vast and vague theories were being elaborated on the basis of little more than speculation, while crucial matters like the condition of the body, its height and weight, its temperature on recovery, and the temperature of the river water had simply not been taken. In that regard, the conduct of the investigation was eighth-rate. And this was an investigation into the gravest crime in the criminal calendar.

If that sounds as if we're being a little hard on the police, let me offer in return a fairly disastrous cock-up that we brought upon ourselves. When we came to reconstruct the prosecution's theory, on the last day of filming, we trooped down to the river bank. It was a misty and overcast morning, after a night of thunderstorms. I was going to declaim to camera the prosecution's account, retracing the absurdly unbelievable steps of Aunt Flo's supposed last walk. What we hadn't realized was the effect those thunderstorms would have – they had raised the level of the River Brede by a good two feet. So my reconstruction was going to be problematical – much of it was under water. It being the last day, we were well and truly stymied – bringing the crew down for an extra day at some future time would wreck the schedule and cause grievous budgetary harm.

It's at times like this that producers have to think fast. 'Waders', said Steve Phelps; and, under protest, I squeezed myself into form-hugging rubber, and completed my piece-to-camera by jumping, up to waist height, into the brown waters of the Brede.

The pathological evidence, then, looked fairly shaky. We went to see the doctor who examined Aunt Flo's body for the defence. Dr Vesna Djurovic told us that there was absolutely nothing on the body to suggest forceful treatment. The 'grip marks' on the arm could perfectly well be the result of helping a frail old lady out of bed – old people bruise very readily. As for the 'encouragement blows', Dr Djurovic said that the term had no validity; no scientist could apply a motive to a wound. Everything was consistent with an accidental fall. We conducted the interview in the mortuary of Guy's Hospital, a room of slabs, sluices, hose-pipes and sinister-looking buckets. In the course of it, one of the friendly mortuary staff popped his head round the door and asked us if we could be as quick as possible: 'I've got a young doctor here wants to come in and fiddle around with a leg.' Of course the pathology didn't prove Mrs Bowler innocent; nothing ever did, and nothing ever will, just as there is nothing to prove her guilty.

With the sightings and the pathology destroyed, the Crown's third pillar was the business about the tyres – the attempt to prove that Mrs Bowler had cunningly let the tyre down to provide herself with a cover for the whole murderous exercise. For this theory to hold water, they had to show that the tyre had not been driven on while it was deflated; in other words, that the tyre had been fine until Mrs Bowler had driven Aunt Flo down Station Road, killed her, returned to the main road, and let the air out of it.

Once again, the Crown's expert witness came to grief. The Crown contended that the tyre could only have been driven, while deflated, for at most a couple of revolutions, so that Mrs Bowler's story of a developing deflation, and presumably driving the tyre when it was flat, must be untrue. But when the expert witness was called, it emerged that he had been wrongly briefed; his report referred to the effect of sustained driving on a totally deflated tyre. Then the driver of the recovery vehicle was called, and showed that the tyre had revolved a considerable number of times as the car was manoeuvred on and off the breakdown truck. The whole evidence about the tyre was further tainted by clumsiness on the part of the constabulary. A policeman had called to collect Mrs Bowler's car on the morning after Aunt Flo's disappearance. He had found her trying to pump up the tyre – she intended driving it down to the garage where Lofty, the mechanic at Rye Harbour, would check it over. The policeman, however, inflated the tyre himself, and drove it away for tests. Any innocent evidence of débris, like a piece of grit in the valve, would have been destroyed. Interestingly, the tyre – supposedly intact until the wicked Bowler tampered with it – deflated significantly of its own accord during that very journey with a policeman at the wheel, at least according to the evidence of those policemen who checked the pressure before and after the journey, Yet, by now, the police blinkers were so firmly on that they failed to take account of the evidence of their own eyes. The judge was clearly exasperated by the state of the tyre evidence. 'The tyre tells us nothing', he said; the evidence 'adds nothing to the sum of human knowledge.' Once again, basic evidential rules had been overlooked by the East Sussex Police; no one noted or photographed the state of the car at the Bowler house on the morning after Aunt Flo's disappearance, and no record was taken of whether or not the wheel had a dust-cap on it.

'There is no single element in each of these three pillars of evidence about which the prosecution can legitimately address the jury and say "there is evidence about which you can be sure," ' the defence submitted. 'My learned friend has set out a theory, and the evidence to prove that theory has been lacking. . . . My Lord, the evidence has fallen away, and what we are left with is a collection of witnesses who have been called in pursuit of a theory, the theory which is shown to be faulty, and cannot be supported by the witnesses and the facts.'

Collapse of case? Well, if it had been a third-rate burglary in Catford the case against the accused would almost certainly have been abandoned. Mr Justice Garland agreed that 'the evidence actually given did not support all of the assertions' made in the Crown's opening statement. The tyre tests, for instance were 'all based on wholly false premises.' The pathological evidence was flawed, and, far from Mrs Bowler being a callous and uncaring woman, there was ample evidence of her concern and care for her late husband's aunt. And yet he concluded that 'there are issues to be left to the jury.' And, principal among these issues, was the question: 'If not the defendant, then who?'

All this argument took place with the jury dismissed. The professionals were agreeing that the evidence was in tatters – but this information was not for the jury's ears. Having lost the battle of the submission of 'no case to answer', the war was lost. It is very hard to prove someone innocent, to prove the negative proposition that someone did not commit a crime. Yet, that – a classic reversal of the burden of proof – is what led to the conviction of Sheila Bowler. It was Friday afternoon, and the jury were finding it hard to reach a unanimous, or even a majority, verdict. The judge knew that if their deliberations were to continue, it would involve the court sitting over the weekend. A hotel would have to be booked, and the hotel's deadline for reservations was looming. The judge explained the situation to the jury. Minutes later, the jury filed back in to pronounce their verdict of guilty.

'A typical Sussex jury,' a lawyer at the heart of the administration of criminal justice told me. 'Ever since' . . . and he went on to quote an infamous case in which a local jury had acquitted a man of murder, who then went on to commit an attempted murder – 'you can usually rely on a Sussex jury to convict.' These local traits are an open secret among lawyers. Liverpool juries, for instance, are notorious for taking their time over reaching a decision, if it means a night in a hotel, while southerners don't take so kindly to the idea of being away from their beds.

Logically, however, it is hard to see how the jury could have come to any other conclusion, given the judge's decision and the police's lack of independent investigation. By leaving the jury with the question of who else could have led the immobile old lady to her death, he had left them with an unanswerable riddle. A Libyan assassin? An alien invader? There was no evidence of anyone else's involvement – but how could there be, if the police had never looked for evidence of such an eventuality? The Bowler conviction is a salutary experience for those who believe that an accused can only be found guilty beyond reasonable doubt and on the basis of the evidence set before it in court.

The branchline from Ashford, with its rattletrap two-coach trains – pensioned off, one suspects, because they were too old even for the London commuter lines – adds to the Agatha Christie feel of the case. You almost expect sepia photographs of Worthing on the compartment walls, or the train windows to be operating on the old strap-and-buckle principle. Sue Walker had been on the case for some days, and Stephen Phelps had immersed himself deeply into the paperwork, before I made my first visit to Rye and checked in at the Mermaid Hotel.

As journalists, we spend a lot of time in hotels. We can predict the pictures on the walls of our room in every Forte Crest; we could take 'Complimentary Bathroom Accessories' as a specialist subject on Mastermind. We have all stayed, some time or another, at the nightmare hotel with the yellow nylon sheet through which you can see the floral print of the mattress. The plywood veneer of the bedside surround is scarred with cigarette burns. A built-in radio has five buttons, only one of which works – and it cannot receive Radio Four. When you run the bath a torrent from the shower hits you on the back of the head, because the chambermaid has used it to rinse out the bath and has not bothered to flick the switch back to bath mode. A more than usually boisterous social evening organized by the junior chamber of commerce is taking place in the room immediately below, and it sets the wire coathangers in the wardrobe jangling. Next door a couple are involved in a lengthy argument in which, tantalizingly, you cannot quite make out the words, but which later climaxes in a rumbustious, rhythmical reconciliation. There is a worrying scrubbed patch on the carpet near the head of the bed. The alarm call does not come through.

All we really ask for is somewhere warm, quiet, with access to a telephone; the restaurant doesn't matter – we are hardly ever back before last orders, because the evening is the best time to catch people at home. The Forte Crest at Gloucester, unpromisingly sited in the middle of a business park and next to an out-of-town Sainsbury's, was ideal. But the Mermaid at Rye – 'Rebuilt in 1420' as the sign on the wall declares – was a delight; genuine creaky timbers, every piece of furniture an oaken antique and – joy of joys – no kettle for home-brewed tea, but a real, old-fashioned, room-delivery, early-morning-tea service. The telephone worked. A log fire the size of a small ballroom blazed at one end of the bar. Breakfasts were a riot of cholesterol, with the life-prolonging option of haddock as well as kippers. One woke to the sound of birds rummaging under the eaves; or they might have been rats. It didn't matter. It was an unexpected and blessed haven – in a town, as we were to find, bitterly divided by the case.

It made the contrast with Sheila Bowler's accommodation all the more poignant. You get to Bulwood Hall Prison down an unobtrusive lane in suburban Essex. Within yards, it seems, you are in the depths of the countryside. When we went the countryside was positively bulging with springtime: buds were fit to burst, daffodils pumping through like roman candles. The prison comes as a shock, as you round the corner from this bucolic idyll. Twenty-foot high, vomit-coloured mesh surrounds the squat, damp brick buildings. The very climate seems to drop by five degrees. The prison officers are friendly enough as the visitors are processed, but there's a nervous, edgy atmosphere in the little gathering of boyfriends, parents, and bewildered toddlers who have made the journey to Bulwood Hall. Suddenly, we felt very lucky to be there by choice.

As the fourth door was unlocked I caught my first sight of

Sheila Bowler. A commanding figure, she was fussily arranging the chairs in the visitors' room, for all the world as if she was setting up the seating for the AGM of the village-hall committee. We bought her tea from the WRVS counter – one cup only per inmate per visit, warns the notice, for some pettifogging reason. At neighbouring tables couples spent their pent-up passion in a manner acceptable to the burly, bald prison officer on the raised dais who supervised the visits; fevered fondling, voracious kissing. Matter-of-factly, Sheila Bowler answered the fifty-six questions we had prepared for her.

Why, having collected Aunt Flo at eight, had she driven all the way to Bexhill and back, breaking down at 9.45 p.m., instead of taking the old lady straight back home? After all, her aunt's bedtime was eight o'clock. Nonsense, she prickled, that's what staff at the residential home may have said, but in fact Aunt much preferred to stay up late. As for the food, Aunt Flo had already been fed at the home. 'They feed them early, don't they?' I said. 'I suppose it's for the convenience of the staff.' 'We get supper at five o'clock here,' she shot back. 'Still, it's better than Holloway – last meal at a quarter past three!' Prison had already begun to leave its stain on this game, starched matron, inklings of the worldly-wisdom of the old lag. 'Not much going on between the ears of that prison officer,' she remarked conspiratorially. 'The only qualification she has is knowing how to lock doors.' Then back to business: 'I can see how it looks bad that I didn't have any food in the house; but then, if I had been planning to kill her, I'd hardly have made my intentions so clear!'

The same, of course, was true of Mrs Bowler's attitude to the zimmer frame, which Greyfriars had suggested she should take for Aunt Flo's convenience. Her refusal to take it was interpreted as evidence of murderous intent – after all, Aunt Flo wouldn't need a zimmer frame for much longer. Studying the paperwork later, we found that one of the care assistants who saw Aunt Flo off that night heartily agreed that taking the frame would be a waste of time. In fact, Mrs Bowler reckoned that the last thing she wanted was her aunt tottering round the house with the frame; she would be easier to deal with if she stayed put. 'She was a bit of a wanderer, you know.'

That took us a bit by surprise. The entire case had been

179

founded on the fact that Aunt Flo could not have left the car unaided, while Mrs Bowler went off to get help. When Mrs Bowler returned to the car, she had specifically told the search party not to range too far because of her aunt's relative immobility. Now, apparently, Aunt Flo had a history of independent locomotion. 'A few months before she went into Greyfriars, when she was living at home, I suddenly saw her on Rye Station; she'd taken herself off for the day to Hastings, for a look round the shops.'

So had Aunt Flo deteriorated so fast in the six months or so since this little escapade that she was virtually incapable of movement on the fatal night? The question intrigued us. Certainly we would have to take a closer look at Aunt Flo's medical records. A chat with the local GP might pay dividends. Yet even her niece assumed that she was virtually chairbound; but could that attitude have more to do with the way all of us regard old people? Of course no one had seen Aunt Flo walking by herself – because by definition you go to the assistance of an old lady. We want to think the old are dependent upon us, and the old, in turn, do nothing to disabuse us of this.

There was another intriguing aspect to Aunt Flo's health. During the drive to Bexhill, Mrs Bowler said that Aunt Flo had been in pain from her stomach. 'I assumed it was a symptom of her stomach cancer,' she said. We probed further. 'Yes,' she said, 'she'd been in to hospital several times for tests. I was shown the X-rays by a doctor – can't remember his name – but he said "It won't be long now." He said it right in front of Aunt Flo – I remember thinking at the time how tactless it was.'

Why murder a woman who is going to die anyway? We edged the conversation, as discreetly as we could, round to the subject of euthanasia. 'I disapprove of it intensely,' said Mrs Bowler. With that out of the way, we looked further into the matter of motive. It would be financially advantageous, the police had argued, for Aunt Flo to die before her Greyfriars bills had eaten up all her capital, which was in the form of the small flat she owned and which Mrs Bowler stood to inherit. 'But we were making plans for that,' said Mrs Bowler (shortly after I had struck a blow against the system and bought her a second cup of tea). 'We were going to let her flat, and, with her pension, that would have gone a long way to meeting the bills for the time that was left to her.'

Why present the police with the wrong shoes, first time round? 'I made a mistake,' she shrugged. 'Anyway, if I was guilty, why would I have corrected my mistake and shown them the right ones later?'

As we left, we saw her once again tidying up the interview room, marshalling the chairs and rounding up the errant teacups. We drove back to London. Had we just spent two hours in the company of a murderess of infinite, double-bluffing cunning? With a woman who simply could not come to terms with the enormity of her crime? Or an innocent woman trapped by suspicion and circumstance?

We had no very clear answer to that question. But we had looked her full in her clear grey eyes and Stephen Phelps had asked her bluntly: 'Did you do it?' 'No, Mr Phelps,' she said. I am no psychologist, and my instinct is as flawed as anyone's; but I had spent most of the time watching her, watching the way she took her foot out of her shoe to scratch her calf, watching the impatience in her face as we asked questions 'to which you already know the answers.' How she must have annoyed the police, as she bristled at their impertinent, importunate questioning.

But whatever we may have thought of Mrs Bowler was not going to alter matters – the case was already bedevilled enough with subjective judgements. There were no other witnesses to what went on that night; the owner of the caravan park had seen a car at the pumping station, but not at the relevant time, and it was almost certainly one of Rye's romantic young couples. The answer had to lie in the six-hundred-odd yards that separate the pumping station from where the car was parked.

We began by deciding we had to know all there was to know about the behaviour of the River Brede. Aunt Flo had been found only a hundred yards or so downstream from the pumping station. If she had walked just half the distance, she would have come to a bridge across the Brede. The railings along the side end abruptly; anyone feeling their way along them in the dark would then have plunged down the forty-five degree bank to the river below. This scenario would mean that Aunt Flo would only have to walk a more manageable three hundred yards.

It also meant that she would have had to float *upstream* to the position where she was found.

A few days later saw the Bowler team – Stephen Phelps, Sue Walker and myself – heading west along the M40 to the Hydrology Research headquarters at Wallingford. We had spoken to local experts at the National Rivers Authority; we had even dredged the expertise of the Inland Drainage Board, and everything had pointed us towards the experts at Wallingford. Rivers do strange things – but do they ever flow uphill?

The Brede very nearly does. In fact, we had a heady moment when we analysed the twenty-four-hours charts logging the water levels at various points along the river. They revealed that the level of the River Brede where it entered the sea at Rye sluice was a good metre higher than the point, several miles upstream, where we were hypothesizing that Aunt Flo might have fallen in, after a comparatively short walk. Could this be true? Sadly, it could not. There was, the expert told us, almost certainly a calibration error in the recording equipment. But the river's proximity to the sea, as it meanders through the Romney Marsh, does make it behave differently from waterways further inland, because of the action of the tides. Twice a day, at high tide, the sea wants to come charging up the River Brede. Lockgates at Rye sluice are closed to prevent the inward flow. In effect, then, the water moving down the river backs up from the sluicegates. 'It virtually ceases to be a river, and becomes a pond,' explained our expert. 'There might even be, for a time, the very slightest upstream flow, but it would be negligible.' As we pored over the Ordnance Survey maps, we noticed that a canal fed into the Brede; if that water was flowing strongly it could add to the upstream current. We would need accurate measurements of the Brede flow from the nearby gauging station. Sadly, however, a few more minutes' research revealed that the station had been closed a couple of years earlier – part of the economies of our national infrastructure.

We left Wallingford with our heads buzzing with statistics and jargon: the ordnance datum (a vertical Greenwich meridian taken from a point in Newlynn Harbour) of the riverbed, the offset factor for tides calculated from Dover for Rye; we also wondered how carefully the police had analysed the workings of the River Brede. We got the answer from a police statement, which I reproduce for its innocent simplicity: 'At 3 p.m. I went to the scene on the River Brede and conducted an experiment with one of the walking sticks I had obtained from the Greyfriars Home. For a period of six minutes I placed the stick into the water. The stick floated. However it travelled a distance of about five metres before becoming lodged in the river bank.' No tidal analysis for this honest East Sussex copper, no calibration of the mean flow rate for comparison with that relevant to the night in question. I suspect, however, that, in the end, his game of forensic pooh-sticks may have been just as valuable as our hi-tech, top-level research.

That experiment had helped buttress the police against Mrs Bowler. She had told the police that there was a walking stick in the car when she left it, but no trace of the stick could be found. It wasn't to be found in the river. If the police could prove that the stick should still be in the river, and would not have floated away downstream, this would suggest that Mrs Bowler was lying about the existence of the stick. The experiment satisfied the policeman conducting it that any walking stick would have stayed put. Now, thanks to Wallingford's experts, we can inform the Sussex Police that their experiment was desperately flawed; their walking sticks couldn't have floated away, because at exactly the time that they threw them in the water, the tidal conditions downstream were causing maximum stagnation. I repeated the experiment, in similar tidal conditions, and actually got the sticks to voyage upstream at a fair rate of knots, under the influence of a brisk easterly wind.

Forensic Access, the Newbury-based team of independent forensic experts, were surprised at the bias and amateurism they detected in the do-it-yourself detection of the police. The walking stick experiment wasn't the only example; when the police had restaged a walk in slippers, to assess the effect a six-hundred-yard walk would have had on the scuffing of the soles, no assessment was made of how scuffed Aunt Flo's slippers already were. The problem, we discovered, lies in Home Office economies. Police forces, instead of being able to call on the central resources of police laboratories, now have to bear the actual cost of forensic experiments themselves. The internal market, it seems, has spread from the Health Service to the police, with equally problematical results.

Our own amateur efforts, I have to admit, would, in turn, have amused the police. We wanted to see what would have happened to the second slipper – the first had been found on the bank close to where Aunt Flo's body was found. Steve Phelps set off into Rye to buy a pair of slippers. The quest was to prove problematical in more ways than one. First of all, there were not many shops open. When, eventually, Steve found a shoe shop, he found himself suddenly at a loss for words when asked what style and size of slipper he was looking for. The answer 'it doesn't really matter, because I'm going to throw them into the River Brede as soon as I've bought them' would clearly be confusing. Ever conscious of budgetary constraints, Steve asked for a small pair. He had the misfortune to stumble upon the most assiduous, attentive and patient shop assistant in East Sussex – just when he was in a hurry and could not, frankly, care less about the quality of the merchandise he was buying. He was subjected to a gentle lecture on the importance of getting the size of footwear exactly right, especially, as was clearly the case, if he was buying for a child. He picked out a pair of pink fluffy slippers. 'Wouldn't you like to see some of the other styles?' asked the concerned assistant, as aware as Steve himself of the hideous quality of the slippers. Steve assured her that these were indeed the very pair he wanted most in the world, and asked how much they were.

Seven pounds fifty is not a great deal of money for a pair of children's slippers, but it is a lot of money for a pair of slippers you are intending to throw away in a few minutes. 'Seven pounds fifty!' Steve couldn't help exploding. 'Well, you did say they were just the ones you were looking for,' said the assistant, 'and I have to say that it's a very reasonable price.' As this abyss of mutual misapprehension grew wider, a flustered Phelps proffered the cash. But the shop assistant, ever solicitous, said that she would make a special exception, and take only five pounds. This made Steve feel even worse, of course; especially as he left with the kindly assistant's words ringing in his ears, 'do feel free to bring them back if they don't suit.'

It was with quite a sense of relief that Steve threw a slipper into the Brede, to observe the effects of the current. But as it drifted ever further downstream, Sue Walker, the principal researcher on the case, became agitated. 'Aren't you going to fish it out?' she asked. It then dawned on Steve that the discovery of a child's slipper down by the sluice at Rye Harbour could trigger a major emergency inquiry. At worst, the team could be prosecuted for wasting police time – Steve had made such a fuss that the shop assistant would certainly be able to identify him to the police. So the next half-hour was spent in a frantic chase downstream, Phelps dangling precariously from the bankside undergrowth to intercept the serenely fluffy slipper as it floated by, maddeningly, out of reach. Eventually, his linen suit more than fashionably crumpled, he managed to retrieve the thing.

We had learnt a lot about rivers, and we thought we knew all there was to know about the River Brede – until a local man assured us that things actually did float upstream: 'Happens all the time with dead sheep'. But in the end we had to acknowledge that Aunt Flo probably fell into the river near the pumping station, where one of her slippers was found. Study of the police scene-of-crime photographs, and comparison with the record of when they were taken, convinced us that the slipper could not have been 'planted', nor accidentally placed there by police activity.

On another front, however, our researches were making better progress. We went to Aunt Flo's flat, to see what sort of a motive for murder it represented. It is a sad little place, left very much as it was when Aunt Flo went to Greyfriars. It can't be sold until the lawyers work out who it belongs to, because, although Sheila Bowler is named in the will, no one may benefit from committing a crime. While we were there, we were struck by the layout of the place; it's a series of rooms, all leading off one long corridor. Quite clearly, Aunt Flo would have had to be fairly mobile before she went into Greyfriars.

Neighbours confirmed this. 'I'm not saying she could do the Highland fling,' said one, 'but she was well able to get around, albeit in a limited sort of way.' We went back to Aunt Flo's GP, Dr Jeelani, who told us that in his view, as her GP, she was reasonably mobile – indeed later nursing notes describe her as 'mobilizing well'. 'From what I knew of her, I can well imagine her getting out of the car and walking . . . but no one ever asked me.' We amassed a great deal of evidence about Aunt Flo's ability to walk, but all of it referred to the time before she went to Greyfriars, five months before her death, and the staff at Greyfriars – who, to a woman, refused to talk to us – were adamant that she could not walk unaided in the time that they knew her.

But would they actually know? It sounds a preposterous question – of course those intimately involved with a patient's welfare would know the limits of her mobility. In fact, the reverse is true. When an elderly person is taken into care, we learnt from experts in geriatric medicine and from leading physiotherapists, it often happens that they lose their independence, their motivation for mobility. The atmosphere of care conspires to keep them immobile. Meals are brought to them, they are escorted to the lavatory, they are carried out of bed – in part because no one wants to tax their energies, but also because it is, frankly, handier for the staff. The staff, indeed, had said that they took Aunt Flo to bed in a wheelchair. 'Well, of course they did!' one professor of geriatric medicine chuckled. 'Last thing in the evening, when you are going off shift, and there are only four of you and a lot of them, you want to get the old dears into bed as quick as you can, and if that means using a wheelchair, that's what you'll use.' A local physiotherapist allowed us to film her unit at the Conquest Hospital in Hastings, and told us how her patients, given encouragement and confidence, are capable of far more than even the nursing staff or doctors assume.

Further checks with the pathologist confirmed that there was nothing structurally wrong with Aunt Flo which would have inhibited mobility. There was no particular muscle degeneration, or skeletal infirmity. Indeed, we discovered that whatever had been causing her intestinal bleeding, including the vomiting of blood which precipitated her move to Greyfriars, seemed to have gone away. Examination had revealed no trace of cancer, and, if she had been suffering from a stomach ulcer, a recent course of pills seemed to have cleared it up. Aunt Flo had also, after years of looking after herself in a fairly random manner, been enjoying regular meals and bedtimes at Greyfriars for the past five months; in other words, she was probably in better condition on the day she died than she had been for years.

But if she could have walked – would she? Why leave the safety of a car, on a busy road, late at night, when you've been told by your niece that she won't be long? It's one of the luxuries we enjoy that we know where the top experts are to be found, and have the resources to borrow their expertise. Another thing we enjoy is their confidence that we are serious about our work. Professor Brice Pitt is Professor of Psychiatry for the Elderly, and from a study of Aunt Flo's medical notes he was able to make a diagnosis of mild to moderate dementia. So how would she have reacted to her situation, that dark midsummer night?

'I think she might well have reacted catastrophically,' said the Professor. 'We know that she was afraid of the dark, we know that she was afraid of being alone, she wouldn't have known if it was five minutes or five hours, and I think she would have found her isolation there quite terrifying. There would be a sense of terror, of awful loneliness, a sense of total bewilderment – she would be strongly motivated to get out of the situation if she possibly could and try to find help.'

The jury had to choose between two unsatisfactory alternatives; either Sheila Bowler took her aunt to her death – and there was no evidence for that – or it was some other, unnamed, mystery killer. The court was never given a third possibility – that Aunt Flo could have gone out into the night by herself. Everyone assumed that she could not have walked – even Sheila Bowler herself. If the jury had known that old people in homes are more capable of movement than their carers can know; that Aunt Flo was a relatively sprightly soul before she went into Greyfriars; that there was nothing physically to inhibit her mobility, and that she was healthier than she had been for some time; and that, given her mental condition she would have done almost anything to get out of the situation she was in – would they have found Sheila Bowler guilty beyond all reasonable doubt?

I don't think we'll ever know what happened on the banks of the River Brede that night, but I know that there's nothing to prove Sheila Bowler guilty – nothing, actually, even to suggest that she is. The strangest things ring true, things which I would not expect any court in the land to take seriously, nor an investigating detective sergeant to appreciate. Jane Bowler, Sheila's daughter, said that her mother would never have done such a thing – 'and certainly not during my exams, when she knew how much I'd be upset by Aunt Flo dying.' Another friend said: 'Even if I could imagine Sheila doing it, she'd blurt it out the next day – she couldn't keep anything to herself.' Another friend, the former vicar of Rye who knew her churchwarden husband as well as Sheila Bowler, refuses to believe her capable of the crime; she was too saintly and – with a twinkle – 'she's simply too intelligent to do something so obvious.'

Filming at the scene of the crime had its problems; it's not the easiest thing to film on a busy main road in the middle of the night. In one particularly busy reconstruction – with actors playing the parts of emergency-breakdown-vehicle drivers, policemen, dog-handlers, and search-teams – a man in a policeman's helmet asked me what it was all about. I explained the background to the case, how police suspicions had fixed upon Mrs Bowler, and the general shortcomings of the enquiry. 'But shouldn't you be being filmed?' I ended by asking him. 'More than my job's worth, sir,' he replied – I had been talking to a genuine member of the Sussex Constabulary. I remember that night well; my night-time pieces-to-camera, to be filmed with dramatic midnight lighting, slipped further down the schedule. We only just managed to get them in before dawn broke – if you listen closely you can hear a morning cuckoo. The night also took its toll on Laura, who had left the office to run itself to come up and lend a hand. In one particular scene, we had to coordinate five cars driving round the hairpin bend. Laura, however, did not respond to the walkie-talkie order 'Action'. Her car remained immobile. Laura, bless her, was asleep. It was, after all, three o'clock.

If you want to kill an eighty-nine-year-old woman, there are easier ways to do it; damp sheets and an open window on a chilly night would probably do the trick. Of course it's less exciting a prospect than taking an old lady down a precipitous path on a dark night, hurling her to a watery death, and then arranging an elaborate plan involving artfully deflated tyres. It's no comfort to the wagging tongues of Winchelsea – who at one time organized an *ad hoc* vigilante squad to spy and report back on our activities – but truth is usually a little bit drabber than fiction. In real life, widowed piano teachers do not plan the murders of elderly aunts for the sake of inheriting small and dingy flats. In real life, there is disappointingly little dirty work at the crossroads, still less at the hairpin bend. There is not much murder at the vicarage these days, and, dull as it may be, the Cinque Ports Murder Mystery was in all probability no more nor less than a sorry little accident.

12
Mark Cleary
Day of Judgement

It's a bright early spring day, the first day after the May Day
bank holiday, the day that has hung over the long weekend full
of threat and promise. It is the day of Mark Cleary's appeal.
Ever since we heard that the Court of Appeal had consented to
look again at Mark Cleary's case, we've been on the rack. I
remember the moment well, receiving the news on a mobile
phone and breaking into an ungainly and embarrassing jig in the
middle of Farnham High Street while we were filming the Fell
case (see chapter 4). It means that our work is finally going to
be judged. If things go wrong, we will have raised Mark's hopes
only to dash them to ultimate despair. If it is judged to be right,
we will have achieved our ultimate goal – the freeing of an
innocent man.

I've always thought that the occupational vice of journalists
isn't cynicism, but sentimentality. Lawyers need to keep a professional distance from their clients, but we get hopelessly
involved in our cases once we have committed to them. That's
why I find myself doing stupid things as I prepare to go to court,
like rootling out my lucky underpants, avoiding (naturally) the
lines on the paving stones on the way to the Central Line Underground Station, and making extraordinarily rash deals with God
in exchange for a favourable result.

Outside the Royal Courts of Justice there's the usual disconso-
late knot of television cameramen who know they've got at best
a long day, at worst a wasted one, ahead of them. Central Television ask me if I'll go back and walk in again so that they can
film me. Today I'll do anything for anyone – if only . . . Besides
which, Central were helpful all those months ago, in letting us

191

look through their regional archive on the Cleary trial.

Through the cathedral nave of the cold palace of justice which is the Law Courts, and up the stairs on the right, is the appeal corridor. Court Six is where we're booked in. David Martin-Sperry, his own sunken eyes attesting to the homework he's been doing, and with a razor mind behind his languid Harrovian mien, checks a final fact with Ron Birkett, Cleary's campaigning solicitor, who has come up from Nottingham to see the culmination of his for so long single-handed fight for justice. Martin-Sperry reminds me of the bargain I've struck – that I'll take him to dinner at Cipriani's in Venice if we win. And of course there are the people to whom it matters infinitely more – Mark's parents – sitting on the narrow, marble sills that serve as benches. Christine, tugging on a cigarette, asks me if I know where the Ladies' is to be found. We get in a flap over whether there's time for her to go to the loo before the appeal begins. Bill Cleary sits, crouched forward, gazing into space.

We enter the court minutes before half past ten, taking up the back pew facing their Lordships' bench. The lady usher fusses around, placing the carafes of water in place. I notice, for no particular reason, that the glasses do not have little paper hats on them as they do in the Lord Chief Justice's court along the corridor; is that one of the special perks of the job? Here in the very Olympus of the law, there are some strangely mundane features; in the witness box, for instance, sits a very large industrial vacuum cleaner which the night staff don't seem to have put away.

The three judges appear, and as always I'm reminded of a colleague's remark, that judges wear wigs to make it look as if they've got their brains on the outside of their heads. Lord Justice McCowan has the face of a dissipated cherub. To his left sits Mr Justice Buckley, whose wig looks almost as if it were his own hair. He has brought his own quarter bottle of Vittel. Mr Justice Morland makes up the trio. They make fidgety little adjustments of the green-shaded brass lamps which illuminate their patch of desk.

A door opens to the right of the court, and two prison officers escort Cleary into the dock. My heart sinks. Cleary has aged and hardened during his time in jail. Not surprisingly, he looks like a prisoner. We have done everything we can to get him to look presentable. I have written to him in prison begging him to shave his Mexican bandit moustache: 'Olympic runners shave their legs to get that extra millionth of a second; it would be a shame if we lost by a whisker.' But he's wearing a ponytail. It's understandable, of course; he doesn't want to change his prison persona too drastically, for fear of the reception he'll get back in prison tonight if the appeal fails. We have bought him – courtesy of Channel Four – the jacket his hard-up parents could not afford. It looks good on him. But he's wearing sunglasses ... The effect is hopelessly, undeniably, sinister. Mr Justice Buckley gives him a long, appraising look. Then McCowan nods. The appeal has begun.

David Martin-Sperry doesn't stand in the front row of the court, because he is not yet a QC. He opens with the courteous diffidence characteristic of him. He reminds me of a Victorian curate nervously, but with ineffable grace, asking the irascible squire for his daughter's hand in marriage. The bench beams benignly on his unfailing good manners; when they get in a muddle Martin-Sperry apologizes for not having made things clear, and when McCowan agrees with something he has said, he has the trick of making it appear that it's the judge himself who has, in his infinite sagacity, lighted upon a truth which had hitherto not dawned upon the humble advocate.

He explains that, all those years ago, it was not perceived that there were any grounds for appeal; but that now the case must be seen in a whole new light. This is the dangerous point. If the court is so minded, it can abort the whole process now. For cases to succeed, they have to meet that arcane formula that either there is new evidence which was not available at the time of the trial, or some 'other consideration of substance'. Their Lordships could argue that the defence, all those years ago, could have done what *Trial and Error* managed to do – excavate and analyse the evidence which, albeit buried, was there for the finding. Martin-Sperry has to convince the court that there was no reasonable way in which the defence, on the facts known at the time, could have known what we know now.

Things begin to look bad. McCowan isn't just sitting back, listening to Martin-Sperry's argument. He's actively intervening, threatening to push Martin-Sperry off his carefully planned course. But at least it shows that the bench has done its homework; McCowan seems to know the case inside out, with an impressive command of the detail, immaculately briefed, no doubt, by the backroom staff at the Appeals Office. Martin-Sperry has to think on his feet, adjusting his tactics and strategy to absorb the interventions from the bench. Gradually, he coaxes the argument back on track. Partly, that's his skill; but equally, as it becomes clear to us, the bench has already formed much of its own view of the merits of the case over the long bank-holiday weekend. Martin-Sperry isn't exactly pushing at an open door; but their Lordships have clearly not left it locked.

The argument unfolds, as a clear, incandescent ray of sunshine pierces the skylight of Court Six, picking out the white cardigan of Mrs Cleary, slumped beside me. We hear how Atherton's first confession was true in every respect – except that he lied about the time of the crime. The police, faced with such a frank admission, had no reason to doubt its least contentious element, the timetable; if a man admits to murder and buggery, you don't question what time he says he committed the crimes. The net effect of this, the court hears, is that the police and the Crown excluded the evidence of any witnesses who gave the lie to Atherton's timing of the fatal night's events. When Atherton, seven weeks later, decided to shed a lot of the guilt onto the hapless Mark Cleary, the confession extracted from Cleary mirrored the facts as they were then known – but facts which we now know could not be true. They are merely a regurgitation of what the police believe, from Atherton, is the chronicle of that night.

McCowan is joining in with a will, at this point. Why couldn't Mick Ryan, Cleary's key alibi witness, remember clearly enough what happened that night? Was it simply the passage of time, or Ryan's tender years? 'Maybe he took fright because of the pressure of local opinion?' McCowan offers. 'Precisely,' David Martin-Sperry replies, through the smile of one who knows the court is with him. (I scribble out a typically smooth and gracious Sperryism: 'Your Lordship's thought process is one that is entirely correct now, but had not occurred to anyone at the time.') He deftly praises the police for taking contemporaneous notes during their interview with Atherton – and then we realize that his tactic is to contrast that process with the failure of the police to take proper notes during Cleary's interview. The earlier praise for the police means that he does not need to condemn them – something the court is never very keen on – but the condemnation is tactfully implicit.

Throughout it all, Mark Cleary, the man at the centre of the argument, seems strangely detached. Does he simply not understand? Has he closed his mind to the ordeal, and is he just waiting for it to end? Sometimes he looks in my direction, but I cannot tell what is going on behind those dark glasses.

Sometimes the court itself seems oddly detached from the mundane details it is analysing. 'Wayne was doing wheelies,' says Martin-Sperry, and, after hesitating for a moment, 'that is, performing tricks with only one wheel of his bicycle on the ground.' Deep down, I suspect Lord Justice McCowan knows what wheelies are, but it's as well to have the t's crossed, I suppose. Suddenly, the almost church-like atmosphere is shattered when Martin-Sperry drops a bulky lever-arch file. The clatter of the accident breaks the growing tension.

Stephen Phelps sits next to me, on the other side from the Cleary family. If I can fault my colleague in any way, it is his habit of filing his nails in public, which sets my teeth on edge. Out of the corner of my eye I see him gently stroking the emery board along a hangnail. Gently, I confiscate it. He passes me a note – the court has made a mistake over the timing of the call for help that Mrs Burgess heard, putting it at 11.10 p.m. instead of 11.23; should we send a note to Martin-Sperry to correct them? On the whole, we decide not; courts are touchy about journalistic trespass on their preserve, and it's more diplomatic to sit quietly. Indeed, although Martin-Sperry has told us that it was the best-prepared case he's ever seen, he never alludes to the television programme. We've agreed that that's the best policy.

It is now 12.47 by the unticking courtroom clock housed in its own little wooden Gothic niche. Things are happening fast. The court is clearly impressed by the fact that the judge attached too much weight to the alibi that failed; it's a point we made, but clearly the court gives it greater weight than we did, because it's exactly the sort of procedural, legal detail that is the daily diet of the Court of Appeal. There's clearly disquiet about the circumstances of Mark's interrogation, especially the absence of a solicitor; their Lordships seem, thank goodness, to be applying the principles of the Police and Criminal Evidence Act, which protects suspects, to a case which happened long before the act was passed. I give a large wink to Steve Haywood, sitting on the bench in front of me; this is clearly good news for a raft of cases on our books, where confessions have been extracted by dubious, but not at the time illegal, tactics. And the court has grasped the point that we found so difficult to put across, that a confession which echoes another confession in details which we know to be false must, of itself, be a false confession; in what we have now been able to demonstrate was an entirely circular process, the version of events that Mark Cleary stammered out was the one the police believed, because they themselves had believed Atherton.

David Martin-Sperry sits down. He turns to me with a satisfied smile on his face. He's always known that if he can just get the court to listen to the argument, we're on to a winner. He passes me a note, reminding me of my Venetian bargain: 'How many l's in gondola?' it says. I pass him back a note saying the Cipriani's I was referring to is a Cypriot restaurant in Stoke Newington. Schoolboy stuff, but the stuff of relief.

A red-faced QC who has said virtually nothing all morning stands up. He is the Other Side – representing the Crown and resisting the appeal. For weeks we have been trying to discover what the Crown's attitude to this appeal will be. Sometimes they make no effort to contest the appeal. But we gather that there will be at least a formal attempt to oppose. Red-face has got about five minutes to outline his case before judicial stomachs begin to rumble for the lunch adjournment. He has none of Martin-Sperry's fluency – it's a mumble, with sentences left abandoned halfway through, like the lines dying on the lips of a superannuated actor. Does he realise that the court is not with him, and that it is impolite to stretch their Lordships' patience with a lost argument? Or is he himself half-hearted about his case? So much of what goes on seems to be as much to do with etiquette as with justice.

McCowan decides that it is time for the lunch adjournment. We blink our way out into the sunshine of the Strand, crossing

196

the road to a pub. Martin-Sperry joins us. He is beamingly confident. We agree that it couldn't have gone better, the court readily taking on board most of our new evidence. We can't of course, resist asking Martin-Sperry how he assessed the chances, as we chew nervously on our prawn sandwiches. We want the time to pass. We want to be back in court. We want to know what's going to happen. We rehearse all the options. There are a number of things the court can do; it can, of course, either grant or refuse the appeal. It can also decide to order a retrial. It could defer judgement to another day, leaving us all in an agonizing limbo. It could release Mark Cleary pending judgement, which would be a strong hint that things were going to work out successfully, but would not enable us to break open the champagne. It could decide that it wanted to call some of the witnesses, and examine them; we had argued, the day before, over whether we should bring some of them down to stand by. Or the court could take an entirely literal view of the legal situation; technically, we are asking for leave to appeal, because Mark Cleary has long exceeded the time limit for lodging an appeal – his original counsel, Desmond Fennell QC, having advised that there was no realistic hope of success. So the court could simply grant – or refuse to grant – permission for a full-dress appeal another day.

We return to the court, and I am delighted to see that the entire staff of Just Television has turned up for the afternoon. Emma, the secretarial lynchpin of *Trial and Error*, has been involved with Cleary as much as any of us; she monitors and logs all the correspondence with prisoners, and develops a keen sense of the ebb and flow of the morale of those behind bars. To scores of prisoners, Emma Coghlan is the unseen link with the world outside. Laura, who we hired as a telephonist in the early days, before we realized how well she could run the office, is paying her first visit to a court – any court. Olwyn, one of the four founders of Just Television, and the only one who understands the finances, has deserted the computer to be with us. No one, apparently, is looking after the shop, but we all feel we all should be here.

The Crown never gets into its stride. Who knows what has happened during lunch? Has Red-face calculated that the mood of the court is irretrievably against him? McCowan is making his impatience obvious, by shaking his head at some of the arguments put forward. He refers to some of our evidence as 'dynamite' – not a word, in its metaphorical sense at least, that often trips from the tongue of an Appeal Court judge. His two fellow judges have caught the mood, openly agreeing that Atherton, the man correctly convicted of Wayne Keeton's murder, is 'a liar'. Since Cleary's conviction depends utterly on Atherton, this augurs well. There's an awkward moment when it looks as if the court is going to ask to hear the witnesses, which will mean a delay of at least several days – but the moment passes. For no apparent reason, the Crown sits down. McCowan announces that he and his fellow judges are going to retire for a few minutes. When they go, it's as if we have been holding our breath all afternoon.

I know that it is going to be a very long quarter of an hour, for the parents above all. I chatter about anything, everything but the appeal, to keep Christine Cleary's mind off the final verdict. I don't think I succeed, but at least it doesn't seem long before the red-robed judges return. We cannot read the result in their expressions.

But from the moment McCowan returns, at 3.24, to begin his judgement, we know that things are looking good. There is a heart-stopping moment when, in the first words, he says that he will 'grant' the application, but we quickly realize that he is merely giving technical permission for the appeal to be heard. Now the judgement proper begins; it starts with a recital of the known facts – the sad fate of Wayne Keeton, Atherton's arrest and his implication of Mark Cleary. He quickly grants the point that the judge should not have given so much weight to the failure of Cleary's alibi: 'In my view this was a misdirection.' We are home – but home so far on a judicial technicality. But there is better to come. The circumstances of Cleary's interrogation are severely criticized: 'We have considerable doubts as to whether this interrogation should have been allowed in evidence . . . and there is not a shred of evidence other than this.' Finally, he accepts our evidence of the sightings of Wayne Keeton at a time which proves Atherton a liar and Cleary innocent. 'We have become increasingly anxious about this case, and have decided that the original verdict is' – we all tense for the magic formula – 'unsafe and unsatisfactory.' There is a brief moment when McCowan seems to be considering a retrial, until he accepts that too long has passed. Mark's father is fiddling with his tie; he is suffering, I find out afterwards, an angina attack. In the commotion the final words float over us: '. . . we therefore grant the appeal and quash the conviction.' Christine Cleary looks blank; she cannot take it in. 'What does it mean?' she asks me. 'It means we've won,' I tell her. She jumps up and buries her weeping head on my shoulder. Mark, by now, realizes what has happened; he stands up to give a victory sign to the court. A vast hubbub erupts – until we realize that the judges haven't left the court; Ron Birkett, ever the professional solicitor, has got Martin-Sperry back on his feet to ask for costs.

At appeal, one plays for the biggest possible stakes. If their Lordships turn you down, the two prison officers take you down the stairs to face the rest of a life sentence. If they find for you, within ten minutes you are out on the pavement, a free man. Those ten minutes are spent in formalities in the jailer's office, on the ground floor. Here, the prisoner receives his discharge papers, and his property – sometimes in plastic sacks, sometimes the old, cardboard suitcase he first took to the remand centre all those years ago. I well remember Paul Darvell turning up at the Hilton Hotel reception desk with his sacks, stamped 'Property of HM Prison Department', leaving the reception staff a little uncertain as to whether the legend was a piece of designer chic or the real thing. Mark Cleary emerged with a couple of crates – the sort of thing used to transport paperwork and files when people move office.

The team had been hovering round the jailer's gate, but as Mark emerged we withdrew to leave him alone with his parents. There'd be plenty of time for us later, and this, above all, must be a precious and private moment. We've only ever had two pictures of Mark – one of the gawky teenager peering out from his identity pass at the Shire Hall where he worked, and the other, a dreadful photograph taken in jail, when we had asked for a more up-to-date picture. In the latter, with his lank hair, droopy moustache and bandanna he had looked for all the world like the founder of some exotic paraChristian cult irredeemably doomed to dissolve in mass suicide. Here, in the dusty daylight of a spring morning in the Royal Courts of Justice, he looked desperately older than his thirty years. His twenties, which he had spent behind bars, had hardened and strengthened his small physique, giving him a wiry, pinched and almost ferret-like look. Prison had made him look like a jailbird, sly, pale and wary.

He came over to us, shook my hand and gave me a suitably inarticulate hug – there are no words for such a time. I explained to him the abrupt baptism into freedom he was about to experience; the press and television were massing outside the precincts of the court. And we walked out.

Mark stood in front of the scrum, and, on the pavement of the Strand, spoke movingly. He graciously thanked *Trial and Error*: 'I wouldn't be here without them; their research was fantastic; I couldn't fault 'em.' Then a touch of iron entered: 'This should have happened ten years ago . . . I've spent ten years in jail for a crime I never committed, and should never have been found guilty of.' I could see his eyes beginning to redden, and so could his father, Bill, for he embraced Mark and took over the impromptu conference. 'We're a family again,' he said, 'we just want to put this behind us and go back to being a family again.' I stayed behind to mop up the requests for quotes and interviews from the papers and television, and to give the family time to get away; we bundled them and our own Just Television crew – the crew who had filmed the original story and were now to chronicle the victory – into a fleet of black cabs.

Because of the London traffic, we all arrived at Just Television's offices, among the Dickensian warehouses of Emerald Street, at about the same time. There was spontaneous applause for the Cleary family as they reached the airy, open-plan, top-floor office. We had decided to take them to the office rather than to the hotel where we had – optimistically – booked them in, to provide them with an environment where they could make the telephone calls and give the interviews they wanted to the local press in relatively peaceful surroundings. We also wanted to have a party. I had telephoned from the Appeal Court that we should lay in the champagne, but unfortunately the petty cash tin was empty and we came back to a dry office. That was quickly put right – though there were very reasonable requests from Christine Cleary for a reviving cup of tea.

It was a great party. Friends, well-wishers, lawyers, journalists working in the same field, assaulted the office with messages of support. There's no professional envy among those who share the obsession about miscarriages of justice, and recognize it as a special, and different branch of journalism, though sadly, if perhaps predictably, we heard nothing from the BBC's *Rough Justice*, over whose disappointments we had genuinely grieved. Stephanie Rawden, one of the young wives on the Bestwood estate with the courage to speak out for Mark, telephoned to say she'd be on the next train down. Mark hopped from telephone to telephone, giving his 'how does it feel' interviews to radio stations up and down the country. Just for the day, the lowering Calvinist ban on smoking in the office was relaxed; this wasn't a day when Bob Duffield should have to loiter by the landing window for an apologetic puff. For a moment, I thought of faxing a copy of the judgement to the whimsical television critic who wrote a 'silly me' review of the original programme, saying how hard it was to understand, but decided that this was not a day for recriminations. I was too busy, anyway, trying to stop one of the press's more enthusiastic photographers from killing Mark. Having done his bit to drain the European Moet and Chandon lake, he had taken Mark up on to the flat roof overlooking London. 'Back a bit, back a bit more,' he exhorted Mark, to try to get his subject into some sort of focus – with the very real danger that Mark's first hour of freedom would be marred by a three-storey backwards flip over the parapet.

I won't say that it's moments like this that make it all worthwhile. It's all worthwhile, anyway. Every case is an intriguing detective story, with its own surprises and frustrations; every story brings us into contact with extraordinary people and is an education in itself, whether it teaches us about tidal river flows, the incidence of idiom in Derbyshire dialect, or the *modus operandi* of a particular crime squad. Compared with teaching, mining, or checking-out at Tesco's, television is an extraordinarily privileged way of earning a living, even though you sometimes have to remind yourself of the fact at four o'clock in the morning, when you are standing in a damp field, your brain numbed into an incapacity to remember your lines. What's more, it is television with a point to it, so that those of us who never have a totally convincing answer to the question 'why don't you get yourself a proper job?' can at least mumble something about there being a purpose to it all. We may not achieve the big things like toppling presidents or revealing famines, but almost without exception, those who have done this sort of work and who have gone on to grander things in television look back upon their miscarriage-of-justice days as the most fulfilling. Everything else, as we say, is just television.

At last Mark and I get the chance for a quiet word, as the hubbub subsides. Yes, he had a feeling this was going to be the day. At the lunchtime adjournment, his warders had told him 'You're going to walk, son'. How desperate it would have been if that assessment had been wrong. He told me he had met Atherton, his accuser, in jail; 'Philip looked across the landing and said "you shouldn't be in here." Well, I could've told him that.' I can't help asking him the fatuous question about how freedom feels, and his eyes mist over again. 'You have to be in my situation to understand.' I say I hope I'm never in his situation, and the remark temporarily diffuses the tension I can see growing within him. He is beginning to realize that freedom is not an absolute; he'll never be free of the memories, never be free of the sly accusations of those who believe him guilty. It is as if he suddenly realizes that it's not just the last ten years, but the rest of his life which will have to be spent persuading others of his innocence. I try to reassure him: 'Mark, you always were innocent; we know you are innocent, you know you are innocent, and now the highest court in the land has agreed that you are innocent.' Yes, he agrees, but that's easy for a judge to say. But a judge cannot cancel the memory of ten years, ten desperately wasted years in a young man's life.

The celebration has become a little solemn, and somehow it seems fitting. Mercade has entered to set our revelry in context. It's time to send Mark and his family off to the hotel, to start putting their lives together. We can't do much to help there. A few days later we get a beautiful Thank You card. We will also soon receive a Well Done card from Stuart Egdell, the boy actor who took part in our reconstructions. I hear later that Mark has not found the first weeks easy, wandering in graveyards late at night. It has been hard for his parents to understand that the teenager they lost has returned to them not as a youth, but as a man hardened and tautened by time and adversity.

For the moment, though, we let the telephones ring, and take the entire Just Television team round to Two Brydges Place, and the club where we hold the dinners of our eminent advisory group. It's a joyful and raucous occasion. We all make speeches, whether we're asked to or not, which will be related back to us next morning, to our amnesiac astonishment. David Martin-Sperry, who has spent most of the evening calling his family in Oxfordshire with details of ever-later trains, throws in the towel and spends the evening with us. Later, he is to write a most moving and generous letter, which, with his permission, I reproduce:

Dear Just Television,
Congratulations on the magnificent outcome of your investigation into Cleary. This was your result. You turned the case from a unanimous 57-minute murder conviction, as to the correctness of which the jury and virtually everyone else could not have been more certain, into what was, by the time it reached me, an almost unloseable appeal. You put right an appalling historical error, not on the basis of any technical mistake made at the trial or by discovering evidence previously unknown about, but by reconsidering all the material known at the time of the original investigation. You succeeded in showing that Mark Cleary had nothing to do with the killing of Wayne Keeton with precisely the same material as had led the Crown to argue successfully for his conviction in 1986.

It was a pleasure and a privilege for me to have shared in your victory.

Yours,
David Martin-Sperry
May 1994

Index

205